Shaston

Marlott

Stourcastle

Hambledon

...antridge

...CHASE

Chaseborough

Knollingwood Hall

Lorton Inn

...ORE

Bulbarrow

Shotsford Forum

Middleton Abbey

R. Stour

Yewsholt Lodge

Warborne

Millpond

Kingsbere

Welland

Cheve Manor HEATH

EEgdon

Greenhill

Sand bourne

...N HEATH

Puddle

Haven- pool

...ickleford

Well- bridge

Holm- stoke

Inglebury

...ether Moynton

Bindon Abbey

R. Froom

Lord's Barrow

...worth

Chaldon Down

Corvsgate Castle

10

9

...gs- ...orth- ...ay

Lullstead Cove

Enchworth

Knollsea

8

7

6

5

St Aldhelm's Hd

4

ENGLISH CHANNEL

3

Miles

2

1

10 9 8 7 6 5 4 3 2 1 0

Hardy's Wessex
Reappraised

CASTERBRIDGE FROM THE LONDON ROAD

DENYS KAY-ROBINSON

Hardy's Wessex
Reappraised

They are great trees, no doubt, by now
That were so thin in bough—
That row of limes—
When we housed there; I'm loth to reckon when;
The world has turned so many times,
so many, since then!

THOMAS HARDY

ST. MARTIN'S PRESS : NEW YORK

Library of Congress Catalog Card Number: 76–186155

First published in the United States of America in 1972

*AFFILIATED PUBLISHERS: Macmillan & Company, Limited,
London—also at Bombay, Calcutta, Madras and Melbourne. The Macmillan
Company of Canada, Limited, Toronto*

Contents

6 *Contents*

List of Illustrations

PLATES

Preface

Since the publication nearly sixty years ago of Hermann Lea's *Thomas Hardy's Wessex*, no book has been exclusively devoted to a comparably detailed survey. Yet several hundred of Hardy's poems were not yet composed when Lea wrote, and in the years since Hardy died research has considerably extended our knowledge of his topographical sources. Meanwhile, time and man have wrought changes in many of the prototypes, even eliminating some altogether. On several counts, therefore, a fresh survey is long overdue, and the present volume, completed exactly a century after the publication of the first Wessex novel, is an attempt to supply the need. Every point in Wessex mentioned in Hardy's prose or verse, and known or believed to have a basis in fact, is here covered, and where Hardy goes into details, such as describing the individual rooms of a house, the details are examined accordingly. Settings outside the South West have not been considered, nor, for the most part, have I mentioned places that are purely imaginary. I have visited every established scene at least once, in addition to many other regions in quest of settings not hitherto located. As a result, this book corrects various errors in previous concepts, and postulates a number of new identifications.

None of the maps has appeared before, and the Wessex, South Wessex, and Casterbridge maps contain many names not previously shown. The smaller maps mainly clarify new findings in the text. For permission to reproduce the sketches by E. H. New I owe thanks to The Bodley Head Ltd, and to Macmillan & Co Ltd for leave to use the many Hardy quotations in the text and the verses at the head of each section. In order to make the book as pleasant as possible to read I have avoided all but a minimum

11

of footnotes, and also the interpolation into the text of data concerning works and authors mentioned, about which full information will be found in the bibliography on pages 257–62. No author who has previously written on Hardy's Wessex has failed to make errors, and while aiming at a high standard of accuracy I have no illusions that I shall prove the first to be infallible. As most Hardy students know, many of his texts vary considerably, not only between the magazine version and the first book edition, but from one book edition to another. Since it is impossible in the compass of this volume to notice all the variants, with a few exceptions I have confined myself to the final reading. Some of my 'new' findings will doubtless arouse controversy. Recent activity in other fields of Hardy research has shown what can be done with gossamer evidence, non-evidence, and even counter-evidence, given sufficient obsession with a preconceived idea; and it may happen that I shall be thought by some to be guilty of similar disingenuousness. I can but plead my acute awareness that there remain many topographical enigmas in Hardy's prose and poetry to which I no more than my predecessors have found the answer.

It remains for me to thank the many scores of people who have helped me in my four-year task; and I hope none of them will think me less grateful for having decided to name no names. If I named them all—and there are some whose names I never found out—each individual would be lost in the great tally; and if I tried to single out those who gave more help from those who gave less, injustices would be unavoidable. My helpers have included librarians and archivists, parsons and publicans, shopkeepers and schoolteachers, builders' foremen, the owners of stately homes and homes less stately, dairymen, bailiffs, engineers, farmers and mill-owners, curators and caretakers, professors and prison governors, railway experts, and of course, that most valuable first-hand informant, the village ancient. To all these, from Reading to Truro and Gloucester to Portland, I am deeply indebted.

Burbage
near Marlborough   Denys Kay-Robinson
Wiltshire

SOUTH WESSEX: *Casterbridge*
(*Dorset: Dorchester*)

And midnight clears High Street of all but the ghosts
    Of its buried burghees,
From the latest far back to those old Roman hosts
    Whose remains one yet sees,
Who loved, laughed, and fought, hailed their friends, drank their toasts,
    At their meeting-times here, just as these!

AT CASTERBRIDGE FAIR

Most of the characters introduced to 'Casterbridge' from outside approached it over Grey's Bridge; and the panorama they saw before descending from Stinsford Hill ('Mellstock Hill', 'Mellstock Rise') or Rushy Pond is astonishingly little changed. A 'new' spire here and there, a late-Victorian mock-keep in the background, the vast red bulk of the 1884–5 prison toward the right: not much else would puzzle those Hardy ghosts. Only on the flanks of the town and in the foreground—alongside the road linking the two bridges, and where 'Mixen' Lane was—are modern buildings conspicuous.

The spread of houses out to the nearer bridge, Grey's, means that the avenue of trees bordering the main road now stops short of this point instead of continuing more than halfway to Town or Swan Bridge as shown on the older maps and in New's delightful frontispiece (reproduced here) to Windle's volume.* The descendants of the romantic young ladies in the poem 'Sitting on the Bridge'—Grey's, that is—very seldom sit on it today, and even the bench now provided alongside it is patronised mainly by the heirs of the 'Crusted Characters'. But an iron notice on the new wall (the bridge was widened in 1927) still threatens with transportation for life anyone found causing damage. Of the 'dace, trout, and minnows' noted by Parson Maybold among the 'long green locks of weed' below, only the dace, I am told, have ceased to be evident.

To the north of Grey's Bridge Ten Hatches still stands, in surprisingly good repair, and Ten Hatches Hole in which Henchard was so narrowly prevented from drowning himself has barely altered, nor has the Blackwater (still willow-fringed) further upstream. (Earlier in *The Mayor of Casterbridge* the prison reach of the Frome is misleadingly termed *Schwarzwasser*.) It was by the 'eve-lit weir' of Ten Hatches that Hardy sat, as he recalled

* For full details of all authors and works mentioned in the text see bibliography on pages 257–62.

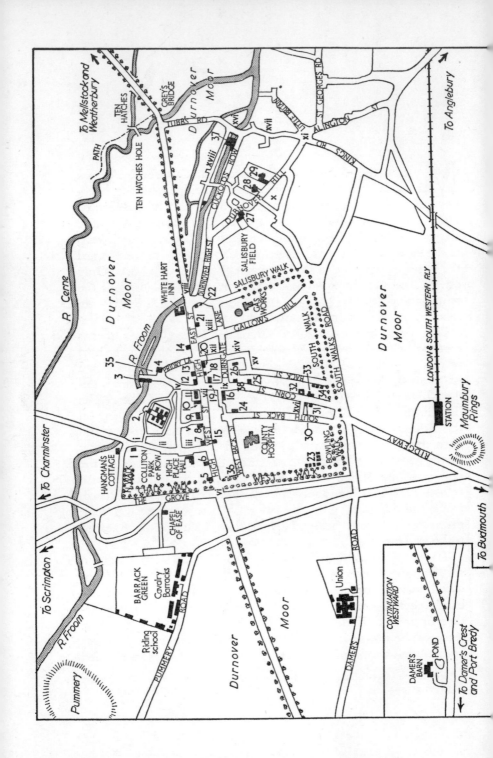

B

in the lines 'Before My Friend Arrived', on the day before the body of Horace Moule was brought back from Cambridge for burial in Fordington churchyard. And in widely different mood here the disgusted candidate for the workhouse in 'The Curate's Kindness' wished he could do away with himself on finding he was not after all to be rid of his wife. Between the Cerne that flows under Grey's Bridge and the Frome that flows under Swan, only a strip of allotments hugging the Frome today lessens the extraordinary desolation that still characterises the marshy expanse, a fit setting yet for 'The Fight on Durnover Moor'.

There are now public conveniences beside Swan Bridge, and the parapet on which Sergeant Troy sat to await Fanny Robin is not the one there today, for in 1954 the old bridge collapsed and had to be rebuilt. Up-river, on the right bank, is the site of the Priory Mill. The walls of one of the mill buildings have been left standing up to garden-wall height, with a small, very new house looking self-conscious inside them. Outside, the 'cascade which had raised its terrific roar for centuries', together with the Priory (or Friary) ruins on which Henchard looked out from Jopp's cottage, are no more. Indeed, the cottage itself, so rich in 'scraps of tracery, moulded window-jambs' and other stones from the Priory, has vanished as though it never existed—which perhaps it did not.

Just to the north, and above the cliff, towers the large factory-like brick façade of the 'new' prison. One feature of the older building is left, the 'classic archway of ashlar' prominent in 'The Withered Arm', and through which Boldwood passed after shooting Troy. But the words 'County Jail 1793', once incised over the doorway, are now missing; possibly they were removed when the government took over prison administration from local authorities in 1877. The other entrance mentioned in 'The Withered Arm', fronting the Bull Stake (now North Square), was replaced by the present iron gate in 1899.

Hangman's Cottage, in which the resident executioner still lived during Hardy's boyhood, is today a very neatly kept private residence. The outside staircase noticed by Gertrude Lodge has been removed, and there is a garage, but otherwise little external change. The wicket in the prison wall, pointed out by the hangman to Gertrude, has so completely disappeared that it is difficult to judge where it was, for the cottage is not really opposite the prison. The steep rise in front of the cottage, reached by a bridge across the stream, is Glyde Path Road, formerly divided into Glyde Path Hill—the 'Glyd'path Rise' of 'The Burghers'—Colliton Row, and Shire Hall Lane. The poem mentions a pleasaunce, a door in an outer wall, and an arch. The house was therefore probably Colliton House, the door the arched one with the mask above it described in *The Mayor of Casterbridge* (see below); but just possibly the scene was the old house (originally divided) that still stands beside the Rise itself, and which also exhibits a filled-in arched doorway in the garden wall.

Colliton (or Colyton) Park is now given over to the buildings and car-parks of the new county administrative headquarters. Lengths of the old boundary wall and a few trees, surrounded by new lawns and flowerbeds, alone remain from the past. Colliton House is the 'High Place Hall' occupied by Lucetta Templeman; Hardy varied its position, however, not merely with each new edition, but within any single edition. The 'little-used alley' to which the door with the mask gave access must surely have been Glyde Path Road, and the allusion to 'the Town Hall *below* Lucetta's house' [my italics] also suggests this site. On the other hand, the reference to the house overlooking the market, and to the nearness of the Town Hall archway where Henchard's waggon upset, seem to suggest a position in Cornhill. Windle identifies 'High Place Hall' with great precision as the corner building at the junction of Cornhill and Durngate Street, maintaining that the gateway with the mask was 'borrowed' from Colliton House. But all the Cornhill houses formed then, as now, a continuous terrace, and that makes nonsense of Hardy's remark that Lucetta's house 'had the characteristics of a country mansion' and 'dignity without great size'. These epithets, however, apply perfectly to Colliton House.

The mansion is now part of the County Council offices, but has been left freestanding, and cleaning of the stonework has restored its original tone. On the south side a one-storey canteen has been added—fortunately where it is not too conspicuous, except to those looking for the original site of the door with the mask. This door once stood in a stone wall that ran alongside Glyde Path Road from the corner where the canteen now obtrudes, past the forecourt of the new brick County Laboratory to the back of the nearest house in High West Street. Today the arch and mask frame a library doorway in the County Museum.

The north-west corner of the park is formed by two of the tree-lined walks that mark the line of the ancient town walls: North Walk and Colliton ('Chalk') Walk. Here Henchard made his fateful plea to Farfrae not to leave the town; and after more than a century the only difference in the scene is the asphalt underfoot. Just beyond the southern end of the walk, almost at Top o' Town, stands Eric Kennington's memorial statue of Hardy, a seated effigy whose dignity has long recovered from the placing in its lap, a few hours after the unveiling in 1931, of a large portion of fish and chips.

North of Colliton Walk and the Yeovil road (the Grove) Fordington's great vicar Henry Moule built in 1846 a small chapel of ease, Christ Church, to spare his parishioners in this outpost of his sprawling parish the necessity of tramping to Fordington St George. This is the chapel of ease alluded to in *A Changed Man*. It has recently been demolished, together with some cottages, to make room for the residential part of the Grove Trading Estate; but it had already outlived its purpose with the formation in 1910 of St Mary's parish out of north Fordington and the building of St Mary's, Victoria Park.

The barracks in which Captain Maumbry was quartered before he exchanged his cuirass for a cassock, where the narrator in 'The Revisitation' lay sleepless, and from which the 'King's-Own Cavalry' sallied forth to hold their memorable 'Dance at the Phoenix', were mainly on the south side of a huge grassed square, the Barrack Green. Here, in the opening pages of *A Changed Man*, the band played on Sunday afternoons. This green still survives, but except on a football pitch in the middle its grass is long and untended. The buildings themselves, later called the Marabout Barracks, have survived in part, and during the army reorganisation of the 1950s and 1960s one section became a Territorial Army centre. Some of the cookhouses, storehouses, and part of the hospital are among the units still standing. The Riding School, where Moule preached before he built Christ Church, is now a garage. The Infantry and Militia Barracks, south of Poundbury Road, including the keep or gatehouse that now harbours the regimental museum, were all built after the events in Hardy's relevant works.

North of the barracks the development of the trading estate means that once-isolated Poundbury ('Pummery') has become virtually part of the town; there is even a small caravan colony on its eastern flank! The earthwork itself has not altered perceptibly since the last of the sheep marts evoked in 'A Sheep Fair'; but south of it, too, the solitude is vanishing as the space between Poundbury and the Bridport road becomes filled in with new streets and houses. The railway (Great Western, 1857) is another intruder since the period of Henchard and Maumbry; thanks to Brunel it passes through a tunnel under the great square mass instead of cutting across it.

The residential development flanking the Bridport road has obliterated Damer's Barn which, together with its 'slimy pond', used to stand opposite the junction of Damer's Road and this thoroughfare. One or two fine water-colour sketches of the barn are to be seen in the Dorset Museum. 'Dammer's Crest', referred to in 'The Burghers', is where the tree-bordered road breasts the top of the hill a furlong or two farther west.

These trees lining the Bridport road, and their fellows along the Wareham, Weymouth and Puddleton roads, give the Dorchester approaches the longest tree borders of any public roads in Wessex, except for a few round Wilton. But their age makes them dangerously susceptible to storm damage and disease. Already by the turn of the century the trees, mostly elms, along the Puddletown road had suffered many casualties, from which the avenue has never recovered. Today it is the turn of Weymouth Avenue; its trees were felled in 1969. They have been replaced, but the first replacements were destroyed by vandals.

Looking down the two High Streets, East and West, one sees few buildings that would be unfamiliar to the characters in any of the later-set works, and many that would be recognised by the protagonists in those set earlier. Hardy's principal allusion to this view occurs at the beginning of 'A Changed Man', in the description of what the invalid saw from his first-floor oriel window. Some have fancied the 'old, substantially built house' with the oriel to be Top-o'-Town House, but Hardy himself revealed that he had in mind 51 High West Street. This stands on the north side, quite a distance down from Top-o'-Town; but the oriel, rather deceptively, does command approximately the view ascribed to it. Number 51 has been given a shop window (now frosted), and has been retained. The oriel has not been altered. On the same side, the uppermost house in High West Street, now a dentist's premises, appears from Hardy's rather odd description to have been the residence of Laura and her uncle in 'A Changed Man'.

At the corner of the former Shire Hall Lane there stood, until the 1840s, the Trenchard mansion so much admired by Hardy. This may have been the 'noble pile' of the poem 'A Man'. The balustraded house in Glyde Path Road is perhaps a surviving fragment. The grey Shire Hall, scene until 1955 of the Assizes and Quarter Sessions (but not Petty Sessions, which were held in the Town Hall), is also outwardly unaltered. Hardy wrote in *The Mayor* that sheep could be heard bleating without the Shire Hall while a sheep-stealer was being sentenced within; these sheep must have been in Colliton Park—for Fordington Field, the nearest extra-mural pasturage, would even in the pre-motor age have been out of earshot. Now we have the court (from 1972 a Crown Court), not the sheep, in Colliton Park, and the Shire Hall is, mainly, a quiet memorial to the Tolpuddle Martyrs.

Between the hall and Holy Trinity church was the little seed shop that housed Henchard's last business in Dorchester, and himself and Elizabeth-Jane overhead. This is borne out by the following details. When Henchard decided to leave Casterbridge, Elizabeth-Jane accompanied him down to Grey's Bridge, and while returning from there met Farfrae, with whom she walked up High East Street as far as the Bow. Here she turned off with him into South Street instead of going 'straight on to her own door'. This places the shop firmly in or just off High West Street. Elsewhere we are told that the shop occupied a 'pleasant, sunny corner', which appears to preclude the north-facing side, and that it stood 'overlooking the churchyard'. That name would surely not have been applied to the tiny space on the west and south sides of St Peter's, and in any case the building immediately north of it (where the County Museum now stands) was the George Inn. But at that time Holy Trinity—the predecessor of the present building—was bounded on the west by a small extension of the churchyard, with a tree in it, west of which again lay the alley still to be seen, Grey's School Passage. This ran then, as now, past the main churchyard, which it separated from the present terrace of cottages. The corner building with its frontage on High West Street, was the house to be seen today, consisting of two storeys above a double-fronted shop. This shop is a good deal larger than the 'cupboard' with which Hardy compared the seed shop; either, therefore, Hardy deliberately made it smaller, or he may possibly have pictured Henchard in one of the cottages, which are sunny enough during the first half of the day. 'Corner' must in this event be interpreted in its wider sense of 'nook'.

East of Holy Trinity—which was rebuilt, and the area with the tree obliterated, in 1875—stands the Dorset County Museum, built in 1881 (with galleries added in 1903) by Hardy's then recent employer G. R. Crickmay, on the site of the George Inn. This was therefore not the museum recommended to Elizabeth-Jane by Lucetta, though the great mahogany table still in its library is probably the one around which Hardy envisaged the narrators of the stories in *A Group of Noble Dames*. In 1969–71 the museum was enlarged and a Rural Life section added.

St Peter's Church features in *The Mayor of Casterbridge*, *The Trumpet-Major*, and the poems 'The Dance at the Phoenix' and 'The Peace Peal'. The tower has long since recovered from the dilapidated state described in *The Mayor*. The whole church was restored in 1856 by John Hicks (apprentice-assistant, Thomas Hardy), and again before the end of the century by C. F. Ponting. There were repairs in 1961, and a further repointing in 1967. The tenor bell that so pleased the Trumpet-Major is still there, more than a ton of it, along with its seven colleagues, three of which were recast during the nineteenth century. The 8 o'clock curfew mentioned in *The Mayor* continued to sound, except for an interval during World War I, until the outbreak of World War II. The chimes that 'stammered out' the Sicilian Mariners' Hymn were not, despite the implication in some versions of *The Mayor*, those of another building—no other building within earshot had the eight bells needed; they were the chimes of St Peter's itself, as is borne out by the poem 'The Chimes'.

In front of the church, the curve of the 'Crossways or Bow' has recently been flattened for road improvement and the wall taken back some five feet nearer the church. The railings that topped the wall during most of the nineteenth century were removed and not subsequently replaced, since it was felt they would look wrong so much nearer the building. The gate and pillars, however, have been resited. The plate bearing the name of The Bow was put on the wall at Hardy's expense after the council had refused to affix one. It was here that the long-suffering woman in 'A Wife Waits' (part of 'At Casterbridge Fair') waited for her husband to emerge from 'the Club-Room below'—according to Hermann Lea, a building facing into the Bull Stake and already demolished.

Until 1847 the old Town Hall abutted on to the wall surrounding St Peter's and an arched throughway under it gave access to the 'large square called Bull Stake'. Here stood the post to which bulls were tied and baited by dogs to make the meat tender—in those unenlightened days calves were not yet reared in little dark boxes. The stake has long since vanished, and the square (North Square) has been mostly rebuilt. It was by the church wall at the entrance to the archway that Henchard's waggon capsized after the clash with Farfrae's. When the present Town Hall was erected in 1848 a narrow road was left between it and the church. At first there was no clock turret at the corner, but a small cupola in the centre of the roof ridge. The cupola was removed and the corner tower added in 1864, and a new Corn Exchange was built at the back of the building in 1867. The Gothic entrance was constructed in 1876, since when the Town Hall has remained externally unchanged. Hardy probably thought of the Town Hall and the Corn Exchange in their present form when he put Bathsheba Everdene among the corn merchants, and also in writing 'After the Fair' with its reference to 'Clock-corner steps'.

Externally unchanged over a somewhat longer period is the King's Arms in High East Street, which was last rebuilt between 1800 and 1820. The front room in which the commissioners dealt with Henchard's bankruptcy may have been either the front bar now on one side of the entrance or the coffee lounge on the other. In the room behind the first-floor bow Henchard himself, dining with the other dignitaries in his heyday as mayor, had been surveyed through the opened sash by Susan and Elizabeth-Jane from the crowd on the top of the waggon office steps opposite. These steps, as old photographs show, used to jut out from the doorway of 21 High East Street, now a branch of the Victoria Wine Company. There appears to be no record of a genuine waggon office, although it turns up again in 'The Waiting Supper' as the place where Nicholas saw Christine.

In his speech on being presented with the freedom of Dorchester Hardy named various buildings, once known to him, whose disappearance he particularly lamented. Among them was the Three Mariners Inn of *The Mayor* (in earlier editions the King of Prussia). This seemingly most agreeable Elizabethan stone building with mullioned bow windows was pulled down, and its successor of the same name built on the site, before the end of last century. It is now a British Legion club.

Hard by Swan Bridge is the White Hart where Sergeant Troy and Pennyways discussed their plans, but it has been so extensively redecorated within and without that all sense of antiquity has gone. It stands well back from the road, leaving a forecourt for customers to park their cars where once the carriers' carts loaded up with their goods and passengers, including the storytellers of *A Few Crusted Characters*, and where Gertrude Lodge dismounted from her carthorse at the end of her ride over the heath.

The third bridge within the town limits is Standfast or Prince's Bridge in Fordington, mentioned in 'The Dance at the Phoenix'. It belongs to an area much redesigned, that of the once notorious Mill Lane ('Mixen Lane'). The original bridge remains—with repaired parapets—but it has lost its importance, for most vehicles now cross by the newer bridge a few yards downstream. The adjacent confluence of roads formed Standfast Cross. Fordington Cross is rather more than a cross, being the point south of Fordington Green where King's Road is converged upon by High Street, Fordington, Alington Road, St George's Road and Little Britain. Many street names in the area have been changed since Hardy wrote. The stretch of the present High Street between Holloway Road (formerly Cuckolds Row) and Fordington Cross was Fordington Hill. North of the cross the present King's Road was called Standfast Road; south of the cross it was King Street.

Between Standfast Bridge and Grey's Bridge the present King's Road was called Tubb's Road.

Although it still contains a few fine old houses and streets of Victorian cottages, Fordington has altered much more than Dorchester. Not only have the low-lying slums vanished, but the 'congeries of barns and farmsteads' on Fordington Hill has now been transformed for the most part into a region as urban as the rest of Dorchester. It is therefore fortunate for us that in a tiny rural pocket east of the churchyard a muddy rustic enclosure containing pigsties and a small shed (thatched until 1971) can reasonably be regarded as the remnant of the 'Durnover Barton' that Hardy bestowed on Henchard, and where Susan arranged for Farfrae to meet Elizabeth-Jane.

The church of St George in Fordington has had a curious history during the last 200 years, for it has regained in the twentieth century the medieval outline it lost in the eighteenth when the old chancel was pulled down and a new and much smaller one built in the Georgian style. This was the chancel that existed during the period of *The Dynasts* and 'Enter a Dragoon', the poem 'No Bell-Ringing', the comings and goings of Lucetta and Elizabeth-Jane, and the activities of the Reverend John Maumbry in 'A Changed Man'. It was pulled down and rebuilt in the old proportions by the Reverend Richard Bartelot shortly after he became vicar in 1906. Hardy strongly opposed the plan to rebuild and was greatly distressed by the removal of the Georgian structure. He agreed with Bartelot, however, about the demolition of another addition, a galleried aisle put up alongside the nave in 1831; and when the same vicar went on to enlarge and improve the nave, Hardy himself designed new Gothic pillars for the north aisle. In the churchyard the principal changes are the disappearance of the thatched wall (or at least the thatch) and promenade noted in *The Mayor*, and the comparatively recent removal of nearly all the tombstones, including some of considerable interest; only the far enclosure where the Moules lie has been left undisturbed.

Fordington Green has been preserved, and indeed improved, Bartelot having planted a septet of trees to which the borough council has added. There is a scene in *The Dynasts* in which Napoleon's effigy is merrily burnt on 'a patch of green grass on

Durnover Hill'. This refers not to Fordington Green but to Fair-
field, formerly Salisbury Field, close by, on to which the garden
of the Old Vicarage abuts: the vicar watched the burning from the
garden gate. The old house, outwardly little altered, is now converted into flats. On the western side of Fairfield the tree-lined
path—Salisbury Walk—that leads down to the Town Bridge is the
'deserted avenue of chestnuts' into which Fanny Robin turned to
reach the Union without going through the town.

Maumbry, we are told, lived at or near Fordington Cross. The
Mill Lane of his day, so graphically conjured up in *The Mayor*,
where its squalor is in no degree exaggerated, has now given
place to demure squares and blocks of council flats. Nothing to
suggest the former overcrowding in this little island of 'free'
land in the midst of the huge Duchy of Cornwall estate remains.
Even the mill has given place to a block of flats, its pool partly
overgrown.

But the river continues to flow, and those who recall how the
poachers, on their return across Fordington Field, would whistle
to those in the houses to bring out their plank bridges, must
often be puzzled by the modern scene; for the river is, and clearly
must always have been, on the wrong side of the street: beyond
the water lies, not the open moor, but Fordington village on its
height. The explanation is that the back gardens and courts of
the Mill Street houses, all of which were on the north side of
the road and river, were divided from the stretch of moor that
lay between them and the London road by a lesser channel of
the Frome, forcing the poaching fraternity, if they wished to
enter their houses from the back, to call for some means of
crossing. The channel was covered over at the beginning of this
century. Lea's photograph of the Mill Street backs was taken either
after this or from inside the islanded area: some of the back courts
were very long.

With the destruction of the slum dwellings went also the
tavern immortalised in *The Mayor*, the 'Peter's Finger'. Its real
name was the King's Head, but the more colourful title was
borrowed by Hardy from an inn, still extant, at Lytchett Minster
('Flytchett', page 74), near Poole. Peter's Finger is a corruption
of St Peter ad Vincula—St Peter in Chains.

On the Fordington–Dorchester boundary, close to the Town

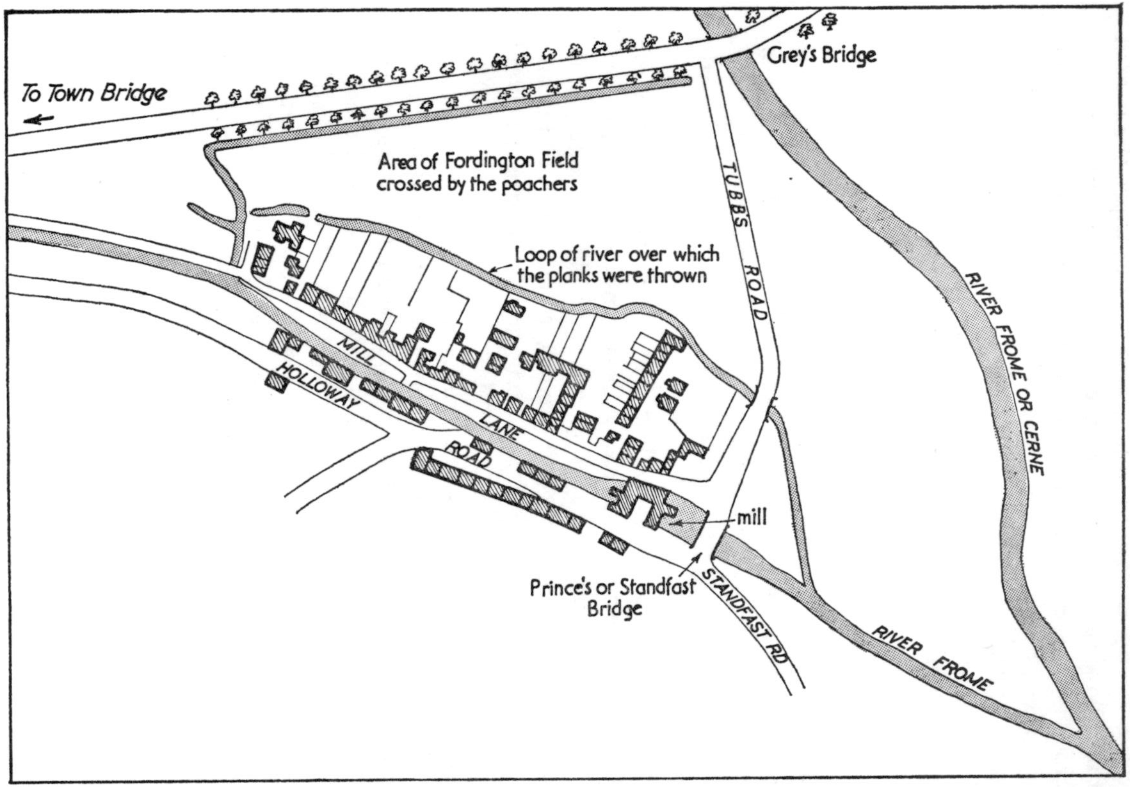
To Town Bridge
Grey's Bridge
Area of Fordington Field
crossed by the poachers
TUBBS ROAD
Loop of river over which
the planks were thrown
RIVER FROME OR CERNE
MILL
LANE
HOLLOWAY
ROAD
mill
Prince's or Standfast
Bridge
STANDFAST RD
RIVER FROME

The Mill Lane area of Fordington

Bridge, a building now used by the Jehovah's Witnesses is the former 'Dorford' Baptist Church, the setting for the factually based poem 'The Chapel-Organist'; and a short way up High East Street from the Fordington turning is the Phoenix, of 'The Dance at the Phoenix' fame. In spite of its distance from the barracks, the Phoenix was a favourite with the military. It still stands, but, like so many other inns, it has been drastically rebuilt and given an ugly twentieth-century ground-floor frontage.

All Saints church, also mentioned in 'The Dance at the Phoenix' and in *The Mayor*, has a curious association with the poem 'The Casterbridge Captains'. The sub-title of the poem is 'Khyber Pass, 1842', and it tells of three lads who had carved their names on the back of one of the All Saints' pews. All three become soldiers and fight in India, where two are killed. The survivor returns to Dorchester and finds the names still on the pew. But between 1842 and 1845 the seventeenth-century church was pulled down and a new one built—Dorchester's finest piece of Victorian architecture. Contrary to nineteenth-century practice, the pulpit, choir stalls, and some of the pews from the old church were retained; so that the soldier who, with his friends, had carved his name in one church, returned to find the carvings in another. They were still there for Hardy to sketch for the first edition of *Wessex Poems*, but during subsequent repairs the panel was removed. In 1971 All Saints was put up for sale.

In the centre of Cornhill the town pump manages to survive, though no longer operative as in Henchard's day. Just beyond Durngate Street is the site of the Greyhound Inn, where in *The Trumpet-Major* Bob Loveday waited for Matilda Johnson. One fragment of the inn remains, the sixteenth-century arched stone doorway. Preserved and reset, at Hardy's suggestion, in the new building on the site, it was again reprieved when that building was in turn demolished, and today it spans the passage connecting South Street with the municipal car-park that has replaced Old Greyhound Yard.

At the back of the car-park is a group of stone buildings, now occupied by Ling's printing works but which originally housed a brewery; the actual brewing was done in the low structures beside Acland Street, and the long, very tall building next to them was the malthouse. It originally had only two storeys, a lofty ground floor and an attic level reached by a wooden staircase in one corner. Near the centre of the attic floor was a large trapdoor, through which an apprentice once fell—luckily, on to a pile of shavings. In the east wall of the attic a doorway, surmounted by what Hardy called a cat's-head, opened into the void. In spite of some discrepancies (Hardy put in extra floors, for instance) there can be no doubt that the malthouse was the model for Henchard's corn-store in which he had the fight with Farfrae. After it had ceased to be a malthouse the building was taken over by a building company, and later by a heating-appliance firm which inserted an extra floor and modified the doors and windows. But the filled-in attic doorway remains visible, facing Acland Street. In the magazine version of the story an illustration of the fight shows, through the doorway, a roof strongly resembling that of Wollaston House opposite.*

Nearly lost amid towering brick walls, and largely paved over, a remnant is left of Henchard's long garden. Two lime trees that grow there are said to date from the days when the house was a private residence. Today a branch of Barclay's Bank, the mansion itself, fronting South ('Corn') Street, is one of the finest and best-kept mid-eighteenth-century buildings in Dorchester, and externally lacks only a balcony to accord with Hardy's description; the green railings were removed for salvage during World War II. 'Back Street', in which lay the commercial entrance to Henchard's premises, and in which Abe Whittle lived, is now called Charles Street. Much of it has been rebuilt—some of the South Street shops extend right through to it—but toward the lower end there are still some small terraced cottages that preserve the atmosphere of a residential street for the community's humbler members.

A short distance below Barclay's Bank is Napper's Mite, now

---

* According to a strong tradition in the family that for more than a century has owned Upwey Mill (see p 159), near Weymouth, the mill building was the model for Henchard's granary. Hardy, a frequent visitor, is said to have pointed to a lofty trapdoor and said it was the one beside which Henchard and Farfrae fought. However, apart from the fact that they fought beside the door in the wall, not the trapdoor, there seems no reason why Hardy should have gone to Upwey for a setting when one that exactly fitted his needs stood exactly where he needed it. I suspect that in fact on one occasion he indicated the Upwey Mill trapdoor and remarked on its similarity to the one in the building he had used for the fight scene. But the millowners' belief is held in very good faith.

a café and offices, but almshouses when Hardy referred in both *The Mayor* and *Far from the Madding Crowd* to the striking of the ancient clock over the entry. The clock is still going, though at present its voice is silent. In contrast to the survival of Napper's Mite is the fate of its neighbour, Hardye's Grammar School, which after various rebuildings—the last by Hardy's early employer, Crickmay—was finally demolished in 1966 in favour of a shopping arcade. This was the school attended by Frank Troy, who would have been there during its pre-Crickmay phase. The school is now established in the south-eastern suburbs, with a junior section in Wollaston House.

Opposite the Hardye Arcade and next to each other, are two buildings that played an important part in Hardy's early years, and about which he wrote in *The Life*. These are the former home and offices of the architect John Hicks, and the house in which William Barnes lived and taught before he exchanged a pedagogue's life for a parson's. On each house a plaque beneath the first-floor window records the historic importance of these otherwise insignificant terrace structures. The Hickses' house became a small temperance hotel; then the ground floor was occupied by a bicycle shop; and today, the final indignity, it is a snack-bar. Barnes's house has fared rather better, and is now an estate agent's offices.

Returning to Cornhill, the Antelope Hotel, where Henchard waited to return Lucetta's letters, has hardly altered since it acquired its twin-bow frontage early in the nineteenth century. The yard goes right through to Trinity Street, where from 1851 to 1883 the museum occupied a handsome house (number 3) still very little changed within or without, except for the upper part of the façade. Today it is a dentist's premises.

The china shop over which were 'the only lodgings fit' for Susan and Elizabeth-Jane was either at the corner of Trinity Street and High West Street (the site of the former theatre, now a restaurant called 'The Horse with the Red Umbrella'), or a short distance along High West Street, where Mabb's the men's outfitters now stands. Along here also is Judge Jeffreys' House, the first home of the museum, and today a fashionable tea-room; and further west, the Old Ship Inn, where Norbert told his story of the great battle in the poem 'Leipzig'. Only the stone-mullioned first-floor windows remain from the original building; any picturesqueness, however, has been completely destroyed by clumsy refacing earlier in the present century and rather styleless redecoration within. Which of the bars was the 'Master-tradesmen's Parlour' no one now seems to know.

One can place only approximately the cottage that Henchard procured for Susan 'in the upper or western part of the town, near the Roman wall and the avenue which overshadowed it'. The reference is to West Walks and the surviving length of Roman city wall near the northern end. But the nearest houses are large town houses, and nothing else in the area qualifies fully as the cottage Hardy had in mind. It is certain, however, that Susan would no longer be able to look through the trees of the West Walks at the 'tumuli and earth-forts of the distant uplands'—the open country west of Dorchester—because the view has been closed by much red-brick residential development in Cornwall Road and beyond. Furthermore, between the avenue and Cornwall Road there has existed since 1900 a small and leafy public park, the Borough Gardens.

It was amid the trees of the West Walks that Farfrae organised the entertainment that proved so much more successful than Henchard's at Poundbury. Regular and straight-boled, the sycamores would serve him today as they served him then.

After the junketings Farfrae escorted Elizabeth-Jane home (she was then living at Henchard's house) down West Walks and round the corner along Bowling Alley Walks ('the Bowling Walk') to the Junction, as the point is now known where South Street, Trinity Street, and several other roads meet. The southern part of West Walks, together with Bowling Alley, were also known as the Old Walk, the term used by Benjamin Grower when directing the two constables during the skimmington affair. In Bowling Alley Walks there are now lamps, but Farfrae escorted his partner through darkness to the first street-lamp in South Street. Buildings herabouts have altered considerably, and some of the trees have been removed.

Westward from the Junction runs Damers Road, in which, on the north side, stand the buildings of the Damers Road Hospital. This was formerly the Union or workhouse in which Fanny Robin died, and to which went the ancient protagonist of 'The Curate's

Kindness'. Built in 1836, it has had some additions, but the principal block, of brick and pale grey rubble, differs from the building seen by Fanny only in lacking the ivy that made it 'look like an abbey'.

The Damers Road area was once on the brink of the town, and it is here, to westward and southward, that the greatest modern spread shows. The urbanisation has meant an immense change in the surroundings of the two railway stations, Maumbury Rings, the cemetery, and even Max Gate.

The first railway station, built in 1847 by the Southampton & Dorchester Railway Company (soon bought up by the L & SW), is substantially as it was at first, even to the need for up-trains from Weymouth to reverse into it, although the down line now has a platform on the spur that connects with the Great Western. Maumbury Rings ('the Amphitheatre', 'the Ring'), once as solitary as it was sinister, became not only surrounded by roads and houses, but very nearly enclosed by railways. The Great Western line—then the Wiltshire, Somerset & Weymouth—was originally planned to pass through the Maumbury earthwork as through the Poundbury, but here too, public pressure and Brunel's enlightened policy saved the day.

Notwithstanding its changed environment, Maumbury must remain the grimmest spot in Dorchester, its black story culminating in 1706 in the hideous execution of nineteen-year-old Mary Channing. Hardy used this event in his poem 'The Mock Wife', and recorded some of the grislier details in his notebooks. But his chief use of Maumbury is in *The Mayor*, where he makes it the meeting-place of Henchard and Susan, and in 'Her Death and After', where it is the scene of the interview between the lover and the husband. Except that the earthwork is no longer lonely, Hardy's detailed pictures of it remain completely valid. Long thought to have been built by the Romans, it was proved by excavations begun in 1908 to date from the New Stone or Early Bronze Age; the Romans merely adapted it. The corner in which, as Hardy confirms, the gallows stood, was the southwest; earlier it had stood in the centre. Ironically, the entrance to the Rings now faces, at short range, the County Police Headquarters.

Earliest of the gallows sites was Gallows Hill, where South

c

Walks Road crosses Icen Way; Buzzford, in *The Mayor*, refers to the Monmouth rebels hanged there. Until the last century 'Gallows Hill' applied to the whole road between the gallows site and King's Road.

South of Maumbury Rings lies the municipal cemetery, the setting, with its gates and lodge, of 'The Supplanter'; it is also 'the Field of Tombs where the earthworks frowned' in 'Her Death and After'. It looks what it is, a large well-kept town burial-ground, with little new about it except the latest graves. East of it, and of the railway, is a labyrinth of new residential streets; east of these again, an expanse still unbuilt on; and then Alington Avenue, notable now for the new inn called The Trumpet Major. In the angle between the avenue and Syward Road is Max Gate, Hardy's home from 1885 until his death, and the setting of a number of poems.

Now a National Trust property, it remains structurally very much as he left it, an ugly, oddly gloomy house, hardly visible behind its much-needed screen of tall trees, the planting of which is recorded in the poem 'Everything Comes'. The last of the three studies he occupied there has been recreated, with the original fireplace and furniture, in the Dorset County Museum, but it is not clear whether this is the room referred to in 'An August Midnight'. Sad to say, Emma's piano on which—in a last-minute attempt to re-establish an understanding?—she played the old tunes of their early years just before she died (as related in 'The Last Performance' and used for the theme of 'Lost Love'), has vanished. Was it in prophecy or to record what had already happened that in 'The Strange House' Hardy wrote of the ghostly piano-playing:

> There's no piano to-day;
> Their old one was sold and broken:
> Years past it went amiss . . . ?

This piano is also the instrument in 'At the Piano' and one of the household features alluded to in 'Ten Years Since'. 'The Little Old Table' is the one now in the replica of Hardy's study at the museum.

'The Spell of the Rose' is another poem inspired by the Hardys' estrangement. If what it tells us be true, the rose could conceivably be a pink, sweet-scented one, clearly of great age,that continues to flourish beside the house; this is the only old rose in the garden. Not far away the 'Druid' stone of 'The Shadow on the Stone' is still to be seen, and the tenants of Max Gate until 1971 recalled the disintegration of what seems to have been the original 'Garden Seat'. Other survivals are the headstoned graves of Moss, the black labrador, and Wessex, Florence Hardy's terrier, who may have moved Hardy to eulogise him as 'A Popular Personage at Home', but who was singularly unpopular outside it and with visitors. His passing is commemorated in 'Dead Wessex, the Dog to the Household'.

Further afield, Conquer Barrow—scene of 'The Death of Regret', 'The Clasped Skeletons', and 'Evening Shadows', in which it is the 'Pagan mound'—swells majestically under its dense cover of bushes and tall trees on the very edge of a new council estate; and a short way further still, where the West Stafford road breasts Frome Hill, the Frome Hill tumulus rises as conspicuously as when Angel Clare looked across the vale from it (for surely this was the 'detached knoll a mile or two west of Talbothays'), and the companions walked thither in 'Seeing the Moon Rise'.

Down the Wareham road (A352) stands the little pink-and-thatch doll's house, Came Rectory, that was the last home of William Barnes. Hardy used to walk to the rectory from Max Gate by a path—it is still usable—that cut off the sharp elbow in the highway; and he was taking this route to his fellow-poet's funeral when he saw a sudden gleam of sunlight on the distant coffin as it was borne to the church. He commemorated the incident in the poem 'The Last Signal'. Came Rectory, just after Barnes's successor had moved in, is the scene of 'The Old Neighbour and the New'. The nearer water-meadows in the vale, with their tracks and weirs, are those of the poem 'Paths of Former Time'.

Came House, home of the Damers, stands south of the rectory, off the main road, with the church close by; and at a little distance to the west of it, in a meadow, is all that is left of St German's church at Winterbourne Farringdon, the 'Farringdon Ruin' of *The Trumpet-Major*. The remnant today is precisely as Hardy described it.

A mile to the west lies Maiden Castle ('Maidon', 'Mai Dun'), from whose 'many ramparts' Henchard, with his telescope trained on the Weymouth road, watched Farfrae's meetings with Eliza-beth-Jane and saw the return of Newson. But the finest picture of the huge fortress occurs in—indeed, *is*—the short story 'A Tryst at an Ancient Earthwork'. As an evocation of place and mood this is unsurpassed by any of Hardy's descriptions in the great novels. Safe under the protection of the Ministry of Public Build-ing and Works, Maiden Castle today conforms to his word picture in every respect save one—there is no longer a notice board warning of prosecution for removing relics or cutting up the ground. Despite the nearness of Dorchester and the main road, within the 60ft-high multiple rampart complete quiet reigns, save for the occasional lowing of the cattle pastured there and (on my last visit) the singing of an exceptionally large exaltation of skylarks. Harper states that at the beginning of the century the place swarmed with rabbits. Since myxomatosis this is no longer so.

The huge ramparts thrown up to replace a previous single earth-wall were stormed, probably in AD 45, by the famous Second Legion. Nearly 2,000 years later, well after the date of Hardy's story, excavations have revealed (by chance) a huge cemetery containing the bodies of men and women killed in this contest. But it was the earlier discovery of a Roman temple that apparently inspired Hardy's slight tale. Today the Dorset Museum contains, if not the bronze-gilt figure of Mercury in the story, at any rate a number of figurines in silver-bronze and other materials, found on the site.

Inside Maiden Castle itself all trace of the British cemetery and Roman temple have now vanished again beneath the grass, and the great green expanse belongs once more to the cattle and the larks.

SOUTH WESSEX: *Mellstock*
(*Dorset: Stinsford*)

And then, when the night has turned twelve the air brings
From dim distance, a rhythm of voices and strings:
'Tis the quire, just afoot on their long yearly rounds,
To rouse by worn carols each house in their bounds;
Robert Penny, the Dewys, Mail, Voss, and the rest; till anon
Tired and thirsty, but cheerful, they home to their beds in the dawn.

WINTER NIGHT IN WOODLAND

Stinsford is a curious entity, being made up of three distinct hamlets, four large houses, several riverside and downland farms, and not a shop (except the post office) nor a tavern to the entire parish. Hardy's description of 'Mellstock' in *Under the Greenwood Tree* shows that its component hamlets have altered very little. Nor has the air of remoteness been lost, a phenomenon the more remarkable because the parish boundary actually marches with that of Dorchester.

Stinsford Farm, between the church group and the Tincleton road, has acquired the familiar quota of concrete and steel modernisation. Behind it a cluster of cottages now occupies the 'green-wooded meadow' known as Boucher's Close, across which, as he records in *The Life*, Hardy used to walk home from Dorchester to his birthplace, pausing on the farther side to sit on the now vanished stile where on one occasion he read *The Spectator*'s crushing review of *Desperate Remedies*.

Close to the church is a very modern glass-and-timber structure, a new addition to the school at present occupying Stinsford House. This house (almost wholly a reconstruction, following the fire of 1892 recorded in *The Life*) was the setting for the poem 'The Widow Betrothed', but the lodge has been replaced by a villa and the drive is disused. Here also lived Lady Susan, *née* Strangways, and her actor husband, William O'Brien, whose memorial with two overlapping hearts can be seen on the south chancel wall in the church, and whose story is told in the poem 'The Noble Lady's Tale'. The 'last dark mew' in this poem is the vault built for the O'Briens, at Lady Susan's order, by Hardy's grandfather. In *A Pair of Blue Eyes* Hardy transfers this to Cornwall, making it the prototype of the Luxellian family tomb (see page 247).

Stinsford church has changed much since the days of the 'Mellstock quire' (disbanded about 1841) and Hardy's own boyhood. Some of the changes, such as the replacement of the fine barrel roof to the nave by one of plain deal, occurred in the 'normal' course of restoration; but many have been made in commemoration of Hardy himself. Another of the more regrettable 'improvements' was the removal of the musicians' gallery pictured in 'A Church Romance', and the stage for the 'Mellstock quire'.

Noting in *The Life* the installation in 1902 of a brass tablet celebrating his family's forty years' service in the Stinsford 'quire', Hardy states that the gallery had been removed some sixty years earlier. This date is supported by Beatty—with reservations in his 1963 thesis, with none in the 1971 *Thomas Hardy Year Book*. On the other hand the Reverend G. H. Moule, in his *Stinsford Church and Parish* (1940) says 'it appears that the gallery was removed before the end of the nineteenth century', which certainly does not imply the early 1840s, and is echoed in the church brochure published anonymously, also about 1940, where the removal is placed 'some sixty years ago'. In support of the earlier date Beatty quotes a number of notes and letters by Hardy, in which, however, Hardy nowhere states expressly that the gallery was dismantled in the 1840s. In support of the later date is the testimony (given to the Reverend L. J. Medway) of a former churchwarden, who died in 1968 aged ninety-five, that he had watched the removal of the gallery when he was a small boy. This too would bring the date to about 1880. If it is correct, Hardy's failure to record any contemporary comment on the removal is strange, though it must be remembered that for several years before and after 1880 he was not living in the Dorchester area. The tall box pews, already twice patched, were removed in 1911, the best panels being saved and incorporated in the present wall-panelling. In the porch there is a copy of a sketch-plan by Hardy himself showing the shape of the gallery and where each singer and player sat. The porch walls have been enriched with Tudor panels taken from Kingston Maurward Old Manor, and seats have been made from oak brought in 1911 from sixteenth-century Parnham House, near Beaminster. The bells (mentioned in *Desperate Remedies*) were rehung and the treble recast in 1927.

A visitor to the church can still see in the north aisle the elaborate monument to the Greys of Kingston Maurward, with the skull that so deeply impressed Hardy as a child and is referred to both in *Desperate Remedies* and *An Indiscretion in the Life of an Heiress*. But that other cause of childish fear, the nearby entrance to the vaults, has been sealed since the renewal of the flooring in 1911. In the south aisle the most conspicuous change is the memorial window to Hardy, inserted in 1930 and incorporating the passage from I Kings 19 alluded to in the poem 'Quid Hic Agis?'.

The chancel shows two important innovations: the memorial reredos given in in 1939 by Mrs Weber, and the organ presented in 1931 by Hardy's sister, Kate. The old musicians were first replaced by a barrel organ operated by Hardy's uncle, James, who continued in this role for forty years until he died at the task. The barrel organ was then replaced by a harmonium and lost sight of, though a similar instrument, in working order, stands in the Dorset County Museum. After the harmonium (played by James's daughter, Theresa) had been discarded in favour of the organ, it lay forgotten in the vicarage loft until the late 1960s, when it was rescued and taken home for resuscitation by a resident of Lower Bockhampton. The museum also contains examples of the home-made instruments used by the 'Mellstock'-type musicians, and copies of their hand-written music.

A number of other alterations were made, mostly in 1911, but all to features not referred to in Hardy's work. His only other allusion in print to an interior feature is to one that never existed. In *Under the Greenwood Tree* he writes of the 'little world of undertones and creaks from the halting clockwork, which never spread further than the tower they were born in'. In reality the church never had a built-in clock, and if Hardy was basing his statement on fact he must have been referring to some movable timepiece that possibly stood or hung at the back of the gallery.

The churchyard receives frequent mention in his poems, including several that do not specify it by name. On entering through the gateway still adorned with the absurdly large urns (sketched by him for the first edition of *Wessex Poems*) the first thing that takes the eye is the row of Hardy graves, and in particular that which, because it contains Hardy's heart (unless we accept the story that this was eaten by the surgeon's cat), was brightened up for the 1968 Festival to outshine those of his relatives in a way that would have annoyed him beyond measure. The festival organisers would have done better to have restored the fast-vanishing lettering on the many gravestones referred to in 'Voices from Things Growing in a Churchyard' and several other poems.

The two yew trees cited by Dairyman Crick to indicate the grave of William Dewy are still there, though not much ivy now covers 'the wall that the ivies bind' ('The Dead Quire'). The whole of this last poem can be followed on the ground. The 'dormered inn' where the revels were being held is said to have been the southernmost cottage on the east side of Lower Bockhampton's 'Lower Mellstock's') main street, close to the bridge. No vestiges of an inn are traceable in this now skilfully restored house, although there are plenty of signs that it used to be a smithy; nor does the existence of an inn here appear among the records. However, it may have been an unregistered beerhouse—blacksmiths often ran these—in which illicit drinking on the premises took place (did it perhaps give Hardy his cue for 'Rolliver's' in *Tess of the D'Urbervilles*?), or Hardy could simply have 'promoted' it. The same cottage seems to have served him for Mop Ollamoor's home in 'The Fiddler of the Reels'.

The pursuers of the ghostly music followed it across the bridge —unaltered save for the tarmac on the roadway—and turned through the 'Bank-walk wicket, brightly bleached' along the Frome path ' 'twixt the hedges twain'. This path, still a favourite walk, is entered now through an opening in a short length of tubular steel railings set in white wooden posts. The 'hedges twain' have become ragged and gapped, while in contrast there is a far greater number of large trees. In this age of polluted streams the 'crystal Froom' still 'crinkles' on both sides of the path. The northern arm borders the grounds of Kingston Maurward ('Knapwater') House, and it is not difficult to visualise Edward and Cytherea, in *Desperate Remedies*, seeing one another's reflections in the clear, shallow water before they clasped hands across it in melancholy farewell. At the 'bottom of Church Lane' the spectral 'quire' turned to go up 'Moaning Hill' to the churchyard. Church Lane is a widish, gravelled way (once wider still) connecting the Frome path with the church, and 'Moaning Hill' is Hardy's name for the area on the right of the ascending lane, where the tall trees inside Kingston Maurward grounds catch the winds blowing across the Frome valley.

Near the top of Church Lane a gate on the east side opens into a small secluded burial ground, the Cecil Hanbury Memorial Garden cemetery. The Hanburys were the last private owners of Kingston Maurward House; the poem 'To C.F.H.' was written for Cecil Hanbury's daughter Caroline. Just beyond this quiet place is Stinsford vicarage, Parson Maybold's home, externally plain but with rather a charming interior. The short drive and circular turning-space in front of the house are still enclosed by a shrubbery, as in Maybold's day.

The brief hill leading north from the church opens into one of the most prominent roads in Hardy's pages, the Stinsford–Wareham ('Anglebury') road through Tincleton ('Stickleford'). This—the scene, with Stinsford Hill, of 'Your Last Drive'—is today a smooth, tarred thoroughfare, the Stinsford sector of it bounded by orderly hedges. But well within living memory it was white, rough, and rutted, and bordered by trees close and thick enough to give the name of Dark Hill (still sometimes used) to the part between the church turning and Bockhampton Cross. The church lane itself is described by Harper (1904) as overhung by enough trees to cause 'a midday twilight'. The description in the opening chapter of *Under the Greenwood Tree*, therefore, is correct, and remained so for many years. The trees were cleared only when it became essential to improve visibility for motorists; some of the trunks are still lying behind the hedges.

Between the church turning and the Cross is the entrance to Kingston Maurward Park, in which stand Kingston Maurward House and its predecessor, the Old Manor. Hardy knew Kingston Maurward House very well from early childhood through his 'romance' with its chatelaine, Mrs Martin. His failure to describe the interior in *Desperate Remedies* is consequently not due to lack of knowledge; indeed, some see certain of Kingston's internal features in Encombe ('Enkworth') House in *The Hand of Ethelberta* (see page 178). His enforced separation from Mrs Martin is the theme of 'In Her Precincts', but again the interior is not pictured. The harvest supper that saw their reconciliation provided the factual material, even to the presence of the soldiers, for the harvest supper in *Far from the Madding Crowd*; and it inspired the poem 'The Harvest Supper' as well as Hardy's various laments for the passing of the old country songs. The barn that was the scene of the real supper (as

distinct from the barn described in the novel, for which see page
129) is still standing, just to the north of the Old Manor: not by
any means one of the more beautiful of its kind, but in good
repair.

The main entrance to the park is still through gates beside a
lodge, but bronze bitterns no longer perch on the piers. The drive,
now tarred, crosses grounds that fully match Hardy's description.
The northern part of the park is Kingston Maurward Eweleaze,
the roadside fringe of which is now occupied by a group of
workers' cottages. Near the house there are one or two pre-
fabricated buildings, discreetly sited.

In spite of the chequered recent history of the house—occupied
during World War II by the army, then sold by the Hanburys in
1948 to Dorset County Council which transformed it into the
Dorset Farm Institute—it has not changed externally to any
degree since Miss Aldclyffe was its fictional chatelaine in *Desperate
Remedies*. Most of the ancillary buildings alluded to in the novel
have also survived reasonably intact, even if their functions have
changed. The grounds and lake, after deteriorating progressively
during the present century, were given a gratifying clean-up when
it was decided to make them one of the focal points of the 1968
Hardy Festival, and there was boating again. The Georgian temple
('the Fane') was restored at the same time.

That it is not possible to follow Miss Aldclyffe's route from
the new manor to the old is due to Hardy's licence in describing
it rather than to change. The waterfall that was 'enough to drive
anybody mad' in the Old Manor is an inoffensive cascade, even
now that weed and other obstructions have ceased to hinder its
flow. The other source of auditory vexation, the water pump,
was modernised in 1925 and abandoned on the introduction of
mains water after the council purchase of 1948. But the pump-
house and some of the machinery, original as well as of 1925, is
still to be seen.

Until a few years ago the Old Manor remained in every respect
as dilapidated as Hardy indicated. Becoming successively a home
for poor widows, a World War II evacuation centre, and a nest
for squatters, it was saved from demolition only by public
agitation and the intervention of a purchaser pledged to restore
it, which he did, in somewhat controversial style, in time for the

1968 festival. Beatty argues that the architecture of the fictional building more nearly resembles the probable design of old Clyffe House (demolished 1842) at Tincleton. One may note the name Ald*clyffe*, and certainly no 'old arched gateway with its flanking tower-bases' ever stood 'ten or twenty yards' from the Kingston mansion. But the *history* of Hardy's manor, the division into cottages, the debasing of the fine windows (now restored) and the use of the top floor (still a single huge attic) as a warehouse, is unquestionably that of Kingston.

East of the Old Manor, and of the large walled garden now used as a horticultural demonstration area for the Farm Institute students, is an old stone cottage, the 'Peakhill Cottage' in which Adelaide Hinton lived. Pleasantly restored and modernised, it has risen in status since Lea wrote that it had 'little else to commend it' but the thatch. A long drive connects the cottage with the main street of Lower Bockhampton. There is also a backdrive from the park into this street. At the junction of street and drive stands the former school built at the instance of Mrs Martin, attended

MELLSTOCK—THE VILLAGE SCHOOL

for one year by the eight-year-old Hardy, and enshrined in due course in his fiction as the academy at which Fancy Day taught. Also the subject of the poem 'He Revisits His First School', it has now undergone some modification to turn it into a private residence, but the school bell still hangs over the porch, and the windows with high sills of Ham Hill stone, on one of which Fancy Day sat to look out across the little green patch called the Grove, have survived, as has the Grove itself.

South of the Grove stands a long, low building, Riverside House, at right angles to the village street. Lea gives this as Farmer Shiner's house in *Under the Greenwood Tree*. Hardy's description runs:

> Farmer Shiner's was a queer lump of a house, standing at the corner of a lane that ran into the principal thoroughfare. The upper windows were much wider than they were high, and this feature, together with a broad bay window where the door might have been expected, gave it the aspect of a human countenance turned askance, and wearing a sly and wicked leer.

Beatty terms this 'Hardy's propensity for distortion'. Riverside House was never at the corner of a lane, has original upper windows that are higher than wide (see Hardy's sketch in the County Museum), shows no ground-floor bay nor trace of one, and is unlikely to strike many people as sly, wicked, or a queer lump. But in the small area between it and the still extant withy bed by the Frome there was once a lane, a short cul-de-sac not displayed on early printed maps, but unmistakable on an undated MS estate map in the country archives. The sketch based on this map and reproduced here shows that where the lane left the 'main thoroughfare' it had a house at either corner, the more northerly being quite distinct from the present so-called Shiner residence, which is seen between it and the school.

What sort of houses were they along this lane? The last buildings hereabouts were two or three brick cottages, not long demolished; but in *The Life* Hardy notes that the area used to contain 'several old Elizabethan houses, with mullioned windows and doors, of Ham Hill stone. They stood by the withy bed'. They were pulled down by Morton Pitt, of Kingston Maurward—some before Hardy's birth, but others long enough afterwards for him to recall their appearance. Was it in one of these at the corner of the lane (which probably vanished when they did) that Hardy installed his peppery farmer? He can hardly have failed to remember that some of them still existed at the time of the story.

The southern end of the village, still containing the thatched post office (said by Bailey to be the post office in the poem 'The Thing Unplanned') and many mellow old cottages, mostly thatched, must

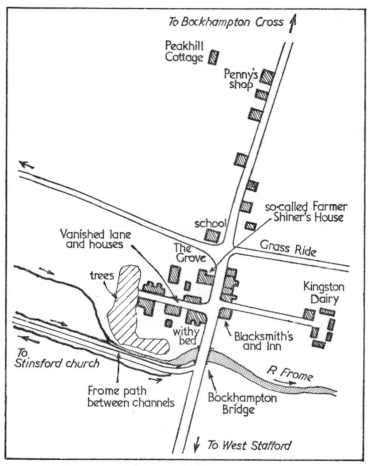

Lower Bockhampton. The vanished lane and stone houses, one of which may have been the model for Farmer Shiner's. From a MS estate map

look much as Hardy knew it in later life if not at the time of
'The Passer-by'. Farther north various unsuitable new villas and
bungalows wreck the harmony. 'Martins', the best of the new
houses, stands on the site of Robert Penny's boot emporium—
the probable scene, according to Bailey, of 'The Night of the
Dance'. There is a pretty sketch of the shop—its real owner was
Robert Reason—in the County Museum. After World War I a
memorial clubroom-cum-reading room was put up on the site,
and opened by Hardy himself. This later became redundant, and
was succeeded by 'Martins'.

Beyond Bockhampton Cross the road—the 'lane' of 'To Louisa
in the Lane'—shorn of its trees, continues toward Higher Bockhampton ('Upper Mellstock'). On the right is an elongated coppice of hardwoods, the Thorncombe Wood of the poem 'She
Hears the Storm'. The same poem mentions 'Mellstock Leaze'
(Stinsford Leaze, to the west of the lane). This is also the 'pasture'
of 'Her Immortality'. East of the lane, between it and Thorncombe
Wood, lies Middle Field, commemorated in 'At Middle-Field
Gate in February'. There is still a gate, though now a broad iron
one, leading from the lane.

At Higher Bockhampton a singularly vile untarred track
branches off toward Hardy's birthplace, which stands at the far
end, at right angles to the other houses. The Hardy house and
its next-door neighbour are all that is left of the original buildings
in the lane. The other cottages are brick replacements (and in
some instances replacements of replacements) of the old cob-and-
thatch structures there at the time of Hardy's birth, and pulled
down as the lifeholds fell in. The cherry trees that once lined the
route have also gone, but the well from which the community
drew its water—mentioned in the story 'Enter a Dragoon'—
survives, with part of its superstructure. It stands about halfway
down the lane, adjoining the roadway in the grounds of a house
called Greenwood.

The Hardy house never had a name, though as the Dewys'
house in *Under the Greenwood Tree* Hardy called it 'Lewgate', a
title that also crops up in *A Few Crusted Characters*. The Dewys,
in fact, were modelled on the Dart family who lived in the house
already mentioned, at right angles to the Hardys'. This, formerly
subdivided into several cottages, is a place of many dormers, as

age 49 Casterbridge: (*above*) Damer's Road Hospital, once the Union or workhouse.
ere Fanny Robin died, and the subject of the poem 'The Curate's Kindness' was
smayed to find that he would remain united with his wife; (*below*) Henchard's granary,
reality a brewhouse at the time and now part of a printing works. The loft door (long
led in) beside which Henchard fought Farfrae is discernible on the right, between the
arest top window and the drainpipe. The windows and door in the front wall are
cent modifications

Page 50 (*left*) Casterbridge: Colliton Walk, the 'Chalk Walk' of *The Mayor of Casterbridge*, looking toward Top o' Town. Inside the wall on the left are the grounds of Colliton House

(*right*) Shaston: Old-Grove's Place, the temporary home of Richard and Sue Phillotson, now once more known by its correct name, The Ox House. The rendering of the upper storey is part of the modernisation

may be seen in a watercolour that hangs in the hallway of the Dorset County Museum. It has now been given a new porch and metal casements.

Hardy's home, as he recorded in his 'Notebooks', was used as a change-over point in the northward conveyance of smugglers' goods. There is a tiny window in the porch said to have been inserted for the purpose of watching for excise officers. Once certain deliberately misleading phrases in the first edition of *Under the Greenwood Tree* had been amended, the description of the Dewys' home became a faithful portrait of the Hardys' house as Hardy knew it in childhood. In less detail, it appears in several other works. Pinion argues that it is the 'cottage-residence' of 'Enter a Dragoon'; the description in the story does not entirely fit, but this could be another instance of deliberate disguise. The house also figures, anonymously, in a crop of poems, including 'On One who Lived and Died where he was Born' (Hardy's father), 'The Alarm' (about his grandfather), 'The Self-Unseeing', 'Concerning his Old Home', and—quoted in *The Life* but not included in the *Collected Poems*—'Domicilium'.

From 1913 to 1921 this was the home of Hermann Lea, who assented to Hardy's request and somewhat disguised the house in his Wessex volume as Hardy had done in the earlier version of *Under the Greenwood Tree*. In his closing years Hardy was distressed by the shabbiness of the house, but since 1948 house and garden have been National Trust property and excellently tended.

There have been changes since the days of Dick Dewy, of which the more important are that the cob walls are now protected by bricks or cement, the parlour chimney has lost the bread oven and inglenook-seat it had when the Dewys held their Christmas party, and the central staircase has been removed, involving also the removal of the cache for smuggled liquor. Outside, the stables have been pulled down and the small orchard abandoned, together with some of the garden. In 1969 there was a project to restore the original appearance of the house, but nothing came of it.

On every side except that of the lane the cottage and garden are bounded by the trees of present-day 'Egdon Heath'. This part of the heath was in fact always well-wooded, the trees formerly encroaching more upon the house than they do now:

D

It faces west, and round the back and sides
High beeches, bending, hang a veil of boughs.

Near the back of the building a granite monument to Hardy was
set up in 1931 by 'a few of his American admirers'.

At the other (Bockhampton Lane) end of the miserable track
stood Elizabeth Enderfield's cottage, one of those later pulled
down and not replaced. The northern part of Bockhampton Lane,
between this point and what is now the A35, retains its old name
of Cuckoo Lane. Like the southern part, however, it is a good
deal less leafy than when Fancy encountered Dick upon it, the
big hedgerows having been much reduced to improve visibility.
Close to where the roads meet, a footpath which leads directly
over the hill from Hardy's cottage also debouches into the A35
and continues on the north side flanked by a long, narrow wood.
This is Grey's Wood, and the path is the Snail-Creep alluded to
in *Under the Greenwood Tree*. Like its larger neighbour Yellowham
('Yell'ham', 'Yalbury', 'Great Yalbury') Wood (see page 63),
Grey's Wood consists of mixed timber, and can have changed
little since Dick went nutting there. North of it Stinsford parish
extends as far as Waterston ('Climmerston') Ridge, thus including
much of Slyre, Slyre's or Slyer's Lane. The latter turns off the
A35 a few hundred yards east of Grey's Bridge, and is the route
by which Carrier Burthen conveyed his passengers in *A Few
Crusted Characters* to Piddletrenthide ('Upper Longpuddle').

The Hardcomes, whose sad fate was recalled by one of the
storytellers, lived at 'Climmerston', and past 'Climmerston Ridge'
the sporting Parson Toogood and his clerk followed the hunt.
The 'rugged ridge of Waterston' and the 'grey, gaunt, lonely lane
of Slyre' lay also on the cavalryman's route in 'The Revisitation'.
The description of Slyre Lane still fits. Almost devoid of bordering trees or houses, its tarred surface now makes it literally grey,
and only the grid wires crossing it strike a modern note.

Waterston Ridge is similarly devoid of buildings, most of this
stretch of the Ridgeway consisting of a grass ride between
hedges that in parts nearly choke it. The 'Sarsen stone' of 'The
Revisitation', alongside the Ridgeway half a mile east of Slyre's
Lane, is in reality a rough slab of naturally fused flints from which
the surrounding chalk has been washed away.

In the western angle formed by the lane and the A35 stood the turnpike house to which the coachman drove after his vain wait on Stinsford Hill for Lieutenant Vannicock and Laura Maumbry; the traces of its garden are just discernible. All along the A35 hereabouts (extending further on the south side) straggle, battered and bent, the iron railings by which Fanny Robin supported herself on her journey to the Union. Nearly opposite Slyre Lane they are interrupted by a kissing-gate, the first of the succession in 'The Third Kissing-Gate'. The topography of this poem is hard to follow, for there were in fact four gates, of which the second also survives. The 'gray garden wall' (actually lichen-covered red brick) belongs to Stinsford House, and fringes the path (with the stream in between) before the last gate is reached. Close to this gate was the 'waterfall', formed by the descent of the stream over a low stone ledge before it entered a culvert under the foot of Church Lane (page 42). Ledge and culvert are still there, but except in spate the water now passes through a newer culvert alongside. The path, which remains in regular use, is also the one by which the fleeing Manston in *Desperate Remedies* made his way to Tolpuddle ('Tolchurch').

To the east, where the A35 climbs out of the Frome valley toward Yellowham, it becomes Stinsford ('Mellstock') Hill. Wider and busier now, with a parking-bay and stone-built conveniences at its summit, it is in other respects still the green-verged, unbuilt-on slope with 'high-banked hedges' (*The Mayor of Casterbridge*) where the narrator in 'On Stinsford Hill at Midnight' encountered the strange singer, and Hardy had his blood-chilling vision of the two unknown men seated on chairs as recalled in *The Life*. Not far from where the Tincleton road forks off, standing in the bank as Hardy states, is the first milestone out of Dorchester, on which the defeated Henchard rested his basket at the beginning of his retreat.

The 'lone copsewood' that Fanny entered in order to make herself a pair of crutches was either some small wood that has vanished or the copse still adjoining Birkin House. Before this she had paused to rest against the second milestone from the town, now, like the first, restored to its proper place after both had spent World War II lying discreetly buried under the turf.

SOUTH WESSEX: *Egdon Heath*
(Dorset: the heath)

. . . The outlook, lone and bare,
The towering hawk and passing raven share,
And all the upland round is called 'The He'th'.

BY THE BARROWS

'Egdon Heath' is such a useful collective name for the multitude of heaths between Stinsford and Bournemouth that one forgets it is only a Hardy coinage. 'Egdon' was never the huge, wild moor that he depicted, and the dual encroachment of cultivation and building has since reduced it, while the Forestry Commission has changed its appearance and many of its paths and tracks, though not altogether its character. When the implements of the foresters are stilled and dusk creeps over the plantations, the atmosphere is not very different from that conjured up in *The Return of the Native*, and the heath suddenly seems as vast as Hardy drew it.

There are still unforested tracts (on the western flank, for instance), covered only by heather, bracken, and—a new feature since the novels—rhododendron groves. Except for the wild ponies, the 'heath-croppers', all the Egdon fauna mentioned by Hardy survive, with the addition of deer. The human population, if we discount the areas lost to town-spread or military camp, is actually less. Not only have nearly all the isolated cottages and groups of dwellings such as 'Mistover Knap' disappeared, but many of the heathside villages have shrunk. The population of Puddletown ('Weatherbury') at the 1961 census was 795; at the time of *Far from the Madding Crowd* it was around 1,250. It is now growing again, but it is still well below its zenith.

After his own birthplace, the feature of the heath made most famous by Hardy is 'Rainbarrow'—properly Rainbarrows: *The Dynasts* refers to three tumuli. It is often said that in *The Return* Hardy moved 'Rainbarrow' much nearer the centre of 'Egdon'. A careful reading of the novel does reveal a modest shift eastward, but not nearly as much as is suggested. The path down to the 'Quiet Woman' (the Traveller's Rest, now Duck Dairy Farm), followed by Olly Dowden and Mrs Yeobright in the opening scene, has no factual basis according to the maps of the period, which show the only path to emerge near the inn running well *west* of the barrows, even in their true position. Bracken-covered and hollowed into a cup at the top, the larger of the two tumuli now visible supports a hollybush on its western rim, with another growing near its base.

If one stands hereabouts and looks south of west, the declivity is seen to form one side of a broad valley opening out to the left, its farther, much lower, side bounded by Thorncombe Wood and the meadows of Stinsford. This is the vale Hardy called 'Blooms-End'. About 600 yards to the north-west, at the head of the valley, is a small round pool, Rushy Pond, near which, in 'The Paphian Ball', the Mellstock quire met the Devil, and which is the subject

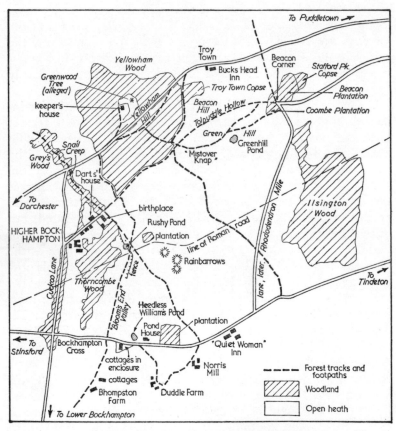

'Egdon Heath' in the nineteenth century

of another poem, 'At Rushy Pond'. The poem, 'I Said and Sang her Excellence' bears the words 'At Rushy-Pond' at its foot. Here, too, Gertrude in *The Withered Arm* paused on her macabre ride to the hangman's cottage, and it is in this tale that the pond is said to be bisected by a railing linking the ends of two hedges. Old maps bear out the truth of the description, though no trace of hedge or fence remains.

Farther down 'Blooms-End' valley the scrub and rhododendrons give way to cultivated pasture, except on the east flank, and the pasture continues south of the Dorchester–Tincleton road until it merges into the Frome meads between Bhompston Farm and Duddle Farm. In the field immediately north of the road lies a large irregular pool, much encroached upon by undergrowth and rushes, but retaining enough clear water to support a few ducks. Here, many years ago, a drunken mail-van driver ran off the highway (not hedged then), overturned his vehicle, and was drowned, thus achieving immortality for his name in Heedless William's Pond. Hardy mentions it only once, in 'The Fiddler of the Reels', calling it 'the familiar landmark by Bloom's End' (*sic*); but in 'A Tragedy of Two Ambitions' he turned to account the legend that William's whip stuck in the ground, took root and became an ash tree. Today an old ash stump and several younger ashes border the pool.

In *The Return* the precise position of 'Blooms-End' *house* is never given, beyond a single reference to 'near Egdon Bottom'. In a letter to the Reverend Perkins Hardy identified it with 'vague recollections of Bhompston farmhouse', though 'the position was a little shifted'. Both Windle and Harper assert that 'Blooms-End' stood where there is now a bungalow just east of Heedless William's Pond, thus bearing out the observation in 'The Fiddler'. Hardy's own map for *The Return* appears to identify the site with his birthplace, a fact into which Millgate reads biographical implications.

The three paths said to radiate from Clym Yeobright's home are not necessarily a close record of fact, and can be visualised in conjunction with all three sites. Thomasin's walk to the 'Quiet Woman', on the other hand, by 'ascending Blooms-End valley and traversing the undulations on the side of the hill', makes little sense whichever point she starts from, birthplace included. Possibly Hardy anticipated here the technique he was to use in *The Wood-*

landers and *Two on a Tower*, writing sometimes with one site in mind, sometimes another.

Pond House, the building where the bungalow now stands, was burnt down early in this century, and although there are still people alive who remember it, the only clue they can furnish as to its layout is that it was spacious and rambling. At Bhompston a new farmhouse was built in about 1934 and the old one converted into two cottages, one of which continued to be occupied until 1968. Thereafter a threat arose that the house would be condemned and demolished, but at present it still stands—and deteriorates. Its features are on the whole consistent with the fragmentary description of 'Blooms-End'. White iron railings bounded the garden until wrecked some years ago by an ineptly felled beech tree. The roof is of slate, but could originally have been thatched. Similarly the walls may easily have been white. The outside door does open into a low-pitched room (the kitchen), which does have a pantry leading off it, a large hearth, and a slightly sunken floor.

There is an interesting allusion to 'Blooms-End' in the poem 'In Weatherbury Stocks', when the youth in the stocks is told that his girl has 'gone to Blooms-End dance'. Both Pond House and Bhompston lay beyond the high heath from 'Weatherbury'. Which, one wonders, had dancing of enough renown to take the girl there? In either case the satellite cottages must have been those that belonged to Bhompston and lay between the two houses. One pair of these survives, halfway down the slope from the Tincleton road, near a newer pair built in the 1930s. Another pair, gone now, used to stand in a small enclosure just south of the road (see map, page 58). One of these was perhaps Fairway's, which had beside it 'an open space recessed from the road'.

Duck Dairy Farm (or Dairy House), Hardy's 'Quiet Woman', was originally the Traveller's Rest—mentioned as such in the poem 'The Weathers'—and later became the Duck. Most of the old buildings were pulled down and a new farmhouse erected, in the 1930s. Only one or two outhouses survive, and none of the old inn trappings. Nor can 'Wildeve's Patch' be traced, for the heath, which formerly extended a short way south of the Tincleton road at this point, has now been pushed back a meadow's depth to the north of it. A footnote in *The Return of the Native* tells us that the real Quiet Woman lay 'some miles to the north-west'—in fact at

Halstock, where it still flourishes, adorned with a modern sign faithfully bearing out Hardy's description. The same footnote states that the fictional 'Quiet Woman' was partly modelled on the Red Lion at Winfrith. Some years ago a fire so severely damaged the Red Lion that in its new and enlarged form only one or two un- expectedly thick internal walls—the old outer walls—are left of the building known to Hardy.

A quarter of a mile east of Duck Dairy Farm a branch lane leads north-east to Puddletown. Since the era of Hardy's prose writings, more than a mile at the southern (Tincleton road) end of the lane has been bordered on both sides with rhododendrons. At this end, in its pre-floral days, first Wildeve and then Venn saw the carriage containing Clym and Eustacia pass, for the road forms the lower part of the route that 'ascended to Mistover by a circuitous and easy incline' and was the only approach to the Vyes' home suitable for vehicles.

The 'easy incline' is not continuous, the early part of it being broken by a number of dips, the first of which is the 'Draats'- Hollow' of the poem 'The Sheep Boy'. Properly called Draats (pronounced Drahts) Bottom, the shallow depression extends for some distance west of the road through what is now the forest. North of the rhododendron avenue the lane bends west, then at Beacon Corner turns sharply east, making for Puddletown. The sharp turn really constitutes two arms of a cross, the other arms being unmetalled tracks. The westward track ascends a shallow vale called Tolpuddle Hollow, between Beacon Hill and Green Hill, until these unite to terminate it. The tableland thus formed is 'Mistover Knap'. To reach the Vyes' home it was probably neces- sary to fork left again a short way from Beacon Corner, on to a track still extant over the summit of Green Hill. Beside the track lies a circular pond of clear black water, out of which grows, in summer, brilliant green vegetation. This is Green Hill or Greenhill Pond, the original of the 'large pool' by Captain Vye's cottage. Rushy Pond and even Heedless William's Pond have been named as the prototypes of this famous spot; but Heedless William is not even on Egdon Heath, and Rushy is too far west. To the watchers at the 'Quiet Woman' Eustacia's signal fire on the bank by the pool ap- peared to the *right* of 'Rainbarrow'. A fire near Rushy Pond would have been visible, if at all, to the *left*, even without allowance for

Hardy's eastward shift of the barrow. Lea, though not naming Green Hill, says the Vyes' pool lay north of 'Rainbarrow'. Afforestation eliminated a number of ponds on the heath, but Green Hill was always the only large one, and the only one with vehicular access.

The 'two converging bank fences', like the house itself, have disappeared, probably when the Forestry Commission prepared the area for the conifers that now cover it. Gone too is the ruined brick-kiln noted by Lea; and understandably the heather has been replaced by bracken and pine needles.

New's small sketch shows 'Mistover Knap' with fir trees on the skyline at the head of an irregular valley. This view, like the reverse one several times mentioned in *The Return*, is unobtainable today because of the afforestation. The trees shown in the sketch were there before the Forestry Commission took over, and according to Lea they perished in a fire. Another disappearance is that of the 'very curious Druidical stone' that Clym told Eustacia about, and which is mentioned in Llewellyn Powys's *Dorset Essays*. Powys quotes an elderly relative of Hardy's as stating that the 'huge monolith' stood in the bracken not far from Hardy's birthplace, and was much beloved of him as a child. Its long existence ended when it was smashed up for building-stone by some vandal.

'Mistover Knap' also figures in 'The Fiddler of the Reels', where its firwoods are described as 'backed by the Yalbury coppices'. The 'Yalbury coppices', otherwise 'Great Yalbury Wood' or Yellowham Wood, formerly extended farther south of that part of the Dorchester–Puddletown road known as Yellowham ('Yalbury') Hill. Over this rise Dick Dewy, Fancy Day and the rest of the party walked on the way to the wedding, which was not at Stinsford but at Puddletown (here called 'Lower Longpuddle', but see page 64), Keeper Day's house being just over the parish border. Here too Fanny Robin on her last journey met Bathsheba and Frank Troy; and at the foot of the hill, Yellowham Bottom or Plain (haunt of the ghost in 'Wessex Heights') Henchard met Farfrae after running to tell him of the 'skimmety-ride'.

At least four poems allude to Yellowham Hill: 'The Comet at Yellowham', 'Old Excursions', 'Ice on the Highway', and the delightful 'The Milestone by the Rabbit-burrow'. This last refers to the third milestone out of Dorchester, near the foot of the western slope. The milestone, like its fellows, was buried in 1940, but unlike them was never dug up, and there is now no official record of its whereabouts. Unofficially, however, the burial was watched by the occupant of 'Keeper Day's Cottage', who maintains that he could still point to the exact spot.

Strictly speaking, most of Yellowham Wood is not part of Egdon Heath at all, but it has far greater affinities with the heath than with the country to the north of it. It figures in fewer poems than the hill, but is much more prominent in the novels and stories, especially, of course, in *Under the Greenwood Tree*. Yellowham remains a wood of pleasantly mixed timber, still conforming to Hardy's description of it as the route of the wedding party; the 'dark perpendicular firs' are also the 'Yell'ham-Firs' of the poem 'The Mother Mourns'. There are still foxes about, as in *Under the Greenwood Tree*, and pheasants, as mentioned in *Far from the Madding Crowd*.

The one house in the wood is that of 'Keeper Day', in real life he was Keeper Browne; his daughter Elizabeth was the young woman of the poem 'To Lizbie Browne'. I found the house less altered than implied by Lea. It stands precisely where Hardy indicates; the front window is still set with thickly leaded diamond glazing, in which one can detect a number of the original thin bottle-glass panes. Inside, the window-bench has been removed. The 'huge inglenooks' and the little window in the chimney-back, on the other hand, are not to be seen because they never existed. The ceilings are beamed. A lean-to extension has been built on, but otherwise the house has scarcely been altered. There is still a side-wicket to the garden, and a flourishing piggery.

Finally, the Greenwood Tree itself, after another century and a quarter, still flourishes—or so one is assured. Hardy refers to it as 'already ancient' and 'horizontally of enormous extent', and pictures it surrounded by a 'carefully-tended grass plot'. Today the tree pointed out is all but invisible amid the bushes and other trees that have grown up over the 'grass plot' about it. What can be described certainly does not suggest a magnificent, or even once-magnificent, veteran. But the tenant of the cottage maintains that this is the tree indicated to him by Thomas Hardy himself, long years ago: an authority not lightly to be challenged.

Less than half a mile from the eastern fringe of Yellowham

Wood, on the main road, lie a farmhouse and its attendant build-ings. These are the modern representatives of Troy Town ('Roy Town'), site of the Buck's Head in *Far from the Madding Crowd* and 'The Waiting Supper'. Once an important coaching stage, the inn's decline was piecemeal. When Nicholas Long in 'The Waiting Supper' stayed there it was 'rather cavernous and chilly', the stable-roofs were 'hollow-backed', and the traffic had gone. When Joseph Poorgrass met Jan Coggan and Mark Clark there the old stabling had been pulled down, and 'little remained besides the habitable inn itself. Harper, writing in 1904, describes the place as not yet pulled down but no longer an inn. And Lea (1913) says it was pulled down a few years previously. It stood on the opposite side of the high road to the present farm. One rather nondescript building still on the site is said to have belonged to it; the cottages nearby were built later.

A mile east of Troy Town the Wareham and Blandford roads part company, and here is Puddletown, the 'Weatherbury' of *Far from the Madding Crowd*. Pinion, evidently relying on a phrase in the novel (last paragraph of Chapter 7) and a reference in *Under the Greenwood Tree*, asserts that Puddletown is also 'Lower Long-puddle', the villages of Piddletrenthide and Piddlehinton together forming 'Upper Longpuddle'. All other authorities identify Piddle-trenthide with 'Upper Longpuddle' and Piddlehinton with 'Lower'. Moreover, a study of the itinerary of Burthen's van and Tony Kytes's waggon in *A Few Crusted Characters*, virtually eliminates Puddletown (see page 125). The only credible explana-tion is that on adopting his standard nomenclature Hardy changed the identity of 'Lower Longpuddle', leaving Puddletown solely as 'Weatherbury'.

Puddletown church—scene of the poem 'The Christening'—is the best example in Wessex of a medieval church that, eluding for once the hand of the Victorian restorers, has retained its high box-pews, musicians' gallery, seventeenth-century wooden altar and altar rails, pulpit, prayer-desk, and fine old timbered roof. Not only did the old 'quire' sing and play in this gallery, but the modern choir still sings there. The battered alabaster effigy in the poem 'The Children and Sir Nameless' commemorated one of the Mar-tyns of Athelhampton ('Athelhall') who lie buried in the so-called Athelhampton chantry off the south aisle. Hardy probably had in mind Sir William, who is accoutred as described and has indeed lost his nose, as well as having initials scratched all over him. The effigy, now restored to its proper place on the tomb, measures nearly seven feet in length.

Outside the church, there is really nothing exceptional about the 'gurgoyles' on the tower; Beatty suggests that Hardy had in mind the gargoyle at the south-east corner of the south aisle of Stinsford church. As though consequent on the flooding of Fanny's flowers, one Puddletown gargoyle is now prevented by a piece of piping from baptising those passing beneath. Inside the north porch is a built-in bench old enough to be that on which Troy passed his uncomfortable night.

There have been some alterations to the fabric since the *Madding Crowd* period, mainly to roofs and ceilings. The present organ was installed in 1906 (New's sketch shows the old one), the chancel was restored and enlarged in 1911, and the pews were renovated in 1966 and later. Less happily, the remarkable triangular-faced clock with its rich chimes, made by the Puddletown blacksmith in 1710, was removed from the tower in about 1865 and disappeared: just why, no one seems to have recorded. This must have been the clock that 'moaned eleven' in the poem 'In Weatherbury Stocks', below the title of which appears the date 1850. The stocks themselves have vanished. Whether the clock was still in place at the time covered by the novel depends on one's estimate of when that time was. Weber assigns the action to the four years 1869–73. The Rev O. D. Harvey's able booklet, on the other hand, which devotes a good deal of attention to Hardy, calls the novel 'a story of the 1840s and 50s'. Mr Harvey is supported by Hardy's preface and by the description of Waterston Manor (page 120), which is depicted as it was before the serious fire of 1863.

Puddletown was extensively rebuilt from 1864 onward, but since the novel supplies no details of any building except the church and 'Warren's Malthouse' little light is shed on dates. The malthouse, which flourished until about 1875, stood some way north of Back Street; one or two lengths of its red brick walls can still be seen. Much more complete is the old mill, which even retains the mill-wheel, now dry, down which the water dribbled in the poem 'At the Mill'. Just below the wheel the water entered a culvert, to emerge again as a shallow drinking-pool, before another culvert carried the stream under Mill Street. The pool was the Mill-tail Shallow of the poem 'The Country Wedding', and like the rest of the millstream it is now dry, though the culverts remain. Four cottages formerly bordered this side of Mill Street, and their gardens, between the road and the mill—now a barn—continue to be tended. But the 'door by the shallow' was probably that of the nearer of two cottages (since replaced) north of the millstream— the birthplace of Tryphena Sparks. Near by, Styles Lane and Front Street, along which the wedding procession marched, retain their names and most of their 1864-period houses.

The gate by which Bathsheba Everdene entered the churchyard is still there, surmounted now by a World War I memorial in the form of a wrought-iron arch and lantern. 'Behind church' referred to the opposite (south) side of the churchyard, but the position of the 'reprobates' ' burial area is today unknown. Gabriel Oak met Fanny Robin beside the graveyard wall 'where several ancient yew trees grew' and there was a wide margin of grass. This must have been on either the south or east side, where the trees still include ancient yews. New's sketch suggests a grass verge along the south wall.

Is the door by which Troy said he attended services an invention? Many indications imply that it is. For one, Hardy is not consistent. Bathsheba tells Oak that Troy went in by the old tower door and thence up to the back of the gallery, yet to assess the truth of this Oak climbs some *external* steps and finds the door—evidently external also—overgrown with ivy. The 'old tower door' in Bathsheba's version is real and remains in use, and there is an archway, long boarded up, linking the tower with the back of the gallery. It is possible that a ladder was once set up in the ringing chamber to allow the bellringers to enter the gallery by the shortest route, but even if this arch had had a door to it such an internal feature would not have become sealed by ivy. Gabriel's version appears at first sight to be based even less on reality, since there is no official record of an outside stair or door, nor any trace of either unless we consider relevant the vestiges of two puzzling stone steps just inside the west window of the north aisle. However, this version receives unexpected support from Hardy's close friend and literary executor, the late Sir Sydney Cockerell, Curator of the Fitzwilliam Museum at Cambridge. Sir Sydney paid no fewer than

age 67 Egdon Heath: one of the few ponds to have survived the Forestry Com-
ssion's tree-planting. Greenhill Pond, beside which stood Captain Vye's cottage, is
another survivor, similar but rather larger

Page 68 (*above*) Weatherbury Upper Farm: the sheep-dip described in *Far from t Madding Crowd* has today lost its sluices but with improvised hatches it still serves tl tenant of Lower Waterston Farm; (*below*) Froom-Everard: in the grounds of Staffo House, the 'Froom-Everard Manor House' of 'The Waiting Supper', one arm of tl Frome still flows over the waterfall that plays so prominent a part in the tale

forty-two visits to Max Gate, and on one of them, according to his biographer Wilfrid Blunt, he called at Puddletown church with his host, who pointed out the window in the south (*sic*) aisle which had formerly furnished the access to the gallery used by Hardy for the Troy incident. This is the word of a reliable witness (even if we concede that he has confused south with north), and taken in conjunction with the two unexplained steps it does furnish a case for believing in a reality of some kind behind the Troy anecdote. Lea also asserts that the 'little gallery door' used by Troy was factual, and still to be seen on the west side of the tower; but he confuses his readers by referring them to a photograph of a door (which exists today) at the back of the nave, underneath the gallery and communicating with the tower through the latter's *east* wall.

Just before the Wimborne road (A35) leaves Puddletown, a lane turns off on the right toward Beacon Corner and the Rhodo-dendron Mile. Alongside this lane is the quarter where most of the new building has taken place, with a network of small new roads to serve it. Further west the lane passes through a deep cutting, beyond which a grassy hill on the right is the Kite Hill of 'The Sheep-Boy'. The poem 'In a Eweleaze near Weatherbury' probably refers to Coombe Eweleaze, south of the lane and now partly covered by the new houses. In former times it was a favourite area for outdoor revels. Coombe Eweleaze has also been suggested by some (Deacon and Coleman; Bailey) as the scene of the poem 'A Spot'. Half a mile to the west, in the south-west angle of the Beacon Corner cross-roads there stood, in pre-Forestry Commission days, a small grove of conifers, Coombe Plantation—the 'Coombe-Firtrees' of 'Yell'ham-Wood's Story'. It is now merged in the general afforestation.

Tincleton, the 'Stickleford' where Car'line Aspent lived ('The Fiddler of the Reels') and where Diggory Venn took a house, re-mains a simple village scattered round a rectangle of lanes, and today, with the shrinking of the heath, belongs more to the Frome valley. In the parish is Clyffe House, the grounds of which include Pallington Clump, the 'Clyffe-hill Clump' mentioned in 'Yell'ham-Wood's Story' and the 'Clyffe-Clump' of 'The Paphian Ball'. Its pines still form a landmark, especially from the Frome meads and the hills south of them.

North-west of Clyffe lies Athelhampton. In addition to its role

E

in 'The Children and Sir Nameless' and 'The Dame of Athelhall' it figures with some prominence in the prose tale 'The Waiting Supper'. The mansion lies north of the Puddletown–Wimborne road, in magnificent grounds that have changed a good deal since the period of the story, let alone the periods of the two poems, the layout of the gardens dating only from the late nineteenth century. Several branches of the Piddle pass through the flat vale north of Athelhampton—the 'Athel Coomb' through which the Dame made her ironical return.

The house itself, mainly Tudor, has been shorn of the portion containing the original gatehouse and experienced various internal alterations. The Great Hall still has its fine timbered roof and musicians' gallery (the latter with a new parapet and sundry changes to the back partition). There is, as Hardy asserted, a spiral staircase in the thickness of one of the walls, but it does not and never did give access to the gallery. (For the link between Athelhampton and 'Endelstow House' in *A Pair of Blue Eyes*, see pages 220, 246.)

To the east is Tolpuddle ('Tolchurch'), which appears briefly in *Desperate Remedies*. Beatty thinks the description of the church and its restoration is drawn from Turnworth, where Hardy himself supervised the work and may even be the 'clerk of the works' sent from Budmouth. But the *site* of the church in the novel is exactly that of Tolpuddle church. The young Grayes lived in 'one half of an old farmhouse' that stood near the church and apart from the 'body of cottages'. This building is still easily recognisable in the Manor House, the long roof-slope of which, on the rear or north side, may indeed once have extended as far as the ground. The house commands a view of at least 100 yards up the main road, and a good deal more of the lane to Affpuddle ('East Egdon').

In other respects Tolpuddle has changed a good deal, but Affpuddle, by contrast, remains tiny, sleepy, and unspoilt. Although its mellow old church is really too far to the east, Hardy treated it as the parish church for 'Mistover Knap'. The parish includes part of the area in which that enlightened industrialist Sir Ernest Debenham tried (and failed) to relieve the agricultural depression between the two world wars with a scheme for modernised farming, better housing for farm labourers, and much else. Many of his cottages and other buildings remain. The Debenham scheme also embraced Briantspuddle (or Bryants Puddle), the unnamed hamlet to which Damon Wildeve went to look for a constable after he had been shot at. Sir Ernest restored much of the old village and doubled its extent with new-built thatched cottages.

Half a mile to the south of Briantspuddle, in a part of the heath displaying much afforestation, an oblong and solitary cottage lies in a dip so abrupt that its roof is on a level with the roadway near by. Rendering and recent retiling belie the age of Brickyard Cottage; but in fact it is of considerable antiquity, the rendering concealing cob above a few lower courses of brick, and the upper windows being of a wooden, many-paned design long since discarded. Inside, the trim parlour shows further evidence of age, although the bread-oven has been filled in. The cottage is 'Alderworth', the marital home of Clym and Eustacia.

Many of the firs that clothe the high ground round the house are recognisably older than the Forestry Commission trees, and there is no mistaking the 'singularly battered, rude, and wild' Devil's Bellows. A few hundred yards away lies Rimsmoor Pond, which young Jimmy Nonsuch said was dry when Clym's mother asked him for water. The other pond that he said was never dry, 'Oker's Pool', does not appear on any map, but may be an allusion to the reservoir, fed by pipes from a distant source, that was installed in 1843 at Oaker's Wood House and (with the substitution of plastic pipes) is still in use. Early maps show a tiny pond across the road east of 'Alderworth', two more at the former brickworks 150 yards down the road, and yet another 550 yards south-east of Rimsmoor Pond; but none of these is near enough to Oaker's (or Oker's) Wood to warrant the assumption that it shared the name.

The Wood itself, a tract of mixed timber contiguous to, but much older than, the Commission's conifer plantations, is the 'fir and beech plantation' alluded to in the description of 'Alderworth', and is also the wood in Grandfather James's story, in *Under the Greenwood Tree*, about the bridegroom caught in the mantrap. Amid so many conifers the beeches now look especially handsome.

Throop ('Throope') Corner presents a problem, because it is given as the point to which Wildeve accompanied Eustacia after meeting her at the open-air dance; a 'short path branched off' to her house 'a few hundred yards' from the corner. The dance, how-ever, was at Affpuddle, and 'Alderworth' lies *between* there and Throop Corner.

The first great change in this part of 'Egdon Heath' came with the establishment of Bovington Camp (1916), barely two and a half miles south of 'Alderworth'. The camp itself is a square mile of unsightliness (making a very poor comparison with, say, Larkhill), and as the headquarters of the Armoured Corps it has been responsible for the despoliation of the heath over a wide area to north and east. However, if we are to have tanks, this is probably unavoidable; the effect is no worse than that of the huge gravel pits strung along the nearby Piddle valley.

Unlike the shapeless and conspicuous camp, the Atomic Energy Research Establishment on Winfrith Heath manages to hide its large and growing spread to a degree one might regard as impossible except in some fold of the hills. If its buildings suggest H. G. Wells rather than Thomas Hardy, the layout at least has design; and at night the constellation of bright lights, suddenly come upon, is not without beauty. On the north-west, west and south sides of the research establishment the heath and its villages remain up to now surprisingly little affected; Winfrith Newburgh village might never have heard of atomic energy. Only toward Wareham is the amount of new housing conspicuous, and here it is increasing rapidly. Hardy's poem 'The Slow Nature' tells us of a tragedy that occurred 'out by Moreford [Moreton] Rise'; in real life this hill is less than a mile north-west of the research station, yet even here the country is quite unspoilt. Change of a different sort from that associated with Bovington or Winfrith overtook the heath slightly farther west, when soon after the outbreak of World War II Mr Noel Paul of Woodsford Farm, one of the truly great agriculturalists of Wessex, reclaimed a vast tract of the supposedly unreclaimable gravel land toward Moreton station and turned it into a wheat prairie.

To revert to the northern side of the Frome: running diagonally across the western half of 'Egdon Heath' like a thread across a tapestry is the Roman road connecting Dorchester with Salisbury and eventually London; and like the tapestry thread, it is difficult to trace in its entirety, since long sections of it are hidden. Hardy knew it well from infancy, as his poem 'The Roman Road' testifies. He mentions it too at the outset of *The Return of the Native*, but misleadingly, stating (and confirming on his map) that the Dorchester–Wareham road overlay much of it. In reality the Roman route runs farther north, passing close to the Rainbarrows.

One of the largest surviving wild heath areas of 'Egdon' lies within the area roughly bounded by Bere Regis ('Kingsbere'), Bovington Camp, Wareham ('Anglebury') and Lytchett Minster ('Flytchett'). This tract has escaped 'development' because it is part of the private estates of Charborough ('Welland') House; a large section is a nature reserve. Much is forested (conifers again), but some stretches, composed of heather and furze-clad heath seamed by narrow, sandy paths and pierced here and there by pools, are of great interest to students of Hardy because they closely resemble his descriptions of the Rainbarrows end of the heath before the trees were planted—though here in the east the contours are much flatter. Somewhere in this area Hardy placed the hovel in which Henchard died; but although Lea professed to have found the site, no trace now remains.

Readers of *The Hand of Ethelberta* will recall the early scene set in the tiny 'Weir House' with its neighbouring weir. From Hardy's statement that only two or three miles separated the 'Weir House' from Bournemouth ('Sandbourne'), and his account of the road-junction visible from the house, we must conclude that he was either evoking a scene that has since disappeared under the lava-flow of bricks and mortar, or, as I think more likely, depicting a genuine group of features, 'moved' to a different locality to suit the story; for a building much resembling the 'Weir House' does exist, and near it are a small stream, several pools, and 'some hatches and a weir' just as described. They all lie, today, within the strict privacy of the nature reserve, a short distance west of the Sandford–Sherford road (B3075).

The building is of brick, oblong (not square), with a somewhat commanding fireplace across one corner, and a rudimentary window. Today it is deeply veiled in trees, though open moorland lies at a short distance on nearly all sides; it is in bad repair, the roof having recently collapsed. If it is not Hardy's little house, it was built by similar people for an identical purpose.

The other pool, the 'whitely shining oval' that Ethelberta came upon when following the 'duckhawk', lies between here and the B3075, from which it is plainly visible.

The heath behind Bournemouth ('Sandbourne') will be dealt with in Section 10. Here we may end with Lytchett Minster, the

'Flytchett' where Sol Chickerel and the Honourable Edgar Mountclere changed horses after their disagreeable journey along the wet
and yielding sand roads of the heath. The cross-roads referred to is
Upton Cross, now a large roundabout at a major intersection.
'Flytchett' is characterised as 'a trumpery small bit of a village'
where a wheelwright kept a beerhouse, a mere cottage with a board
on the wall advertising its function. Nowadays, despite the extreme
nearness of Poole and several main roads, Lytchett Minster remains a 'small bit of a village', though it now has two inns, one a
roadhouse of some pretensions—the true St Peter's Finger (see
page 27)—the other more in the tradition of a village inn. But it is
very doubtful whether either has developed from the humble beerhouse of *Ethelberta*.

SECTION 4

SOUTH WESSEX: *Valley of the Great Dairies*
(Dorset: the valley of the Frome)

Ah! dairy where I lived so long,
   I lived so long;
Where I would rise up staunch and strong,
  And lie down hopefully.
'Twas there within the chimney-seat
He watched me to the clock's slow beat—
Loved me, and learned to call me Sweet,
  And whispered words to me.

   TESS'S LAMENT

Probably the best-known of all Hardy's scenic portraits is the picture of the Frome valley that he sets before the eyes of Tess as she gazes down from the edge of 'Egdon Heath' after leaving her native Vale of Blackmoor (the 'Valley of Little Dairies'). At a first glance, the spectacle remains surprisingly little altered. Yet when one examines the details how much has changed! The 'tribes' of cattle are black-and-white instead of red or dun; there is hygienic, mechanised milking inside the long new sheds; the very pastures, with a few exceptions, are no longer the watermeadows known to Tess; the scores of weirs and sluices are now mainly derelict or dismantled to lessen flood risks. However, the waterways continue to make the landscape look like a gridiron, as it is expressed in *The Return*. One may still, like Angel and Tess, rove along the meads by the paths that creep alongside the brooks and periodically cross them by small wooden bridges. Floodwater is not as liable to cover the road bridges in these days as when Angel did his ferrying of the milkmaids, or when the widow in 'She Hears the Storm' listened on that wild night.

Inevitably, we arrive at the problem of 'Talbothays'. Just where, if anywhere, was the prototype of this, the most celebrated farm in all Hardy's prose or verse? Was it a real farm, or was it, as Lea suggests, merely representative of a type? It is my belief that too much mystery is made of 'Talbothays'. This is partly due to the widespread impression that the place was modelled on Norris Mill Farm, and therefore lay north of the river. The legend seems to have been begun by Windle, and boosted nearly a quarter of a century later by Clive Holland's assertion that during a cycle-ride past Norris Mill, Hardy admitted that he had had this farm in mind when creating 'Talbothays'.*

Yet what are Norris Mill's claims? It is a valid assumption that

* On the other hand, in a series of articles and photographs by Holland published in the New York *Bookman* back in 1899, his picture of 'Talbothays . . . a typical Wessex dairy farm' certainly does not show Norris Mill.

during his early years at Higher Bockhampton Hardy got to know
the farm, and that when he wanted to describe a typical Frome
valley establishment, this nearby example sprang to his mind. But
there is another dairy farm that he knew well as a boy, corresponding much more nearly with his portrait of 'Talbothays', and in a
far more convincing situation. This is Lower Lewell Farm, between
West Stafford and Woodsford. Notwithstanding his failure to say
anything about Tess crossing the river during that celebrated first
approach, the novel abounds in indications that Hardy pictured
'Talbothays' on the south bank.

The brief description of the parish church where Angel and Tess
were married, with its louvred belfry and three bells, tallies only
with West Stafford church, whose parish does not extend north of
the water. When the milkmaids in their Sunday finery were walking
'by the crooked lane winding from their own parish to Mellstock',
they encountered the floods when the church was 'as yet nearly a
mile off'. Not by any stretch of author's licence would Hardy have
represented them as running into floodwater within a mile of
Stinsford church along the Tincleton road, which would have set
them somewhere near Bockhampton Cross! Nor is that road particularly crooked. A mile from the church by the Frome path and the
decidedly crooked West Stafford road, however, brings us to an
area highly susceptible to flooding.

Again, when Angel and Tess were driving the milk churns to
the station the meads 'were backed *in the extreme edge of distance* [my
italics] by the swarthy and abrupt slopes of Egdon Heath'—surely
a description that makes sense only if the viewer is south of the
river. Sometimes Mrs Crick sent the pair to 'the farmhouse on the
slopes' where cows in calf were supervised, and one day, while
returning, the lovers reached a 'great gravel-cliff immediately over
the levels'. The farmhouse could be any one of many, but the only
gravel-pits large enough to qualify are south of Lewell and Woodsford, although Hardy does seem to have brought them unre-
alistically close to the meads and river-channels. Finally, when
Angel returned to 'Talbothays' from Beaminster ('Emminster') he
paused and looked down into the Frome valley from a 'detached
knoll a mile or two west' of the farm. This could perhaps have been
some point in Stinsford Parish, but the most obvious detached
knoll at the west end of the valley is the tumulus on Frome

Hill, beside the road from Dorchester to West Stafford (see page 35).

There are one or two objections to this placing of 'Talbothays' in addition to Hardy's failure to say that Tess on arrival crossed the river. He states that the farm lay on the route from Wool ('Well-bridge') to Puddletown, which Lewell does not (nor, for that matter, does Norris Mill); and Lower Lewell Farm is not strictly speaking in West Stafford, but over the parish border in West Knighton. But against these points Hardy had good reason to feel associated with the neighbourhood. His father had owned a piece of farmland in West Stafford, not far from Lower Lewell, called Talbothays, to which the boy must often have been taken by Hardy senior and his men on their work expeditions. Later, the novelist designed a villa here for his brother Henry, the villa also bearing the name Talbothays. In it Hardy's two sisters were to live and Mary was to die, an event reflected in 'Logs on the Hearth' and 'In the Garden'. Today the villa is very little altered, and in the garden the sundial of the second poem continues to display the initials of the three Hardy residents.

Lower Lewell Farm bears a close resemblance to the 'Talbot-hays' of *Tess*, though not quite so close now as a very few years ago. On two sides of the barton the milking-sheds—long, thatched, and with wooden posts on the open side rubbed glossy by genera-tions of cattle, all precisely as depicted in the novel—have been pulled down in favour of more modern structures, including a huge new steel-framed store filling most of the yard. The third side is still occupied by the old stables, the fourth by a wall dividing the barton from the garden. No longer 'derelict and weed-filled' as when Tess stole up on Angel so appropriately playing his harp, the garden is large enough for her to have kept hidden 'behind the hedge' while stealing up on him. On another occasion she took refuge in the 'thicket of pollard willows at the lower side of the barton'; such a thicket is still there. 'Talbothays' possessed a water-mill; so formerly did Lower Lewell.

The house itself has less conspicuous affinities, although more than Norris Mill, the ruins of which show none at all. The former dairy-house at Lewell is of greater interest. The building is on two floors, the lower divided between the old cheese-room and a por-tion now converted into a residence for farm staff. The upper floor, if one mentally removes a single rough and clearly not original partition, exactly fulfils the description of Angel's room—'an immense attic which ran the whole length of the dairy-house', and could be reached only by a ladder from the cheese-loft. Hardy nevertheless evidently visualised a building of three storeys, for not only does he write cheese-*loft*, but assigns to the milkmaids 'a large room over the milk-house, some thirty feet long' from which Tess *ascended* to slip the note under Angel's door. At Lower Lewell the milk-house was a ground-floor extension (now demolished) of the dairy-house, *alongside* the only possible dormitory for the girls, which was that part of the ground floor now converted into the residence just mentioned.

Prior to the indirect hint contained in Pinion's reference, under 'Talbothays', to Hardy's familiarity with Lewell Mill, no writer as far as I can learn ever suggested Lewell for 'Talbothays'; yet at the farm itself the association has long been firmly accepted, and a window is pointed out as that of Tess's bedroom (if so, it must have been the separate room given her on the news of her betrothal). But with no published basis for the belief, how did it become established unless by Hardy himself during visits to his relatives' villa? *Tess* contains two further hints that this is the region of 'Talbothays'. A farmhand at the dairy is called Bill Lewell; and when Hetty and Marian go to seek some cheer after losing Angel, they walk to a public-house at 'Lew-Everard'. The Everard family, as Hutchins relates, formerly occupied [West] Stafford House ('Froom-Everard House' in Hardy's story 'The Waiting Supper'); and Hutchins appears to have regarded the Lewell area as *East* Stafford. 'Lew-Everard' would therefore seem to be some imaginary spot—or perhaps West Knighton—linking the two Staffords.

Stafford House, at West Stafford, was much altered by John Floyer in 1850. Since 'The Waiting Supper' opens in 1837, this tallies with Hardy's observation that 'at that time of the century Froom-Everard had not been altered and enlarged'. Elsewhere in the story he refers with praise to the Elizabeth design with its mullioned and transformed five-light window facing the lawn. The splendid window continues to be a conspicuous and beautiful feature. The house went through the usual vicissitudes of a manor, becoming (as stated in the story) a farmhouse, and then being

splendidly rehabilitated in the present century as a private residence. Before the alterations of 1850, Hardy tells us, the public lane
passed close under the walls, and a door opened directly into it
from the old south parlour. An early picture in the possession of
the present owner corroborates this.

The church is still surrounded by a low stone wall and possesses
three bells, but has otherwise undergone more changes than are
apparent at first glance. The customary Victorian restoration took
place late (1895–8), well after the period of the story, and included
the extension of the east end to form a new chancel, with various internal rearrangements resulting. A new coloured east window was
put in, and the glass in others was replaced, so that little is left of the
'bottle-green glass of the old lead quarries'. The churchyard is closely hemmed in by roads, but retains enough gravestones for Nicholas
to look on the rows of his friends, side by side in death as in life.

The grounds of Stafford House continue to include extensive
'shrubberies and plantations along the banks of the Froom', and
it is not difficult to identify the willow-grove called the 'Sallows'.
The waterfall above which Nicholas used to wade the river during
his arduous commutings, and where Bellston was drowned, can
still be seen; the reconstruction of it at the end of the story was
probably based on fact. Hardy told Hermann Lea that 'Elsenford',
Nicholas Long's home on the other side of the valley, was either
Bhompston or Duddle Farm. In view of his admission that Bhompston is at least partly identifiable with 'Blooms-End' (page 59) I
prefer to look on Duddle as 'Elsenford'; and it must also be the
'Duddle Hole' farmed by Festus Derriman's crony, Farmer Stubb,
in *The Trumpet-Major*.

The Frome is not always placid and friendly; most sinister, in
Hardy's estimation, was the reach between West Stafford and
Woodsford. Here we have the drowning of Bellston in Stafford
waterfall; the deaths of Eustacia Yeobright and Damon Wildeve
at Shadwater Weir; the attempt of Retty Priddle to end her life at
the same spot (called the Great Pool in *Tess*); and the finding of the
body at Rocky Shallow in 'A Sound in the Night'. This eerie
legend-poem is set in Woodsford Castle, a fascinating architectural
jumble with windows of all periods from medieval to Victorian, a
turret stair and postern as in the poem, and a vast thatched roof
looking grossly out of place, yet not displeasing, above walls that

should (and once did) terminate in crenellations. The 'farmstead once a castle' became a farmhouse earlier than most manors, and by the beginning of this century it was pretty down-at-heel according to Treves, though today everything about it is prosperous-looking.

'Shadwater Weir' (its real name is Sturt's Weir) is situated north of Woodsford Farm, the eastern neighbour of Woodsford Castle. The weir has been shorn of its hatches, but the apertures are still intact, and so also is the flanking stone-work and brickwork. Both above and below the weir the river is wide and deep, justifying the name of Great Pool. Rocky Shallow is slightly farther up-river, 'where the Froom stream curves amid the moorland' at its nearest point to Woodsford Castle. This is forlorn territory; north of the river lies the lush Frome Mead, but south of it, between castle and farm, is a desolate strip of marshland.

Windle identifies the railway station to which Angel and Tess took the milk-churns as Wool; but in *Thomas Hardy and the Lady from Madison Square* Weber quotes Rebekah Owen as saying that Hardy himself had told her the station was Moreton, and that she had seen there the large holly tree under which Tess sheltered. Clive Holland in the *Bookman* (1899) also testifies to the holly tree, calls the station 'a sorry shed', but fails to name or illustrate it. Since neither claimant—both stations, by the way, remain in use—now displays a holly, we have no grounds for contradicting Miss Owen: Moreton let it be. Moreton too is the unnamed 'pretty road-side station' alluded to in 'The Fiddler of the Reels', and Moreton village, tiny and unspoilt, the 'Moreford' where his betrothed lived.

Woolbridge ('Wellbridge') Manor must be the most often-pictured building in all Hardy's works. Even today, when Wool village has enlarged itself along the main road in a dull amorphous straggle, the manor remains isolated in the riverside flats. Hardy accurately describes it as a dilapidated farmhouse in Tess's day; in our own it has become a pleasant hotel. The renowned Turberville portraits, at either end of the small first-floor landing, have been so badly defaced by ham-fisted 'restoration' that one is virtually meaningless, the other just decipherable. Nevertheless, enough is left of the latter to make the original sinister effect credible, whereas the very indifferent replicas in the Dorset County Museum are little better than comic cartoons.

Near the old manor the Elizabethan stone bridge still stands, its parapet battered by the tanks of World War I from Bovington, but otherwise sound. A road continues to pass over it, but the main highway (A352) crosses the Frome by a modern bridge a short distance away. Also near, but less near than Hardy makes out, is Bindon Abbey, originally rescued from its post-Dissolution ruin by Thomas Weld two centuries ago, but in a fairly rough state until after the *Tess* period, for both Harper and Treves enlarge on its unkempt condition and the melancholy nature of the woods and waterways. Today all is vastly improved; the ruins are tidy, the grounds about them beautiful, and the woods and waterways well tended. The celebrated coffin of Abbot Richard Maners, in which the sleepwalking Angel laid Tess, is in good condition. Angel's route on this journey is impossible to trace, perhaps not surprisingly in view of the falsified distance between manor and abbey. The abbey mill, where Angel intended to study, continues in operation, though in the mid-1960s electricity replaced water as the source of power. The mill-house is most gracefully maintained.

Barely a mile farther down the river, close to the north bank, stand the ruins of the church of St Mary, East Stoke, the 'ancient little pile' to which Farmer Lodge and Gertrude repaired in 'The Withered Arm'. The action of this grim tale (based, Hardy maintained, on true events even grimmer) can be fairly accurately placed, from a date mentioned in the text, as between 1819 and 1826; and since the present church was not completed until 1828, there is no ambiguity here. This is an area, extending west up the Frome from Wareham ('Anglebury'), in which much development is taking place, industrial as well as residential. The ruins of the church, creeper-clad and half-hidden by bushes, are on the fringe of an asphalt car-park belonging to the new red-brick offices of the Freshwater Biological Association River Laboratories. Close by is what looks like a covered swimming-bath, but is in fact a fluvarium, only the second such in the world, intended for the study of fish and other river life *in situ*, through a glass floor.

'Holmstoke', the 'white house of ample dimensions' where the Lodges lived, has been variously identified, but the evidence points to its being Hethfelton House, between Bovington and Stokeford: not the present mansion, built only in 1930, but its predecessor, which was white, as the story states, and had farm buildings adjacent. On an estate map of 1828 the house is called 'Heffleton

Lodge', a rare term in Dorset, inviting speculation as to whether Hardy's choice of 'Lodge' for the surname of his chief characters was entirely coincidental.

Despite Windle and Lea, there are several good reasons why 'Holmstoke' should not be situated south of the Frome. The most conclusive is that when the Lodges are driving home from Waring ('Anglebury') they come to a steep, short ascent where it was customary for travellers to walk their horses. There is only one such ascent, Worgret Hill, north of the river on the road to Dorchester (A352). True, Hardy remarks that the road was not a main one, but the absence of any other hill suggests that this statement was one of his red herrings. Nor is it any better justified if we suppose him to have been writing of the road to Dorchester via Tincleton, which forks off the A352 at the top of Worgret Hill, for this, too, was a main road in the first half of the nineteenth century, and furthermore is referred to as the direct route from 'Holmstoke' to Dorchester, which it would not have been if the Lodges had lived south of the Frome.

It is instructive, if not altogether easy, to study the itinerary of Gertrude's secret ride to 'Casterbridge'. She set forth 'in precisely the opposite direction', then 'as soon as she was out of sight' turned left 'by a road which led into Egdon'. From a start on the south bank it is impossible to plot any route consistent with these data, and in plotting one from Hethfelton it has to be assumed that Hardy's description begins at the drive gates rather than the house. From here, on the Wareham road, Dorchester travellers would have turned west, so Gertrude headed east. Her left-turn would be up the track that skirted the eastern edge of the Great Plantation and on to South Heath. At some point she must have crossed the Tincleton road, because she arrived eventually at Rushy Pond, which lies north of it. The 'due westerly' wheel that she made must really have been north-west at first, across South, Higher Hyde, and Bere Heaths, probably as far as Gallows Hill. From that region more than one horseman alive today has made his way to Dorchester by Chamberlayne's and Throop Heaths, Clyffe, South Admiston, Castle Hill, and Rushy Pond; and even now, despite tank-proving grounds, gravel quarries, afforestation and cultivation, it remains true that 'a more private way down the county could not be imagined'.

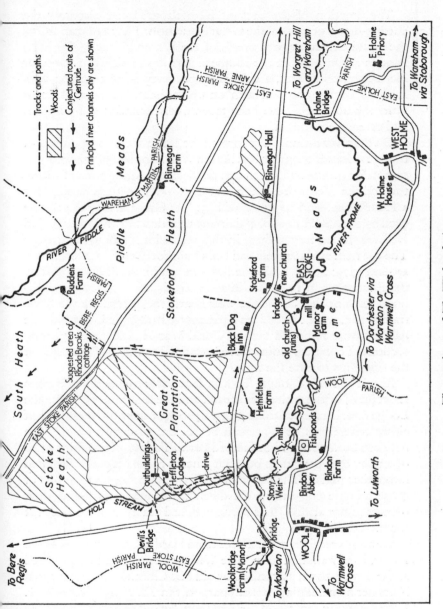

The territory of *The Withered Arm*

The erection of the present Hethfelton House also saw the cutting-down of most of the Great Plantation. The 1828 map shows the estate extending well south of the Wareham road, almost to Bindon Abbey; and in the southern part lies Hethfelton Farm, or Hethfelton Old Farm, a subsidiary property corresponding with Lodge's 'outlying second farm' on which the story opens. In recent years the buildings have been taken over for industrial purposes and extensively altered.

On the river channel that formed the south-western boundary of the estate stands Stony or Bovington Weir. Control of the weir was somewhat quarrelsomely shared between the Framptons of Moreton and the Welds of Bindon, but it would be natural enough for a Hethfelton hand to speak of it as '*our* Great Weir', the phrase used by the old 'Holmstoke' dairyman. (Indeed, at an earlier period Hethfelton had been a farm in the possession of Bindon Abbey.) The old man said the weir had been built forty years earlier, that is around 1779; Stony Weir, medieval in origin, was fully rebuilt by the Framptons in 1749, but in spite of this discrepancy the likelihood remains that this is the weir Hardy meant. Today the stone framework, which resembles a packhorse bridge, is intact, but the hatches were removed before World War II, and more recently sections of concrete piping have been fixed to the upstream side of the openings to ease the flow.

Rhoda Brook's cottage, 'up a by-lane some one and a half miles short [east] of the white farmstead', and the first house outside the Lodges' parish (East Stoke), must be sought over the boundary of either Bere Regis or Wareham St Martin, probably up the lane between Stokeford and Stokeford Farm. Today, after a third or so of a mile, the lane peters out, but a heath footpath could have led into either parish. The cot would have been no more than one of those humble cob-and-thatch dwellings effaced as soon as their owners (if not always their occupants) had ceased to have a use for them.

Wareham receives scant notice from Hardy. Unmentioned in the *Poems*, barely alluded to in 'The Withered Arm', and briefly cited as the market-town patronised by old Mrs Chundle in the story that bears her name, it plays a small part only in *The Hand of Ethelberta*. Here the action centres on the Red Lion, 'an old and well-appointed inn' that had become popular with tourists 'because of the absence from its precincts of all that was fashionable and new'. This would be a somewhat unkind description of the hotel today, for if its exterior still looks old (it is the same building), the interior has been extensively and elegantly modernised. Although Wareham has grown, the fact that it is not on the Channel coast and not quite on the shore of Poole harbour has spared it the hideous development of Swanage and, to a lesser extent, Studland. Built about its four wide streets, it remains Georgian, substantial, and dignified. If he could return now, after nearly two centuries, its illustrious historian-rector, John Hutchins, would not, I think, be distressed.

SOUTH WESSEX: *between Egdon Heath and Upper Wessex*
(*Dorset: between the heath and Hampshire*)

How smartly the quarters of the hour march by
  That the jack-o'-clock never forgets;
    .   .   .   .
Just so did he clang here before I came,
  And so will he clang when I'm gone
Through the Minster's cavernous hollows—the same
Tale of hours never more to be will he deliver
  To the speechless midnight and dawn.

COPYING ARCHITECTURE IN AN OLD MINSTER (WIMBORNE)

After Crusted Character Mr George Crookhill had set out from Salisbury for Blandford and encountered his odd companion on Coombe Bissett Hill (page 217), the pair stopped for refreshment at the Woodyates Inn, just within Dorset on what is now the A354. This roadside hostelry, which in its latter days bore the name Shaftesbury Arms, ceased to be an inn shortly before Hardy, motoring past it in 1919, noted that it still retained its 'genial hostelry appearance'. Treves, on the other hand, earlier in the century, found it deplorably modernised and badly run. The empty buildings were finally razed in the late 1960s, the site at the corner of the turning to Woodyates village remaining a sad patch of weeds and rubble until sold for development in 1971.

The road has improved since 1904, when Harper described it as 'a glaring white road five inches deep in dust and powdered flint, the whole stirred up into a stifling halo of floating particles by the frequent passage of a flock of sheep'.

A very short distance south-west of Woodyates, a cul-de-sac branches off to eastward and leads to Pentridge. This remote and sleepy place, more than a mile from the highway and without an inn, has always been accepted as the prototype of 'Trantridge' in *Tess*, the nearest village to Alec Stoke-D'Urberville's home 'The Slopes' (a fictitious house). It was left for Pinion to point out that 'Trantridge' is also the name of the spot where George Crookhill and his companion put up for the night—at an inn on the main road.

On Hardy's own sketch-map of 'Tess's Country' the position of 'Trantridge' unmistakably indicates Pentridge; yet in the first (magazine) version of *Crusted Characters* what later became 'Trantridge' appears as 'Tranton', surely derived from Tarrant Hinton, a village in the right situation for the story and boasting an inn. I think the explanation is that Hardy used the same name for two different places—as, for instance, he seems to have used 'Lower Longpuddle' for Puddletown and later Piddlehinton. It is conceivable that 'Tranton' was never meant to be changed, but that

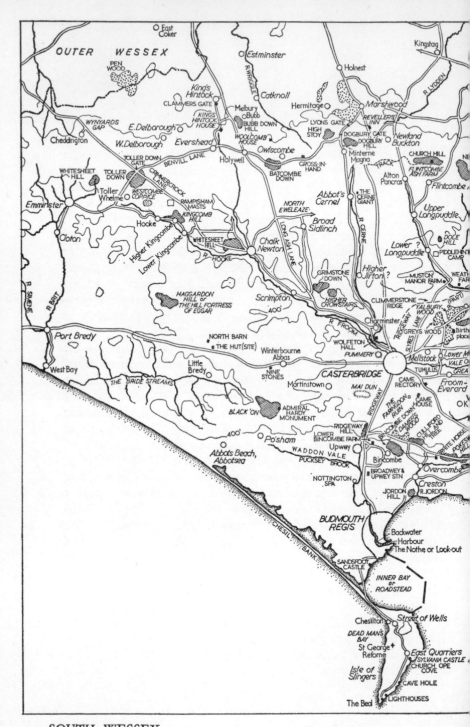

SOUTH WESSEX

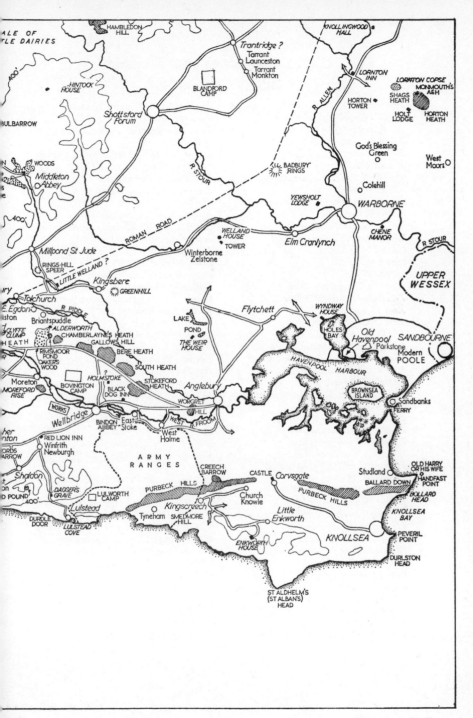

Key overleaf

KEY TO THE MAP OF SOUTH WESSEX

Hardy's names in italics

Abbot's Beach, Abbotsea: Abbotsbury
Abbot's Cernel: Cerne Abbas
Alderworth: Brickyard Cottage
Black'on: Blackdown Hill
Bollard Head: Ballard Point
Broad Sidlinch: Sydling St Nicholas
Budmouth Regis: Weymouth and Melcombe Regis
Casterbridge: Dorchester
Catknoll: Chetnole
Chalk Newton: Maiden Newton
Chene Manor: Canford School
Cloton: Netherbury
Corvsgate: Corfe
Creston: Preston
Damer's Wood: Came Wood
Dead Man's Bay: West Bay
East Egdon: Affpuddle
East Quarriers: Easton
Elm-Cranlynch: Corfe Mullen
Emminster: Beaminster
Enkworth House: Encombe House
Estminster: Yetminster
Evershead: Evershot
Faringdon Ruin: Winterbourne Farringdon church
Flintcomb-Ash: Plush
Flytchett: Lytchett Minster
Froom-Everard: West Stafford
Greenhill: Woodbury Hill
Haggardon Hill: Eggardon Hill
Havenpool: Poole
Higher Crowstairs: Hog Hill
Higher Jirton: Higher Forston (?)
Hintock House: Turnworth House
Holmstoke: Hethfelton (?)
Isle of Slingers: Portland
Kingsbere: Bere Regis
Kingscreech: Steeple
King's Hintock: Melbury Osmund
Knollingwood Hall: Wimborne St Giles House
Knollsea: Swanage
Little Enkworth: Kingston
Little Welland: Roger's Hill Farm (?)

Lornton Copse: Horton Wood
Lornton Inn: Horton Inn
Lower Longpuddle: Piddlehinton (also Puddletown)
Lower Mellstock: Lower Bockhampton
Lullstead Cove: Lulworth Cove
Mai Dun: Maiden Castle
Marshwood: Middlemarsh
Mellstock: Stinsford
Middleton Abbey: Milton Abbas
Moreford Rise: a hill near Moreton
Nether Moynton: Owermoigne
Newland Buckton: Buckland Newton
Nuttlebury: Hazelbury Bryan
Overcombe: Sutton Poyntz
Owlscombe: Batcombe
Oxwell Hall: Poxwell Manor
Port Bredy: Bridport
Po'sham: Portisham
Pummery: Poundbury
Revellers' Inn: Revels Inn Farm
Ringsworth Shore: Ringstead Bay
Roy Town: Troy Town
Sandbourne: Bournemouth
Scrimpton: Frampton
Shaldon: East Chaldon
Shottsford Forum: Blandford Forum
Springham: Warmwell
Stagfoot Lane: Hartfoot Lane
Stickleford: Tincleton
Street of Wells: Fortuneswell
Sylvania Castle: Pennsylvania Castle
Tolchurch: Tolpuddle
Trantridge: Tarrant Hinton (?)
Upper Longpuddle: Piddletrenthide
Vale of Great Dairies: the Frome Valley
Vale of Little Dairies: Blackmoor Vale
Warborne: Wimborne Minster
Weatherbury: Puddletown
Welland House: Charborough House
Wellbridge: Wool
Wyndway House: Upton House (site only)
Yalbury Wood: Yellowham Wood
Yewsholt Lodge: Farrs House

having appeared as 'Trantridge' the name stuck simply through failure to correct it. As for the *Tess* 'Trantridge', it ought to be possible to confirm it as Pentridge by following the girl on her two journeys to 'The Slopes' and back. Unfortunately, however, a comprehensive study of maps, guides, and directories of the period, supplemented by an exhaustive survey of the terrain, fails to reveal any itinerary that can be fitted more than approximately to the description of either of her expeditions. To dispose of the second journey first—that with Alec in the gig—the course is quite impossible to establish, for there neither is nor was a road answering to the story's requirements, and the two genuine place-names included, Melbury Down and Win Green ('Wingreen'), are those of features whose positions only add to the difficulties. All we can say with certainty is that the 'crest' on which the vehicle from 'Trantridge' was to await Tess 'to save the horse the labour of the last slope' was the upper Shaftesbury–Blandford road, that the 'last slope' was probably the one-in-six ascent from Fontmell Magna, and that the description of the first of the hills down which Alec let the gig career exactly fits the western half of the lane to Ashmore from the 'crest' opposite Fontmell Magna. Here indeed is the 'long, straight descent of nearly a mile' between 'two banks dividing like a splitting stick'. They are hillsides rather than banks, today impressively clothed with forest. But once past this descent all close correlation between Alec's route and reality disappears.

On her first journey to 'The Slopes' Tess had travelled by carrier, alighting at 'Trantridge Cross' and walking uphill toward the house, which lay on the edge of Cranborne Chase ('The Chase'). On the obvious road to Pentridge, now the B3081, the crossroads would have to be where this route intersects the A354 at Handley Hill; but except for a stretch of a few dozen yards to the south-east, every direction from the intersection leads downhill, and the entire area is already deep inside Cranborne Chase.

The truth is, the topographical descriptions in *Tess* are in the main so faithful to reality that one is liable to forget that a few owe less to the landscape than to Hardy's fantasy.

As for the picture today, the whole stretch of country belongs to a quiet agricultural region in which change has been minimal in the villages, rather more in the countryside thanks largely to the efforts of one man, Rolf Gardiner. His work belongs properly to another section (see page 211): suffice it to note here that a considerable part of the reafforestation for which he has been responsible covers the heights between vale and chase.

Tarrant Hinton lies just outside Blandford's commercial expansion, and just clear of Blandford Camp. The Crown remains a small and unpretentious inn, probably little different in aspect from that which—if my identification is correct—greeted Mr Crookhill and his new friend. The by-road along which each in turn set out after their sojourn must have been either that leading to Tarrant Launceston and Tarrant Monkton, or some lane that has since disappeared, perhaps obliterated by the army camp.

Despite the nearness of this busy centre, four miles south-east of it the Iron Age fort called Badbury Rings has become a popular focus for summer Sunday outings, yet remains impressive beside a magnificently preserved length of the Salisbury–Dorchester Roman road. The grove of trees crowning Badbury has, of course, been planted since the time of the beacon fire mentioned in *The Trumpet-Major*.

Blandford ('Shottsford') Forum itself, never used as a direct setting but touched upon in 'The Three Strangers', 'My Cicely', *The Mayor of Casterbridge* and *The Woodlanders*, retains its attractive and homogeneous Georgian centre very much as in Hardy's day. A 'cup of genuine' can now be bought at quite a number of places, including the Crown Hotel mentioned in *The Woodlanders*.

Eight miles south lies Bere Regis ('Kingsbere'), a somnolent village in spite of a large watercress industry. The view from the churchyard described in *Tess* now includes a small council-house estate, and inevitably there are a few new private houses, probably less than counterbalancing the cottages that have disappeared. But the place is habitable; in 1904, according to Harper, most of the dwellings were 'very ruinous' owing to the refusal of the estate owner to rebuild them.

The mansion of the Turbervilles stood where there is now a rough paddock—still called Court Green—east of the church. The house was demolished as recently as 1832, Wilkinson Sherren saying that one wall was retained and built into a farmhouse. A pair of cottages on the east side of the paddock does in fact incorporate an area of masonry that probably was part of the house. The last acknowledged Turbervilles were twin ladies who died in 1780 at Putney.

Hardy's picture of the 'D'Urberville' aisle in the church is fully accurate, the inscription Tess read on the door of the sepulchre being completed by the date '24 June 1710'. The diminished legibility of the wording here is virtually the only change wrought by the years. In 1870, when the church was restored, the vault was opened and the skeletons were put into new coffins. It must have been at this time too that the musicians' gallery was removed, in which (in *The Return of the Native*) Yeobright senior had sometimes deputised on the clarinet. Outside, the churchyard is as little changed as a century's growth of trees and shrubs permits, and an outcast family could still (until the authorities learned about it) camp under the Turberville window. The wall against which the Durbeyfields' furniture was dumped also survives.

In *Far from the Madding Crowd* Hardy gives the full name of the town as 'Kingsbere-sub-Greenhill', 'Greenhill' being Woodbury Hill which, rising behind Court Green, was the scene of Woodbury Fair. Here Troy was discovered playing Dick Turpin in the circus. Hardy claimed that the hilltop, which is ringed by a double earthwork, enclosed twenty or thirty acres, the fair occupying the whole of it; in reality it embraces no more than ten acres, of which the fair proper covered no more than four. For comparison, the permanent ground of the Bath & West Show at Shepton Mallet covers 130 acres, exclusive of car-parks. The fairground was not devoid of houses, nor is it now, although they are fewer than the 'sixteen or seventeen' reported by Harper. Near the centre stands the old-fashioned farmhouse. The approaches remain much as Hardy knew them.

We now come to his settings for the main action of *Two on a Tower*. That the mansion on which 'Welland House' was based is Charborough cannot be challenged, for when the artist Macbeth Raeburn was commissioned, under Hardy's supervision, to devise a frontispiece for the novel embodying a real locality used in it, he sketched the house and tower at Charborough. Yet Windle and Harper both identified 'Welland House' with the remnant of the manor house (the greater part had been demolished in 1802) at Milborne St Andrew ('Millpond St Jude' in *The Madding Crowd*). The explanation lies with the tower of the title. Hardy wrote to Harper that this had 'two or three originals—Horton, Charborough, etc). The 'etc' is the column close to Milborne, standing on an anciently-fortified hill called Weatherbury Castle or Ring's-Hill Speer (see plan, page 100); this is not open to doubt, because Hardy uses the latter name in the narrative.

Just how much, in his amalgam of these prototypes, can be identified in the real aspects of Charborough and Ring's-Hill Speer? The *architecture* of the Charborough tower, though certainly not Tuscan—it has been described as Strawberry-Hill Gothic—closely resembles the fictional portrait, except that the windows, which Hardy calls slits, are actually quatrefoil. The lichen-covered tablet is not on the door, but inside, and with the lichen now cleared away the 'letters or words' are revealed as a record of the heightening of the tower in 1839. It is at present judged unsafe because of falling masonry.

The *setting* of the fictional tower follows equally closely that of the monument on Ring's-Hill Speer, except that hardwoods have eclipsed most of the conifers clothing the hill and are now so tall that all but the copper ball crowning the column is invisible from the surrounding meadows. Today this monument of brick, stone-dressed, square in cross-section and solid, is so dilapidated that only the creeper covering one side appears to be holding it up. The fields are grassed at present, and the landscape in which they lie is indeed 'gently concave' (round Charborough it is flat). Sometimes Hardy refers, incorrectly, to a single enveloping field of fifty acres, but near the opening of the book Viviette halts her carriage on the 'old Melchester road' and asks to be driven to the tower across what her coachman calls Twenty-Five Acres, the true name of the field to the south-east of the Speer. The 'old Melchester road' is therefore probably a resuscitation of Hardy's favourite Roman thoroughfare that ran between Salisbury ('Melchester') and Dorchester, since this passes just south of Twenty-Five Acres.

The status of the church as the lone survivor of a demolished village is taken from Charborough. Its surroundings, however, although corresponding superficially with Charborough, have been shown by Beatty to contain several features, such as the wall separating graveyard and house lawn, clearly borrowed from Stinsford. The fabric itself, including the tower, is probably modelled on that of Milborne St Andrew, the *only* church in the area that is 'many-chevroned' (rich in dog-tooth ornament). How many other features Hardy took from here is unascertainable, for the building was drastically restored by Street in 1878—midway through the story—and no account exists of its previous design or furnishings.

Except to remark on its 'long, low front'—Charborough again, before the addition of a later wing—Hardy does not describe 'Welland House', and apart from the position of its church his details of the grounds are wholly imaginary. This is not surprising, seeing that he never entered the gates until the last months of his life. Today Charborough Park and house are immaculate, a stately home in the truest sense.

'Little Welland', the village in which Swithin lived with his grandmother, Mrs Martin, is generally regarded as fictitious, in spite of identification by Lea with Winterborne Zelstone, west of Charborough. There are, however, grounds for believing that Hardy had a real situation in mind, though not a real house (unless it was one he had seen elsewhere). The scattered epithets add up to a picture of a 'little dell', a green and 'bosky' basin, 'Welland Bottom' by name, at the end of the parish remote from the church. Walking to it from Ring's-Hill Speer, Swithin comes upon his home 'quite unexpectedly on the other side of the field-fence'; and on another occasion Viviette after visiting him returns to her mansion 'along a narrow lane divided from the river by a hedge', a lane later referred to as 'flanked by half-buried cottages'.

Perhaps all these details are invented, but it is striking how many of them fit Roger's Hill Farm, one mile south-east of the Speer. It stands at the extreme edge of the parish. The lane leading to it from the north is narrow, and separated from the Milborne or Mill Bourne (a true 'rippling stream') by a hedge that is now close to the road, but used to be equidistant between road and river. As the farm is approached the river basin, called Ashley Bottom, drops lower, so that when one reaches two pairs of cottages midway down the slope from the lane they do appear half-buried, and by the end of the route the farmhouse is low enough to present itself 'quite unexpectedly' and to give the impression of being in a dell, although really on a hillside.

Roger's Hill farmhouse itself bears no resemblance to Mrs Martin's abode, but it is noticeable that although Hardy's normal epithet for this is a cottage, he once (as if by mistake) calls it 'the farmhouse'. The present 'half-buried' cottages were erected by Sir

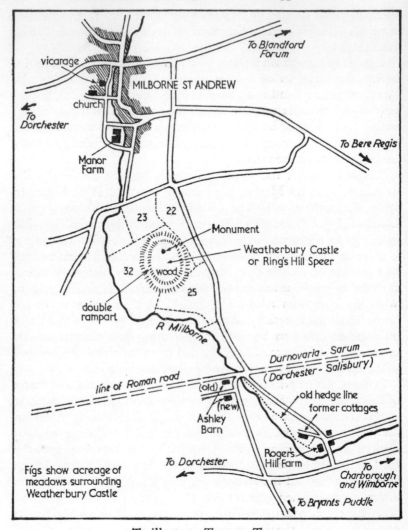

To illustrate *Two on a Tower*

Ernest Debenhan between the two world wars, but they replace a
cob-and-thatch pair set still lower on the slope. It is true that the
lane leads from Roger's Hill in the opposite direction to Charborough, but at more than one point in his novel Hardy appears
to treat 'Welland House' as if it stood in the position of the Mil-

borne manor, as when Swithin and Viviette leave the Speer for their homes 'in opposite directions'. This accords with her use of the lane after calling on him. The 'old turnpike road' linking 'Welland' with the station at Wimborne Minster ('Warborne') mostly followed the line of the present A11, but east of Charborough's Stag Gate it coincided with the now unclassified lane through Sturminster Marshall and Pamphill. Hardy rightly depicts the public highway as at one time running through the park, though it never passed close to the house. It was re-routed outside the park in 1844.

Roger's Hill lies in the heart of the area taken in hand by Sir Ernest Debenham. Dairy and other buildings erected under his aegis are distributed on either side of Milborne St Andrew—a dreary and graceless village, unhelped by lines of dull new cottages in sad contrast to the Debenham designs.

East of Charborough one quickly comes to the fringe of the Bournemouth–Poole subtopia. On the border is Corfe Mullen, 'Elm-Cranlynch' in 'The First Countess of Wessex'. Here in the manor, now Court House, lived Stephen Reynard's rival Charles Phelipson. In real life he was Charles Phelips, the manor being held by a branch of the Phelips family of Montacute ('Montislope', see page 229). Some third of the Elizabethan mansion is now standing: stone-built, mellow, with very tall chimneys.

Almost adjoining Corfe-Mullen to the south-east, on the now defunct railway link between Hamworthy and Wimborne, stand the remains of Broadstone station, originally called Poole Junction. This was the junction, twice alluded to in *The Hand of Ethelberta* when Sol Chickerel and the Honourable Edgar Mountclere were trying to get back to Swanage, at which the Bournemouth spur left the main line. When the novel was published (1876) the spur was barely two years old.

North-east of Corfe-Mullen, across the Stour, stands Farrs House, the original of 'Yewsholt Lodge' in 'Barbara of the House of Grebe'. At first sight the house in its trim whiteness looks later than eighteenth-century; but inside there is no mistaking the 'central hall with a wooden gallery running round it'. After a grim occupation by the military during World War II, and by squatters afterwards, Farrs has been fully and imaginatively restored, and is now a small mansion of great and unusual beauty. Hardy neverthe-

G

less exaggerated the smallness: the rooms are much larger than 'closets'. In the wooded grounds outside there are still many song-birds.

Wimborne Minster retains a nucleus of old-world lanes and houses, but has undergone much expansion. Hardy and Emma lived here for a short time, and there is a note of his that he wandered into the minster one evening in 1875 and sat down to listen, an audience of one, to the organist practising. The organ as it then was remained unaltered until 1965, when the pipes were modified by adding to each a brass tube, like a trumpet, projecting at right angles near the top. Recitals are occasionally broadcast. The building has changed little. Hardy brought it into the poems 'Copying Architecture in an Old Minster' and 'The Levelled Churchyard', which does not identify Wimborne but is known to be about it. The 'jack-o'-clock' of the former poem continues very much in evidence.

In Hardy's prose works the town is alluded to here and there, but the only specific features named, the railway station and Grammar School, appear in *Two on a Tower* (which was written here). Today Wimborne has joined the long list of abandoned stations, and passengers must use Poole, six miles away. The Grammar School, where Swithin was educated, was until 1849 a stone building with mullioned windows and a dormered shingle roof. It was then poorly reconstructed in red brick, and enlarged in the 1930s and again in 1954. If we take the eclipse of 1881 as dating the action, Swithin attended the old school. (The railway situation rules out Weber's earlier dates.)

'The Pedestrian' was said by Hardy himself to have been composed with Colehill in mind, now an elegant but dismayingly huge north-eastern suburb of Wimborne in which the sufferer in the poem could undertake his nightly ten-mile walk entirely under street-lamps.

Canford Park, containing Canford ('Chene') Manor, parental home of Barbara Grebe (really Webb), is so far still in rural surroundings. But only a little is left of the mansion of those days; demolitions were followed by new building in three different decades of the nineteenth century, until in 1923 the pile became a public school. The so-called John o' Gaunt's Kitchen, mentioned in 'Barbara', with its two tremendous hearths and tower-like chimneys, has become a reading-room; and adjoining it is a further fragment of the house that Barbara would have known. An engraving of 1786 shows the old kitchen looking very much as it does today.

'Barbara' also mentions Horton ('Lornton') Inn, where the modern B3078 from Wimborne to Cranborne and beyond intersects the road from Woodley Down to Ringwood ('Oozewood'). The 'solitary wayside tavern' is solitary still, but a far cry from the 'rendezvous of many a daring poacher', having been smartened up as a luxury port of call for the motorist. The building has been doubled in size by the addition of a wing at right angles to the eighteenth-century original, which has virtually disappeared from view beneath elegant modern embellishments.

A few miles to the north-east stands Wimborne St Giles House, the prototype (again in 'Barbara') of 'Knollingwood Hall'. Inside, the seventeenth-century building has hardly been altered since it was refurnished in 1750—shortly before the period of the story. The gallery to which Barbara took Edmond's statue extends round a lofty but smallish oak-pannelled room hung with portraits, and is bounded by a decorative white iron balustrade.

Between Horton village and Horton Heath is Horton Wood, presumably the 'Lornton Copse' mentioned in *Two on a Tower*. On Horton Heath the Ordnance map marks Monmouth's Ash, supposedly the spot where, after the battle of Sedgemoor, the miserable Duke of Monmouth was found hiding in a ditch beside a young ash tree. Betrayed, according to one story, by an old hag, in another version he owed his capture to a young housewife, as in Hardy's poem 'At Shag's Heath'—a local name for the part of Horton Heath where Monmouth was found.

Pace the map, there is now no ash tree at the site marked. The original lived its allotted span and died, its bark, Treves tells us, scored with many initials. Harper says it was finally blown down, and that a new tree grew from the same root. Certainly a new tree did grow, which Treves in 1906 estimated to be between fifty and sixty years old. It should therefore still be in its prime, but according to Harper it was already propped up in 1904, and although it still existed in 1965, today only a plaque marks the spot. The 'Justice Ettricke' of the Monmouth poem was quartered at Holt Lodge (now Holt Lodge Farm) near God's Blessing Green. Perhaps the duke would have fared better had he hidden at this last.

Close to Holt is West Moors, site of the unnamed 'next station' to Wimborne on the way to 'the junction' in *Two on a Tower*. West Moors station (itself a junction for nearly a century) and both the lines it served have been lost to passengers since 1964, although the one-time hamlet is now part of the string of horticultural and dormitory centres that have spread north from Bournemouth. A freight line still connects with Poole.

The last few places I have mentioned have all been in the borderlands between Cranborne Chase and the New Forest ('The Great Forest'). The finest Hardy picture of Cranborne Chase occurs towards the end of *Two on a Tower*, when Viviette's brother Louis takes the train from Wimborne to Salisbury. It is also a very fair description of the Chase today, although the balance is gradually shifting from woods—forest fragments—to more profitable agricultural land. Wholly vanished during the past few decades are the cider orchards that used to be attached to many Chase farms. Yet this remains a quiet and empty area: in the surviving woodlands huge, aged yews and mistletoe-bearing oaks continue to grow, their numbers diminishing, but their tough resistance promising many years of life yet.

At Cranborne the Fleur-de-Lys tavern ('Flower de-Luce' in *Tess*) carries on, the décor of its single bar so little altered that one could fancy the Trantridge folk had left it the previous evening. No one could call it smart, but it would be surprising if any 'maids' today failed to find it respectable.

The road between Salisbury and Poole via Wimborne, 'one of the finest examples of a macadamised turnpike-track that can be found in England' ('Barbara of the House of Grebe'), ran from the Salisbury–Blandford turnpike (A354) at the top of Coombe Bissett Hill along the present unclassified road to Rockbourne as far as the bend at the Hampshire border, then straight along what is today a superior farm track over Toyd Down to the Martin–Cranborne lane at Tidpit. It followed this lane to Cranborne, then the modern B3078 to Wimborne, and finally entered Poole down the line of today's A349 via Fleet Corner. Constructed in 1755, the road cannot have been macadamised from the outset, because Macadam's essay setting forth his system was not published until 1819. But it was among the first macadamised roads in Wessex.

SECTION 6

SOUTH WESSEX: Egdon Heath to Mid-Wessex
(Dorset: the heath to Wiltshire)

I had slowed along
After the torrid hours were done,
Though still the posts and walls and road
Flung back their sense of the hot-faced sun,
And had walked by Stourside Mill, where broad
    Stream-lilies throng.

THE MUSICAL BOX

Not far north of Milborne St Andrew stands Milton Abbey, the 'Middleton Abbey' of *The Woodlanders* and the home of Joseph Damer, first Earl of Dorchester, whose evil conduct is recorded in 'The Doctor's Legend'. He built the celebrated model village and the mansion, planted the woods that grace the surrounding hills, and calmly destroyed the entire market-town of Milton Abbas because he found it an eyesore. This type of conduct was by no means unique, but more than two centuries later resentment at it still lingers, as it does against similar high-handedness on other estates. The new cottages, moreover, were grossly overcrowded, and remained so until long after the period when Mrs Charmond must have seen them. Like the village, the mansion, grounds, and abbey church have undergone very little change since her day, and almost the only additions have been the open-air swimming-bath and playing-field appurtenances incidental to Milton Abbey's current function as a boys' school.

The woods are the 'Milton Woods' of 'The Revisitation'. They are quite unspoilt, and north of them the chalky uplands extend similarly undisturbed to Turnworth, the original of Mrs Charmond's seat, 'Hintock House'. Although Windle had already made this identification, complete with full-page sketch by New, Lea for some reason was mystified by 'Hintock House'; but many years later Hardy corroborated Windle's identification by accompanying Donald Maxwell, the artist, over to Turnworth to make a watercolour of the Charmond residence.

In *The Woodlanders* the position of the house is 'moved' many miles further west, but its setting 'in a hole' is the setting of Turnworth. The description of the building, to judge from New's drawing, which is clearer than Maxwell's watercolour, is also strictly accurate. The illustrations and Hardy's description suggest a fine Elizabethan manor, but in reality Turnworth House was a nineteenth-century pastiche, and jerry-built at that. It was erected by William Parry-Okeden, who became High Sheriff of Dorset in

HINTOCK HOUSE (TURNWORTH HOUSE)

1849. Between the two world wars it was acquired by a young and energetic owner who spent £10,000 on trying to make it sound, only to be killed in World War II before he could learn that all his money and enthusiasm had been wasted; for experts called in by his successor pronounced the building beyond salvation. Behind a thin stone facing the construction was of brick, held together by steel ties most of which had rusted through. Pieces of masonry kept falling off like autumn leaves. The only sound wood in the place was the oak staircase and panelling put in by the late restorer.

So the mansion was pulled down, and on the site was built a low, rambling house of timber, more Alpine than English, yet not inappropriate to its environment. Some stables survive from the former establishment, also a walled garden, a lawn, and the original drive. The 'dense plantation' still grows on the steep slope at the back, and in front the equally steep slope on which Grace Melbury stood remains 'richly grassed, with only an old tree here and there'. One younger tree is also there, planted by the would-be saviour of the mansion in memory of a favourite horse. It may be thought of today as a memorial to himself and his high hopes.

Three miles away across the Stour rises Hambledon Hill, which entered Tess's thoughts during her journey home from 'Flintcombe-Ash', and where Hardy, according to *The Life*, was once lost in a fog. The high triple ramparts of the twenty-five-acre Iron Age fortress surmounting the hill are undamaged, and to stand amid them on a misty day makes Hardy's experience indeed credible. In clear weather there are extensive views to north and west over the Vale of Blackmoor (the 'Valley of Little Dairies'). The same panorama, but looking southward, is to be had from the 'level terrace where the Abbey gardens once had spread' at Shaftesbury. The terrace, asphalted since Jude walked there while waiting for Sue, remains a deservedly popular resort. Behind it the few remnants of the abbey in their mellow garden enjoyed a moment of late glory in 1931, when the bones of the tenth-century Edward the Martyr, which had 'vanished into oblivion' at the Dissolution, were re-discovered.

The 'extensive stone-built' schools continue in operation, and across the street called Bimport, the 'two enormous beeches' (one sadly ailing) tower now over a small car-park. A little farther along Bimport is 'Old-Grove's Place' where Sue and her husband, Phil-

SHASTON—OLD-GROVE'S PLACE

lotson, lived. Curiously built with its floors lower than the outside
ground on all sides, it has been modernised in a manner that is
striking, if not to everyone's taste. The 'wainscotting of panelled
oak reaching from floor to ceiling' of the front parlour is still in
place, but painted white, and under the carved 'Jacobean pilasters
and scroll-work' of the mantelpiece the back wall of the fireplace
has been removed and a pane of glass let in, permitting a view
across the neat garden, recently improved by the removal of various
outbuildings. The 'dismalness' of the room in which the Phillot-
sons breakfasted and were nodded to by passers-by has been al-
leviated by covering the whole of one wall with mirror.

The staircase, which originally rose from the front of the house
towards the back, has now been reversed, causing the disappearance of the cupboard in which Sue slept on one occasion.
Upstairs, the bedroom with the forty-mile view across the vale
'even into Outer Wessex' (Somerset) is the principal room at the
back of the house. From its window, according to Hardy, Sue
took her panic leap. Yet it is 'on the gravel' at the *front* of the house
that he makes her land, close to the 'heavy door' specifically named
as the 'front door'. To compound the confusion, the mullions of
the back-room window are too close-set for even Sue's slender
form to have passed between them.

Hardy's odd name for the house stems from its occupancy, long
ago, by one Grove; the present owner has restored the proper
name, The Ox House. He has also had the upper storey of the
projecting porch rendered and painted white; the rest of the
exterior remains in its natural stone.

A little farther along Bimport, on the opposite side, a large
green garage occupies the site of the warehouse where the itinerant
show people who used to winter in Shaftesbury stored some of their
gear. Farther along still there is a sharp turn to the left and the
name changes to St John's Street, very steep and narrow. Here,
above the high bank to the right, is the burial-ground of the church
of St John, Hardy's 'chief graveyard [that] slopes up as steeply as
a roof (*Jude*). The graveyard is itself level, but the ground on either
side fulfils his description. Today it is a place of weeds, nettles and
unkempt trees, with a few headstones here and there, some with
still-legible inscriptions.

Toward the centre of the town, the other 'venerable graveyard'—

that of Trinity church—where Jude walked after he had missed the bus to the station, remains trim enough, its paths still bordered by 'avenues of limes'. Close by, the tiny former market-place (the new market is on the edge of the town) affords space for one to appreciate the handsome eighteenth-century façade of the Grosvenor Arms, the 'Duke's Arms' of *Jude*. The station referred to in the novel is Semley, two miles to the north: closed now, leaving Shaftesbury travellers with a choice between Tisbury and Gillingham. Ironically, it is toward Semley that Shaftesbury (having no more building-room at the top of the hill) has mostly spread. Except for some new shop fronts, there is not much recent construction in the rather dull streets at the summit.

When Phillotson felt the need to consult his friend Gillingham he walked from Shaftesbury to the town of Gillingham ('Leddenton'), 'leaving Duncliffe Hill on his left'. This is a solitary conical hill in the Stour plain, partly encircled by woods and faintly forbidding. Gillingham is described as 'a little town of three or four thousand inhabitants', and at the 1961 census its population was 3,619, so it has neither shrunk nor grown. The boys' school of the novel (red brick, Victorian) is now a primary school.

Five miles south lies Tess's home at Marnhull ('Marlott'), a 'long and broken village' widely scattered about a network of lanes. Among the inevitable crop of claimants to be the Durbeyfield cottage (which Lea declared 'swept away') all but one can be dismissed out of hand. This building stands at the head of a narrow, bent cul-de-sac ('a crooked lane or street') off the west side of the B3092, a little north of Walton Elm Cross. During the 1920s Barton Cottage, as it was then called, was owned by a Major Campbell-Johnston, who lived one field away by the old Marnhull Brewery in Carraway Lane. A path still connects Carraway Lane with the head of the cottage lane, thus justifying Hardy's references to people *passing* the cottage (although in including Alec on horseback he appears to have ignored the stiles).

The Major employed a factotum named Blake, who on a day in 1924 was tending the garden of Barton Cottage with his assistant when they saw an elderly figure scrutinising the house. On Blake asking if he could be of service the stranger replied, 'No, thank you, I was only seeing where I put my Tess'. It has been said that Hardy was much too reticent to have been so forthcoming. But he had been caught in a situation that he may well have felt demanded an explanation. Whether this answer meant anything to Blake is not recorded, but evidently he amplified it, for Blake ended by asking if he would care to meet Major Campbell-Johnston. The major was away at the time, as he often was, but according to Blake's account the meeting did take place—one imagines, in view of Hardy's age, at Max Gate. Shortly afterwards the deeds of the property were altered, and the name was changed to Tess Cottage.

Such is the version of the story given to me by the Blakes' nephew and virtually adopted son, Mr Ernest Allen, who heard it several times from Blake himself. The account differs only slightly from that given to the present occupants of the cottage by Mrs Blake shortly before her death in 1965 (Blake died in the 1930s). But corroboration is elusive. Neither Hardy nor Campbell-Johnston left any known letter or diary entry referring to a meeting between them. The major's son and daughter, though adults at the time, heard nothing of the matter then or later, but admit they spent long periods away from Marnhull; that their abnormally reticent father was fully capable of considering an encounter with Hardy none of their business; and that their infrequent appearances at home might explain their not hearing of the incident from the Blakes. Professor Geoffrey Cheshire, who with his wife and two sons lived in Tess Cottage for some years, during which he became the major's friend, never heard from him that he had met Hardy, but did hear repeatedly that the cottage was where Hardy had placed Tess. The professor adds that Campbell-Johnston was by no means a literary man, and would have been most unlikely to have linked his property with anything in a book unless he had strong reason. All these informants, together with Group-Captain Leonard Cheshire and his brother testify that the Blakes were an honest, conscientious, and solid couple incapable of inventing or even embroidering their story. It is worth noting that, if Hardy left no record of the episode, *Tess* was certainly in his mind in 1924, for his notes witness that he attended several rehearsals of a new dramatic production of the story that year at Dorchester.

The cottage itself neither invalidates the claims made for it nor tallies with Hardy's snippets of description closely enough to clinch the matter. At the period of the novel it was divided into two, a circumstance evidently discarded by Hardy. No one now alive

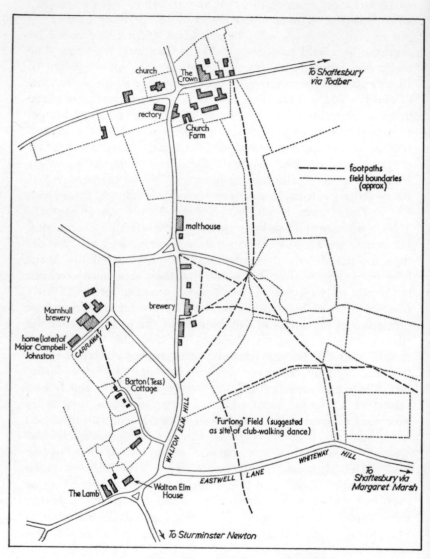

Marnhull ('Marlott') in the Durbeyfields' time

recalls a stable, such as Durbeyfield had for Prince, but where the garage has been built there were outbuildings and pigsties. Apart from the conversion into a single dwelling and the necessary practical improvements, Tess Cottage is substantially as it was in the late nineteenth century, and the great amount of recent building that has changed much of Marnhull has not yet affected the immediate neighbourhood. Just beyond the garage stands an agreeable single-storey wooden structure with large windows, built as a place of recreation for the two Cheshire boys.

How does the position of the cottage and its lane, in relation to the rest of 'Marlott' fit the novel? Ever since Windle gave a lead it has been assumed that Hardy visualised the 'club-walk' dance in the meadow between the Crown Inn ('The Pure Drop') and the crossroads. The walkers 'came round by the Pure Drop Inn, and were turning out of the high road to pass through a wicket-gate into the meadows' when old Durbeyfield was observed driving past in a carriage from the direction of Shaftesbury. However, the dance meadow must have been still a fair distance off, for when the girls teased Tess about her father she 'threatened to walk no further with them', but later 'moved on with the whole body to the enclosure where there was to be dancing on the green', and 'by the time the spot was reached' had recovered her equanimity. All this hardly suggests that they were going to dance in the meadow they had already reached when she was upset.

Let us suppose that 'coming round by the inn' means that they came *down* to the crossroads by the 'Pure Drop', turned *toward* Shaftesbury, and entered the meadows of Church Farm, where until recently a gate gave admittance to a network of public footpaths extending to Eastwell Lane, the eastern arm of the Walton Elm crossroads. Under this re-routing the procession would still have met old Durbeyfield.

But the Clare brothers, walking from Shaftesbury to 'Stourcastle' (Sturminster Newton), also passed through 'Marlott' while the dancing was in progress. After the elder pair had gone on, Angel ran down the lane *westward*, 'passed the hollow and mounted the next rise', and looked back for a final glimpse of the dancers. If the brothers had come into Marnhull by the road John Durbeyfield had just driven along and the dancers had been in Crown Meadow, the Clares' route to Sturminster would have lain south at the crossroads; and if despite this Angel had run west, the church would have cut off his view of the revels almost at once. But suppose the Clares had approached Marnhull through Margaret Marsh and Eastwell Lane, and the clubwalkers had been dancing in one of the meadows beside the lane, Angel would have had to continue westward as far as Walton Elm Cross before turning south. True, the intervening hollow now becomes a piece of author's licence, but a more probable one than a false compass-direction. Again, if Tess's home was in Tess Cottage, the placing of the dance-meadow by Eastwell Lane eliminates any problem of how she could have passed within sight of it during her subsequent return from 'Flintcomb-Ash' through Hazelbury Bryan ('Nuttle-bury').

Like Durbeyfield's home, the cottage is at one end of the village, and at the right end for Tess's backward glance 'at Marlott *and her father's house*' [my italics] when setting out for Sturminster on her way to 'Talbothays'. At the same end stood 'Rolliver's'. There is no inn or alehouse near by today, but just west of Walton Elm Cross stands an old house, The Nook, which was formerly the Lamb Inn. Though it was never, like 'Rolliver's', merely an off-licence, the white palings before its front garden may have been those made use of by Hardy in his picture of the improvised shelf; or, as so often, he may have seen the device elsewhere and, wishing to use it, have downgraded the Lamb. Harper and Lea both mis-identify 'Rolliver's' with the Blackmoor Vale Inn, north-west of the church in a region of many new houses. The inn has itself been rebuilt. The Crown in our day, on the contrary, does not really differ much from the Crown of the 1890s. A gravelled car-park now occupies all Crown Meadow. The church too has altered little, but its neat graveyard shows no trace of the nettle-filled corner once reserved, with true Christian charity, for burying the un-baptised and the ungodly.

South of Marnhull, alongside the old turnpike road to Sturminster, lies Yewstock Farm; a small red-brick cottage flush with the road here used to be the turnpike house in which Tess left her baggage when returning home after the parting with Angel. The 'back lane' by which she then reached home was probably the track from St Mary Hinton past Cut Mill and Yardgrove Farm.

Sturminster Newton is chiefly associated with the group of

age 117 (*above*) Revellers' Inn: now Revel's Inn Farm, the former inn alluded to in *The Woodlanders* contains several traces of its former function, including some fine panelling. stands on the upper Dorchester–Sherborne road; (*below*) Yewsholt Lodge: here arbara of the House of Grebe was to have lived with her young husband Edmond illowes. Situated near Wimborne Minster, the real name of the building is Farrs House

(*above*) Overcombe Mill: despite its modern appearance, there is strong eviden that this house, now the residence of the engineer in charge of the adjacent waterwork is basically the original millhouse described in *The Trumpet Major*. The mill former extended to the left; (*below*) Oxwell Hall: Poxwell—pronounced Pokeswell—House today the antithesis of the tumble-down farmhouse pictured by Hardy. The lawn se here was where old Derriman kept his cattle

poems in which Hardy commemorated the happiest period of his life, the 'Sturminster idyll' or 'A Two-Years' Idyll' as he called it in the title of the poem that sums it up. The centre of the town still has an old-world somnolence and nestles under plenty of the 'thick thatch' mentioned in *Tess*. Thomas and Emma Hardy rented a grey Victorian semi-detached villa, 'Riverside', on the edge of the high town, overlooking the Stour valley. This is the 'dusky house that stood apart', and Emma the lady 'waiting there', in 'The Musical Box'. The house is still rendered in dusky grey, the porch unchanged, the interior modernised with restraint. The room is pointed out in which Hardy wrote *The Return of the Native*. The monkey-puzzle tree he planted in the small garden was removed when it grew too large.

From the windows of this little house one may gaze yet upon the view he delineated in one of his loveliest poems, 'Overlooking the River Stour'; happily, man has not so far driven away the swallows, the moorhens and the honeybees, nor ripped out the kingcups. In the wide ravine beneath can be seen the iron bridge of 'On Sturminster Foot-Bridge'; and farther down the curving river the 'Stourside Mill' of 'The Musical Box' remains in operation, though with electricity now supplementing water-power. In a little-altered quarter of the high town stands the church, and beside it, also little altered, the churchyard that is the scene of 'The To-be-Forgotten'.

In many ways the great tract of lush clay that is the Vale of Blackmoor has changed less than any region in Dorset except the other great clay vale to the south-west, Marshwood. The fields are small and hedged, and with patience one may still find a building on stone staddles, as one will never do on the coastal downs where the staddle-built granary stood in *The Trumpet-Major*. But alas, no patience will now discover the cider-apple orchards so important in *The Woodlanders*.

Some of the vale lanes once constituted through-routes of some importance, among them that which runs between Sturminster Newton and Dorchester through Hazelbury Bryan and Hartfoot ('Stagfoot') Lane—a hamlet, this, not a road—and figures more than once in *Tess*. On her walk home from 'Flintcomb-Ash' she 'passed the village inn' at Hazelbury and was greeted by its creaking sign. Lea thinks this was the Antelope, as it may have been; but

H

there were at least three other Hazelbury inns at the time. How, if 'Flintcomb-Ash' is situated in even the most easterly of its possible positions (see page 126, and map on pages 92–3), Tess can have included both Bulbarrow and Hazelbury in what Hardy calls 'the nearest course' to Marnhull, he does not explain. The 850ft Bulbarrow is now surmounted by a small group of aerial masts. Hartfoot Lane lies about two miles further south, in the parish of Melcombe Bingham or Bingham's Melcombe. This name suggested that of Parson Tringham in *Tess*, who is said to have been indeed founded on a real vicar of the parish.

To the south the long route eventually divides, one branch entering Puddletown, the other joining the B3142 (Puddletown–Piddlehinton) at Druce Farm, William Boldwood's 'Little Weatherbury Farm' in *Far from the Madding Crowd*. The farmhouse is a mellow, antique building, creeper-faced; and the whole farm contrives to look exceptionally prosperous, although its modern additions are almost invisible from the road.

Running NNW from the farm, and forming a cross with the Hartfoot Lane road and the two arms of the B3142, which here makes a turn of 90 degrees, is a track leading up to Druce Higher Barn. The small vale through which it lies, though difficult to reconcile with the account of the pursuit of Bathsheba by Oak and Coggan, is Puddletown or Druce Bottom, the 'Weatherbury Bottom' in which Hardy set the gipsy camp. There are one or two cottages, remnants of a larger number, beside the lane. Halfway up its length the valley forks, and the tree-crowned promontory at the top of the western arm is Dole's Hill Plantation, 'Dole Hill' in the poem 'The Revisitation'.

The true position of Waterston Manor ('Weatherbury [Upper] Farm') is a mile west of where Hardy placed it, which was within half a mile of Puddletown. After being (as in the novel) a rented farm for longer than most lapsed manors, the house and some of the land have reverted to independent ownership; but the long period of subjection explains Hardy's true references to mould, rot, and the ravages of worm. The place was first rebuilt, somewhat inartistically, by the fifth Earl of Ilchester following a severe fire in 1863. Hardy's detailed picture describes the house before the fire. The extent of the damage caused by this fire is the subject of conflicting views. The brochure issued at the manor describes the

BATHSHEBA EVERDENE'S HOUSE

house as having been 'almost completely gutted', yet the present owner is emphatic that the degree of damage has been grossly exaggerated. In part the ambiguity arises because shortly before World War I the gifted architect Morley Horder was commissioned to undo the clumsy handiwork of the fifth Earl, and today the building, more especially the interior, presents so harmonious a synthesis between old and new that it is not everywhere easy to tell which is which.

Certainly the south front, with its tower-like central bow, survived the fire. At the time of the novel the main entrance was still on this side (it is now on the west), and the public road ran close to the house. Hardy's 'fluted pilasters' adorn the Great Gable, a projecting feature of the east front with a most elaborate design. This too is a seventeenth-century survival and little changed; but the rest of the east front was probably rebuilt, and the house has been extended to the north.

Inside the house the lay-out is unorthodox and extremely attractive: I do not think I have seen a more pleasing interior in

Dorset. But how much belongs to the seventeenth century and how much to the twentieth it is almost impossible to say. The uneven, worm-eaten boards have gone from the upper floors—destroyed in the fire, no doubt. But although Lea says that *all* the old woodwork was lost, the panelling in the study and main hall is pre-fire, and, despite some assertions to the contrary, it seems likely that Hardy's great oak staircase, so minutely described, is the one we see today. Its position was shifted slightly during the rebuilding, but the existence of various pieces let in by way of repair, and of replaced balusters, in addition to the general appearance of age, do not suggest a nineteenth-century substitution.

The odd arrangement for the shearing supper, whereby Bathsheba sat in her parlour at one end of a long table, the rest of which extended through an open window so that her staff were outside on the 'grass-plot', is fairly surely meant to refer to the window (now a door) on the ground floor of the Great Gable—if only because this was probably the only window unobstructed by stone mullions. The beautiful gardens laid out by Morley Horder are entirely different from their predecessors.

The fern-brake with oaks and beeches in a swamp beside the road, to which Bathsheba wandered after the opening of the coffin, is either imaginary or lay somewhere between the manor (as repositioned by Hardy) and Puddletown. The sheep-washing pool, however, is not only still in existence, but still used. Improvised gates raise the water-level when needed, but the 'circular basin of brickwork' is just as it was more than a century ago, though the meadow in which it lies is no longer a water-meadow.

The prototype of the great barn in which Sergeant Troy led the alcoholic revels was never at Waterston but at Cerne Abbas, and is dealt with in Section 7 (page 129). 'Nest Cottage', to which Gabriel Oak retired, stood on Chine Hill, between Puddletown and Druce Farm; a row of twentieth-century cottages now stands near the site.

SOUTH WESSEX: Casterbridge to Outer Wessex
(Dorset: Dorchester to Somerset)

And are ye one of Hermitage—
Of Hermitage, by Ivel Road,
And do ye know, in Hermitage
A thatch-roofed house where sengreens grow?
And does John Waywood live there still—
He of that name that there abode
When father hurdled on the hill
    Some fifteen years ago?

THE INQUIRY
(from *A Set of Country Songs: At Casterbridge Fair*)

According to Lea, whom on this occasion there is no reason to doubt, the farm in 'The Revisitation' where Agnette lived was Muston Manor Farm, about a mile south-east of Piddlehinton. In general the surrounding land is little altered, but a bare quarter-mile to the north lies Piddlehinton Camp, dating from 1938, the least obtrusive of the county's army settlements. The road that passes between Muston and the camp, B3143, has always been assumed to be that taken by Burthen's van in *A Few Crusted Characters* and by Tony Kytes in the first of the stories. But on attempting to follow these travellers, we find that Tony's experiences do not fit in with this route at all. There is no 'corner where we *drop down* [my italics] to Lower Longpuddle', whether the latter be taken as Puddletown or Piddlehinton. It is impossible to reconcile the three points at which Tony saw the three girls. In another of the stories the coffin bearing Jack Winter is heard approaching along the turnpike road, which the B3143 was not.

There is, however, another route from Dorchester to Piddlehinton, somewhat unlikely though not much longer, which deserves notice because it unexpectedly solves nearly all the problems raised by the B3143. We know that Burthen set out from the White Hart and crossed Grey's Bridge. Since he certainly did not go to 'Upper Longpuddle' through Puddletown he must have turned into the B3143. But suppose about a quarter of a mile along it he again turned left, into the lane leading back west to Charminster. From here he could have proceeded along the upper Sherborne road and turned right beyond Charlton Higher Down towards Piddlehinton. This route would have furnished (1) a turnpike road, (2) a climb (mentioned by one of the storytellers), (3) the corner and 'drop down' to 'Lower Longpuddle'. Tony's horse overset the waggon by taking the corner too fast, causing the *offside* wheels to mount the bank. This suggests a right turn, which the corner here is, whereas the corner in the B3143 is to the left.

In the *Crusted Characters* tales Puddletown is referred to un-mistakably only once, and then as 'Weatherbury'. All the odds therefore seem against its still being 'Lower Longpuddle' when these stories were written. Hardy gives a list of the names in the fictional churchyard, but they are not names in the registers of the real churches.

'The inn' (where the carrier's journey ended) is used as if there were no other, although there were several inns in each of the three villages. The 'Tinkers' Arms' named in 'Absentmindedness in a Parish Choir' is fictitious, but we do know that the church in which Hardy set this richly comic episode is that of Piddletrenthide (gallery removed about 1850), for its identity is made unequivocally clear in the passages linking the three Satchel stories. Furthermore, Piddlehinton church had no gallery, and at Puddletown the 'quire', unlike its absent-minded counterpart, contained no violins. 'Long-puddle Spring' is identifiable as the spring that feeds Morning Well, a natural beauty-spot north-west of Piddletrenthide church. The manor house at which old Andrey Satchel tried to make believe he was a fiddler is that of Piddletrenthide, a comely eighteenth-century house flanked by beeches. There are some new houses in the twin villages, but even the presence of the camp has produced no major expansion.

The short poem 'The Sexton at Longpuddle' refers to Piddle-trenthide or Piddlehinton, and the Piddle ('Pydel') valley, some-where along its length (Piddlehinton, according to Lea), is the setting of another poem, 'A Sunday Morning Tragedy'.

Within the parish of Alton Pancras lies the most likely site of another much-disputed place, 'Flintcomb-Ash'—in the earliest version of *Tess* significantly called 'Alton Ash'. The poem 'We Fieldwomen' is also set there. Lea considers 'Flintcomb-Ash' to be unidentifiable; Windle and Harper equate it with Dole's Ash Farm, ENE of Piddletrenthide; 'Holland' says it is near Nettle-comb Tout, two miles NNE of Dole's Ash; Pinion positions it north-east of Alton Pancras and south of Church Hill; J. Stevens Cox, who normally echoes Lea, places it very precisely on the site of the Iron Age village 'on Barcombe Down'. The village site is in fact on the south slope of Church Hill—thus tallying with Pinion's version—Barcombe being the next down to westward.

The conduct of affairs at 'Flintcomb-Ash' was unpleasant

enough to bring it under Hardy's rule of avoiding real (or at least identifiable) houses for such events. On this ground alone it therefore seems unlikely that Dole's Ash Farm is the prototype; and a further objection is that Dole's Ash is too far south for the route Tess took to walk to Beaminster. But from Church Hill—on which there is no real farmstead—a bridleway runs almost directly westward to Little Minterne Hill, then along this to Dogbury Gate where one picks up the Beaminster route as given by Hardy.

In their endeavour to locate the farm, most writers have forgotten that 'Flintcomb-Ash' is also a village. Only Harper mentions Plush—somewhat oddly he says that Dole's Ash Farm is there— yet Plush, less than a mile from the Church Hill camp, conforms with all Hardy's few clues. It lies in a depression; during the nineteenth century it was small and poor enough for the novelist, bent on giving the worst impression, to call it the 'remains' of a village; at the period of the novel it was mainly owned by one absentee family; and on the south-western perimeter of the *older* houses the lane has to turn at a sharp angle because the gabled end of a cottage juts into it, exactly as Hardy writes of Tess's lodging.

Modern Plush is still tiny, but no longer poor having begun to attract the well-to-do retired. It also accommodates an unusual industry—an orchid nursery. Nor is there anything 'starve-acre' today about Church Hill, or for that matter Dole's Ash. Gone are the great fields of swede turnips, and new strains of grass have hidden the 'stony lanchets or lynchets'. Much of Church Hill is now wooded, as are most of the slopes enfolding Plush.

Just off the B3145 lies quiet, unspoilt Buckland Newton ('Newland Buckton'), whose clock Dr Fitzpiers heard strike twelve while he watered his horse at 'Lydden Spring'. There is no 'Lydden Spring' as such, but the small river Lydden, a tributary of the Stour, is fed by several headstreams that cross what would have been the doctor's route. The hamlet called King's Stag or Kingstag, up the B3143 north of Alton Pancras, takes its name from one of Dorset's more famous bygone inns to which, as to many another in the county and in Somerset, came the four friends in that most wideranging of Hardy's narrative poems, 'A Trampwoman's Tragedy'. The inn appears too in 'A Last Journey'. It was burnt down in about 1910 and the site filled with the cottages that stand there today. The magnificent sign alluded to by Lea escaped the fire but was shortly afterwards blown down and re-erected in a field called the Brickyard, where it remained until moved in 1921 to yet another position north of the crossroads. In 1959 it was collected by a Bournemouth firm to be repainted; and that was the last that was heard of it, for the firm went into liquidation and the sign was inadvertently sold with the assets. The purchaser has never been traced.

Five miles north is the small town of Stalbridge, and beside it Stalbridge Park, the 'Stapleford Park' of 'Squire Petrick's Lady'. The 'splendid old mansion now pulled down' in which the squire (in real life Peter Walter) lived was demolished in 1822, but the remarkably tall gate-pillars noted by Lea are still in place.

Between Dorchester and Sherborne ('Sherton Abbas') there are two routes for more than half the way, the upper or old road and the lower or A352, with the river Cerne flowing between; the two unite at Middlemarsh ('Marshwood', 'Marshcombe'). Although by the period of *The Woodlanders* the upper road was already little used except by drovers, the 'forsaken coach-road' on which Mrs Dollery's carrier-van plied between Sherborne and Cerne Abbas was in fact the lower road, 'forsaken' because its traffic had been taken by the railways; the failure of the railway-builders to include Cerne, however, left a small opening for the carrier service.

One point on the upper road does figure in the novel—Revels ('Revellers') Inn, where Giles Winterbourne met Fitzpiers on their respective journeys to and from Milton Abbey. Now Revels Inn Farm, the building retains a few relics of its hostelry days, notably the door mentioned by Lea (but not the bench), today stored in a lumber room, and some exceptionally fine carved panelling on the walls of what was presumably the best parlour. Near the southern end of the upper road stands Charminster, now expanding so rapidly that it already fills the half-mile to the converging lower road. The old part of the village, however, preserves an attractive appearance. In the centre stands the church where, according to Hardy in *A Group of Noble Dames*, the Lady Penelope lies, with her third husband, Sir William Hervey ('Hervy'), beside her, 'under the tomb which is still visible'. Lea infers that he saw it, but in truth there is no trace of it nor record of its existence.

The Lady Penelope lived at Wolfeton House, built by the Trenchard ('Drenghard', 'Drenkhard') family, one of whom was her first husband. The 'ivied manor-house', now divided into flats, is ivied no longer, to the benefit of its stonework and great mullioned windows. The two round French-looking towers flanking the gateway are still intact, with the Trenchard arms over the gate between them. But this majestic portal now leads nowhere; beyond it the derelict drive soon becomes lost in a wilderness of undergrowth, and the avenue that continues the drive southward between the imposing trees to the A37 is now a highway of stinging nettles. Access to the house, since the period of the story, has returned to the north. The bowling-green near which Penelope walked was probably the upper of the two lawns, whose well-groomed appearance contrasts with the dereliction about them. The descendants of the nearby willows where basket-makers were cutting osiers, are still to be seen, but not the work associated with them.

Cerne Abbas's fortunes are marked by a long period of prosperity, a shorter one, lasting into the present century, of penury and almost unbelievable dilapidation, then a rise to renewed and still increasing ease. Observing its quiet comfort today, and noting the evidence of bygone riches, it is hard to believe the descriptions given by Treves, Harper and others within the memory of people still alive. The decline set in with the transfer of traffic from road to rail—for the lines stayed remote from Cerne on either side—and the revival came only with the reversal of the trend and, coupled with it, the development of the town for commuters and people in retirement. The lowest population figure, 448, was registered as late as 1931. Today it is double that, and behind the old houses of the main streets lie many acres of new buildings. In view of the condition of the older structures in the depressed days, it is a cause for wonder as well as pleasure that so many could be saved.

Impressed by its roof—for it had little else to commend it above many rivals—Hardy chose the tithe barn at Cerne Abbas as his model for the 'great barn' in *Far from the Madding Crowd*. Despite the widespread impression that the latter is based on the huge barn at Abbotsbury, the claim of Cerne is indisputable. It was first attested in print by Viola Meynell, editor of the correspondence of Sir Sidney Cockerell (see page 66), and confirmed by Wilfrid Blunt in his Cockerell biography. In 1915 Hardy took Cockerell to Cerne, and followed up the visit by sending him a copy of the novel in which he had written the note: 'After a visit to a mediaeval barn typified in the description at pages 164–165'.

With such a wealth of fine barns in the county it is not surprising that so many people mistook Hardy's prototype. Long before his birth the northern end of the Cerne barn had been truncated, and the southern end poorly converted into a residence, which it still is. The roof, however, was as splendid as his description, and it is sad for us that in the 1880s it collapsed. Orders were given for it to be rebuilt to the same design but in a cheaper wood—deal. The deal was certainly used, but the builder preferred a 'modern' design, the ugly and unimaginative results of which we can see today. The non-residential part of the building is currently a garage.

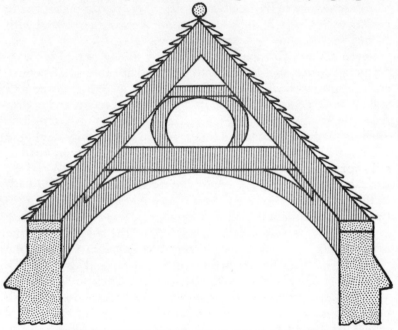

CROSS-SECTION OF ORIGINAL ROOF OF CERNE ABBAS TITHE BARN

To Cerne Abbey belonged the priest of 'The Lost Pyx'. The poem tells us that he later became sub-prior and that his '. . . bones are now bare / In the field that was Cernel choir'. Probably they are, but there is no telling where, for although various fragments of the abbey have survived, not even the exact site of its church is known. The most striking survival is the so-called gatehouse, in reality the entrance porch to the abbot's hall. It contains a turret stair and a porter's lodge in which Betty Reynard, *née* Dornell, and her husband had one of their secret meetings (*A Group of Noble Dames*). In appearance it has changed very little in its now beautified setting—at one time it was surrounded by a farmyard!

On Trendle Hill to the north sprawls the great chalk figure of the Cerne Giant, alluded to in *Tess* and in *The Dynasts*. Miraculously allowed to survive in all its pagan sensuality by monks, Puritans, and finally Victorians, this naughty figure is now assured of preservation by the National Trust. When Hardy knew Cerne, the maypole still flourished in the earth-camp above the Giant's head; and it is said that even today childless couples go in all seriousness to see what the great chalk likeness may do for them.

Just over two miles north of Cerne Abbas is Minterne Magna, a tiny village identified by Hardy in his copy of Heath's *Dorchester and its Surroundings* with 'Great Hintock'. This is the threshold of the country of *The Woodlanders*, the most elusive of the regions in which the Wessex novels are set, particularly when it is realised that Hardy changed many of the locations between editions. A lengthy and careful analysis by Pinion in the *Thomas Hardy Year Book* no 2 (1971) takes the reader effectively through the maze. There is no space here to examine the changes in detail, but they may be summarised by saying that originally, beyond question, Hardy imagined his 'Little Hintock' between Melbury Osmond and Bubb Down, but later shifted it several miles eastward, close to High Stoy; other places were shifted east as well to preserve their relative positions. Pinion gives as the reason for the transfer Hardy's anxiety that the dubious Mrs Charmond should not be identified with any member of the Ilchester family, whose possibly disapproving attention he was about to risk with the publication of the 'First Countess of Wessex'; for in the original landscape of *The Woodlanders* 'Hintock House' occupied the site of Melbury House.

Hardy preferred, to the end of his life, not to have the scenes of this novel too closely analysed. As late as 1926 we find him denying, in a letter, that he knew where 'Little Hintock' was, and the list of hamlets that he names as having helped to supply its features spans the terrain from the old setting to the new.

MELBURY OSMOND

Several names appear not only in *The Woodlanders* but elsewhere. High Stoy and Dogbury were passed by Tess on that journey from 'Flintcomb-Ash' to Beaminster, the trees on High Stoy and Bubb Down 'twanged' at one another in the storm that beset the priest of 'The Lost Pyx', High Stoy was climbed by the four friends in the poem 'Under High-Stoy Hill', and the neighbourhood of Dogbury Gate is the setting for another, 'Life and Death at Sunrise'. So little has the region been modified that even the medieval priest would still find it familiar.

Lyons-Gate is a group of cottages on the main road a mile north of Minterne Magna; Middlemarsh, already mentioned, is equally tiny but boasts an inn, the White Horse, which is ' "The Horse" on Hintock Green' of 'A Trampwoman's Tragedy'. In spite of its main road situation it continues outwardly unpretentious, though some modernisation has recently been effected inside. Faced by a small filling station, which the publican also operates, it is otherwise without a near neighbour. The extensive woods west of Middlemarsh are the largest remaining in the scattered *Woodlanders* landscape. Just clear of their farther flank lies Hermitage, still small, diffuse, very quiet—'This tiny Rip Van Winkle village', Treves called it—but with signs of beginning to be favoured by the well-to-do retired and the Yeovil commuter. No 'sengreens'—houseleeks—grow today out of the thatch.

One of the scenes in *The Woodlanders* that has not been moved east is the last, the brilliant and poignant ending which sees Marty in the moonlight beside Giles's grave in 'Great Hintock' churchyard. We have learnt that before Hardy transposed it 'Great Hintock' was Melbury Osmond; and the reference to the views from the churchyard rules out any substitution of Minterne Magna.

Where the A352, on approaching Sherborne, is joined by the A3030 from Sturminster Newton, there stands in the fork a small dark stone house called West Hill Cottage. This is the former 'Sherton turnpike on the Bath road' where Bathsheba Everdene's faithful employees caught up with her on her flight.

The market-place at Sherborne where Giles Winterborne stood holding his ten-foot apple tree has now become a car-park. The 'Earl of Wessex', the impressive mullioned coaching inn with the central courtyard, which, as correctly stated towards the end of

The Woodlanders, was destroyed to make way for the railway, stood where the station now stands. Its real name was the New Inn. To replace it a new hotel, the Digby, heavy and ugly, was built nearby; but now this in turn has been taken over by Sherborne School, a fact advertised by the construction of a large, pallid new scholastic building at the back. Weber, taking as his premise the change in the divorce laws that came about in 1878 and is prominent in *The Woodlanders*, places the action between 1876 and 1879. But the railway had reached Sherborne in 1860, and the Digby had therefore long replaced the New Inn; indeed, after the final reconciliation of Grace and Fitzpiers it is specifically stated that they visited the hotel 'rebuilt contemporaneously with the construction of the railway'. Yet the description in the account of Grace's earlier visit, which would have been in 1877, is unquestionably a portrait of the New Inn.

'Sheep Street', through which she drove looking for Giles, is Sherborne's smart main shopping thoroughfare, Cheap Street. Midway along it, a structure that looks like a chapel is the Monks' Conduit, which Grace's father was passing when he was hailed by Lawyer Beancock, and behind which the eloping lovers of the poem 'In Sherborne Abbey' hid their horse. Appropriately, the conduit has been adapted to house a public drinking-fountain. Less appropriately, the pleasant effect of its fifteenth-century grace has been ruined by the nearby erection of a large traffic sign.

Looming over the houses west of the Conduit is Sherborne Abbey, the 'Abbey north of Blackmore Vale' in 'The Lost Pyx' as Cerne is 'the Abbey south thereof'. Its glory is the fan-tracery of its roof, yet all Grace does when Giles takes her in there is to regard the tomb of John Digby, third Earl of Bristol, and his two wives. This tomb was doubtless among those noticed by the lovers of 'In Sherborne Abbey' as they waited in the moonlight, and they may have also noticed the resting place of the Horseys, father and son, of whom the son was Hardy's 'Master John Horseleigh, Knight'.

Sherborne Castle appears in *The Woodlanders*, but is more prominent as the scene of the tale of 'Anna, Lady Baxby'. When Anna's husband (in life Lord Digby) was defending it against the Parliamentary troops led by her brother, the Earl of Bedford, it was still intact; but when Grace Melbury went there it lay in the ruined state to which Cromwell had ordered it to be reduced.

Page 135 Christminster: (*left*) St Sepulchre's Cemetery, in the Jericho district of Oxford, can lay a strong claim to being the spot Hardy had in mind as the last resting-place of Jude's and Sue's children. It was closed for general burials in 1954

(*right*) the 'Lamb and Flag', associated with Jude and Arabella: a side view, looking down the 'lane' toward St Giles Street. The original 'low-pitched tavern' is the portion within the bay window and alongside the door

Page 136 (*left*) Jude's mileston‹ awaiting reinstatement, the stor‹ on the back of which Jude is supposed to have cut his inscription is the middle one o‹ these three. The taller figure is the author

(*right*) the Larmer Gardens, Tollard Royal, showing the temple. Hardy made use of his visit with Emma to these lovely Wiltshire pleasure-grounds (closed now) in the poem 'Concerning Agnes'

In 'Anna' the features mentioned owe much to Hardy's imagination. The 'little gate to the south' through which she stole to meet her brother probably did not exist; the 'west terrace' on which she later met her husband's lover may have existed, but if so is now under the turf; and no circular stair is apparent hereabouts, although the remnant of one can be seen elsewhere.

During Bedford's siege Lady Digby was really in occupation of the newer castle, the Lodge, built by Sir Walter Raleigh on the other side of the lake, and still the seat of the Digbys today. It was from here that she rode out, of her own accord, to tell Bedford that if he destroyed the Lodge, not the older castle, he would find her dead body under the ruins.

Pouncy's photograph of 1857 shows the ruins heavily creepered and overshadowed by trees. Grace must have seen them in this state, but today the only plants in the grass-clad bailey are a few ornamental shrubs; for Sherborne Castle is undergoing protracted strengthening by the Ministry of Public Building and Works. Crumbling edges, dangerous cracks, are made good by a kind of invisible mending, using 'secret' formulas and techniques to match the effects of time. The work has already taken a dozen years, and is likely to take several more.

The next radial road out of Dorchester is that route so familiar to Hardy readers, Long Ash Lane ('Holloway Lane' in a few early editions), otherwise the road to Yeovil ('Ivell'), the A37. In both 'Interlopers at the Knap' and 'The Grave by the Handpost' Hardy dilates on the lonely and ill-kept state of Long Ash Lane, and it was not until the 1930s that it was rehabilitated throughout its length. It is lonely even now.

High on the downs in the broad fork by Charminster, where the 'lane' parts company with the A352, is the site of Shepherd Fennel's cottage in 'The Three Strangers'. It is doubtful whether this cottage ever existed, but the 'hog's-back elevation which dominated this part of the down' can be pinpointed as Hog Hill, south-east of Grimstone Down. On the crest a splendid thatched barn of brick, magnificently solitary, can without much effort be imagined as the cottage. The lynchets over which the search-party stumbled are on the eastern or Stratton Bottom side; the Bottom itself is the 'grassy, briery, moist defile' where they searched; and there are still several small areas of woodland.

I

It must have been across Hog Hill or very close to it that (in *A Few Crusted Characters*) Parson Toogood and his clerk set out after the hounds, leaving Andrey Satchel and his bride-to-be locked in Frampton ('Scrimpton') church tower—the same tower that we see today. The hunt proceeded by 'Lippet Wood', 'Green's Copse', and 'Higher Jirton' toward Yellowham Wood; of these only 'Higher Jirton' can be given a possible real identity as Higher Forston. 'Lippet' may derive from Skippet, three miles to the south.

BATCOMBE DOWN—THE CROSS-IN-HAND

From Long Ash Lane a narrow way, once a turnpike, leads under the railway to Sydling St Nicholas, site of 'Sydling Mill' in the poem 'Old Excursions'—in fact there were two mills, both gone now but recalled by older villagers—and the 'Broad Sidlinch' of 'The Grave by the Handpost'. The post stood where the Maiden Newton ('Chalk Newton')–Sydling road crosses Long Ash Lane, and where a newer signpost stands today. The 'North Eweleaze' of the story is North Field Hill, the bare down in the north-east angle of the cross. Long Ash Lane is here at its straightest and loftiest. Where a few houses flank it at Holywell it is crossed by the road from Dogbury Gate to Evershot ('Evershead') and Beaminster, Tess's route. East of Long Ash Lane this road crosses Batcombe Down, and in the roadside grass at nearly the highest point (around 800ft) stands the mysterious stone pillar, the Cross-in-Hand ('Crossy-Hand' locally).

Several guesses have been made at the nature of the now worn-away carving that once decorated it: one is that the shaft showed the figure of a woman with crossed arms, another that the moulding on the south (road-facing) side of the bowl-shaped capital originally represented a hand. Of the many conjectured purposes of the little monument—more even than cited by Hardy—the most charming, and I fear least likely, is that it was a memorial to mark the site of the miracle related in 'The Lost Pyx'. But one authority does postulate a connection with Cerne Abbey, suggesting that the concave capital was designed to receive offerings.

At all events, there the pillar stands, the grass round its base occasionally cut by the authorities, and all around it the country remains as desolate as ever. Batcombe ('Owlscombe') church is a little to the west, close under the hill; here, reputedly, in a very odd tomb still to be seen, lies buried 'Conjurer' Mynterne, one of the curious company of soothsayer-witchdoctors common in Hardy's pages, and collectively discussed by Dairyman Crick in *Tess*.

Evershot is mainly associated with *Tess*, but here too, in 'The First Countess of Wessex', Squire Dornell's man, Tupcombe, sat in the inglenook at the 'Sow and Acorn' (the Acorn) in the hope of hearing news of Betty, and Philip Hall collected Sally's dress from the carrier in 'Interlopers at the Knap'. The small inn has been very little altered outside or in. Neither of the old hearths in the two bars was large enough to possess an inglenook; both have now been partly filled in round small modern grates. Tess breakfasted and supped at 'the cottage by the church . . . almost the first at that end of the village'. This is popularly taken to mean the stone cottage immediately west of the church; even today there is only one other before the open country. The barn in which she discovered Alec ranting stood not far off the road 'near the central part' of the village. Looking much out of place, there is such a barn, down the lane called Tannery; it is of brick, thatched, with very dilapidated woodwork. One end has been extended and made into a garage; other garages face the double doors, which are smaller than implied by Hardy and face north, not west toward the 'three o'clock' setting sun of winter. However, he also said they were on the side away from Tess as she approached from the main street, which they are.

North-east of Holywell cross stands Woolcombe, touched on in 'The Rash Bride': 'I knew him—one from Woolcomb way— Giles Swetman . . .'—a reminder that Hardy's maternal forbears once owned considerable property out here, including Woolcombe House, of which all that remained even when he was born was the stables incorporated into Woolcombe Farm, as may be seen to this day.

The 'obscure gate to the east' of Melbury ('King's Hintock') Park by which Charles Phelipson made off with Betty Dornell continues to stand, nearly opposite Bubb Down Hill. The only parts of Melbury House that would not have been known to Betty are the west wing and tower, both nineteenth-century; since Hardy's day much creeper has been removed. The 'little flowered frock' in which Betty was married is still preserved at the house, just as Hardy says.

Melbury Sampford church, to all intents the private chapel, was heavily restored during the nineteenth century, but its monuments were kept, including Stephen Fox's, from the rhymed inscription on which Hardy applies two lines to Stephen Reynard. Melbury Park is finely timbered, a setting still appropriate to the poem 'Autumn in King's Hintock Park'. One may yet cross the park, as did the enigmatic stranger in the tale 'The Duke's Reappearance', by a private road from Clammers Gate (the real name) in the north to the 'Evershead' gate in the south.

To the west of the park lie the small villages of East and West Chelborough ('Delborough'). It was 'in King's Hintock Wood, by Delborough' that Grace found Giles Winterborne's modest (and fictitious) home 'One-Chimney Hut'. This is a region remote and unspoilt even by Dorset standards.

The extremity of Melbury Osmond nearest to Clammers Gate is called Town's End. Hardy uses the name, spelt 'Townsend', and also the real names of his maternal ancestors, in 'The Duke's Reappearance'. In *The Life* he notes the loss of the stone chimneys and oak staircase from the house involved, which is the one facing Clammers Gate. Hereabouts too, in the opinion of some, stood the old house with the sycamore-root steps to the door featured in 'Interlopers at the Knap' and the poem 'One who Married Above Him'. Neither Hardy's description, in the story, of how the travellers ought to have got there, nor Lea's interpretation of this, can be followed with any certainty; in fact no route that one can work out, on map or terrain, brings one to a point that can be reconciled with the few details we are given about the site of the house: at the top of a slope beside King's Hintock village street, a mile or two from King's Hintock Court, and three miles from where the travellers succeeded in getting to along the wrong road. There was a brook forty yards off. The details of the house were visible far up the road as one entered the village, and the 'little inn' to which Johns and the boy were sent on by Darton (called, in the magazine version of the story, the 'Sheaf of Arrows') lay further away. On his last visit Darton rode 'by a side path to the top of the slope, where riders seldom came'.

The only inn officially recorded is the still-existing Rest and Welcome, not in the 'village street' but in Long Ash Lane itself. There are two conveniently placed brooks, one of which, reached by a path that leaves the road beside the house of 'The Duke's Reappearance', is the Buttock's Spring mentioned in that story. The name is still in local use.

Melbury Osmond church, in addition to commanding a fine view of Blackmoor Vale and High Stoy, is crossed today as formerly by a path through it that would have permitted George Melbury to avoid going round by the road on his way to 'Great Hintock', thus providing further evidence that when Hardy shifted his scenes eastward he retained his original church. The churchyard is the scene of the 'strange interment' that inspired the poem 'Her Late Husband'; neither inscriptions nor registers reveal the real protagonists, but Bailey suggests the two Swaffields and John Swetman (1822).

Chetnole ('Catknoll') lies east of Long Ash Lane, on the railway into near-by Yeovil. It still looks less suburban than one might expect. This is the scene of the poem 'The War-Wife of Catknoll', although it is an entry in the register of baptisms at Melbury Osmond that provides the basis for the anecdote. The Wriggle, the stream in which the 'Catknoll' wife drowned herself, looks too tiny for the purpose, except perhaps after a storm. Even closer to Yeovil and much more suburban despite some fine older houses, is Yetminster, the 'Estminster' of 'The Inscription'. In the church the inscription is now seen to better advantage since in 1890 a Major Harvey caused the brasses to be set in a concrete tablet on the north wall of the nave. The John Horsey commemorated was the grandfather of 'Master John Horseleigh' who built Clifton Maybank ('Clyfton Horseleigh') hard by. Why Hardy should have written that 'hardly a trace now remains' of this mansion is a mystery, for although only the east wing survives, the rest having been demolished in 1786, the fragment, in spite of its now disproportionate height, continues to be 'seductive and picturesque', thanks to careful maintenance and some judicious nineteenth-century restoration. No longer a farmhouse, it is once more surrounded by spacious lawns and gardens. One or two features from the main part of the house were incorporated in it after the demolition, and others were taken away for incorporation in neighbouring Montacute (see page 230). There is still, as in Hardy's time, good timber in Clifton Wood.

Reverting south, at the White Horse in Maiden Newton Darton's bailiff in 'Interlopers at the Knap' took over Helena's orphaned boy, and at the same inn in 'Destiny and a Blue Cloak', Agatha boarded the carrier's van on her way back from Weymouth. The town was also familiar to Tess, but figures most prominently in 'The Grave by the Handpost', which brings in the church, churchyard, 'riverside rectory' and old Ezra's (unidentifiable) cottage. The church, having escaped major Victorian restoration, retains much of its early nineteenth-century appearance. The former rectory, through the garden of which runs the Frome, is a Tudor mansion fit for an archbishop. Largely rebuilt with the original stones in 1844—later than the date of the story—it ceased to be a rectory in 1938.

Alas that similar regard was denied the White Horse! The gracious Elizabethan stone inn, with central archway, diamond-paned mullioned windows and dormered thatch, was pulled down early in this century—not many years after Emma Hardy sketched it—and replaced by a dreary structure in red brick. In the roadway before it the 'stone stump of the cross' remains, dwarfed by the towering proximity of an electricity-supply pole bearing a number of enamelled route signs. Aesthetic considerations have not predominated in twentieth-century Maiden Newton.

The small town is quiet, despite its railway junction, and lacks much evidence of development. The old mill now makes carpets. Just outside the town is Whitesheet Hill, namesake of a hill on

the edge of Beaminster. Pinion suggests that the former is referred to in 'Molly Gone', the latter in 'The Homecoming'. About
the second there can be little doubt, but in 'Molly Gone' it seems
to me either hill may be intended. Both remain open meadowland.

South-west of Maiden Newton, above the rolling downs, rises
Eggardon Hill—'Haggardon Hill' in *The Trumpet-Major* and the
'hill-fortress of Eggar' in the poem 'My Cicely', but *not*, as sometimes stated, the site of Gabriel Oak's 'Norcombe' farm—is a
lonely height, at times strangely unprepossessing notwithstanding
its vast views.

The real 'Norcombe' lies three or four miles farther north,
'near lonely Toller Down' and the stretch of the A356 formerly
called—as in 'A Trampwoman's Tragedy' and 'The Dark-Eyed
Gentleman'—Crimmercrock Lane. The features of 'Norcombe'
are generally dismissed as drawn from the imagination, but in
fact almost every one of them is to be found in the area; all that
Hardy has done is to edit them, as it were, into the arrangement he
required.

The road from 'Norcombe' to Dorchester, 'sunk in a deep
cutting', is the route from Hooke to Lower Kingcombe. Today
this is an unfrequented (and exceedingly narrow) lane with banks
that are nearly vertical; at one time it was part of the coach road
between Beaminster and Maiden Newton. The route, however,
was never turnpiked, and to provide the 'turnpike gate at the
bottom of the hill' Hardy has 'moved' the turnpike from the
crossroads on Toller Down; the true site is still marked on the
map as Toller Down Gate. Originally it was known as Catsley
Down Gate, and on Catsley Down itself there used to be a sheep
fair, now commemorated in the name Fair Field.

The 'featureless convexity of chalk and soil' that was 'Norcombe Hill' would fit most of the hills in the area. The beech
plantation on the northern side was 'ancient and decaying' and
may well have vanished, but there are at least three woodlands
today that answer to the topographical requirements, according
to which hill is picked as 'Norcombe': these are Ridge Coppice,
Westcombe Coppice, and the plantation near Higher Kingcombe.
One may note the simple change of compass-point needed to
make 'Norcombe' out of Westcombe.

'Norcombe' is also the name of a village with a church. The

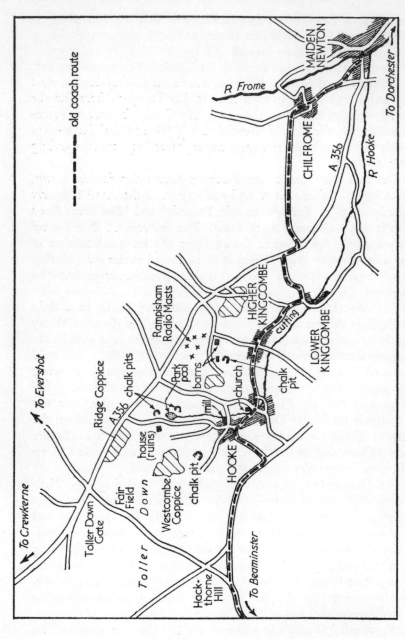

To illustrate the opening scenes of *Far from the Madding Crowd*

likeliest original is Hooke. On its outskirts, at the foot of West-combe Hill, there used to be a mill that we may take for the 'Tew-nell Mill' of the novel. By the middle of the present century it had degenerated into a seedy cottage, but in 1969 it was acquired for restoration as a better-class residence. A little north of it, on the hill, are the remains of a chalk-pit that once employed twenty or thirty panniered donkeys to carry away its product; there are several other pits of various sizes near by, and a very large pit north of Higher Kingcombe, in the shadow of the BBC's Rampi-sham radio masts. No pit is surmounted by the converging hedges that guided Oak's sheep to their doom, but close to the King-combe pit a gate set diagonally across the corner of a hedge-girt field produces a suggestively similar effect. As for the pond, on the east slope of Westcombe Hill there is a pond called Park Pool, and another lies at Toller Whelme. Only Gabriel's rented farmhouse and Mrs Hurst's cottage and cow-byre cannot be related to precise features in a district of less than two square miles. Today this is a sequestered part of the world, and Hooke is a dying village; only its manor, now a Roman Catholic school for 'problem' boys, shows a vitality not always entirely congenial to the other in-habitants. The agricultural land in the area is well maintained.

Kingcombe Hill is another name with two claimants. In ad-dition to the one near Hooke, there is another near Dole's Ash Farm; but the former is the more probable 'Kingcomb Hill' of the poem 'The Pat of Butter'. Toller Down, which features prominently in 'The Homecoming', continues lonely and wind-swept, dominated by the near-by Rampisham masts. The minor road leading east from Toller Down Gate crossroads is Benvill Lane, twice mentioned in *Tess*. To the west the B3163 leads to Beaminster. This pleasant but dull small town appears in 'Destiny and a Blue Cloak', but is mainly known to Hardy readers for con-taining, in its vicarage, the home of the Clares. Despite a fairly extensive programme of new housing nearby, church and vicarage show no departure whatever from Hardy's picture, even to the lawn with its shrubs. The sole innovation is a garage. The road in from Evershot is still hedge-girt as when Tess lost her boots there.

A mile or so south of Beaminster is the pretty village of Nether-bury, suggested by Pinion as the 'Cloton' of 'Destiny and a Blue

Cloak'. Certainly the mill—now a private house—where Agatha lived, conforms to the description of 'Cloton' mill. The stream does form the boundary of a garden, orchard, and paddock, and does separate the property from the 'village highroad'. 'Heavy-headed' trees still grow near. Only the 'little wooden bridge' in its swampy surroundings cannot be found; but there is a stone bridge beside the house. The other house in the tale, Farmer Lovill's, is not identifiable.

The Netherbury–Broadwindsor area has superseded that of the 'Hintocks' as the region of farm-made cider, but Broadwindsor is primarily in dairying country; and one of the places mentioned in 'A Pat of Butter', Netherhay, is a tiny, hoary hamlet three miles north-east of the town.

North of the point where the A356 begins to drop down toward Crewkerne it passes 'the cosy house at Wynyard's Gap', another haunt of the Trampwoman and her friends. The licensee is well aware of the epithet in the poem, and the inn remains cosy. It is also completely solitary and likely to remain so, for the country all about it belongs either to Chedington Court (the manor house) or to the National Trust. Properly called the Wynyard's Gap Inn, formerly the 'King's Arms', it has, to judge from an old photograph, undergone only very slight external changes. Internally, the principal bar has been enlarged and discreetly modernised, and the cellar, with the old hooks still in the beams, has been turned into a cellar bar. The Gap is also mentioned in 'Molly Gone', and gives its name to the long dialogue poem 'At Wynyard's Gap'. The view of 'half South Wessex' (and much more) is as splendid and unspoilt now as when 'He' and 'She' gazed upon it.

Among the places that 'He' pointed out from Wynyard's Gap are Lewesdon Hill ('Lewsdon' in 'Molly Gone') and Pilsdon Pen —Dorset's highest point. The two heights lie between Broadwindsor and the point where Dorset, Somerset, and Devon meet. In appearance they are quite dissimilar. Lewesdon Hill (893ft) is roughly conical and has a thickly wooded summit, but is accessible by public pathways, since from 1943 it has belonged to the National Trust. Most of Pilsdon Pen (908ft) which is much longer than it is wide, is covered with hedged fields, and leave to walk there depends not so much on the courtesy of the farmer as on the co-operation of his cattle. The western end is covered with heather and scrub and is crowned by a prehistoric hill fort, the scene of recent excavations. The views from Lewesdon are limited to what can be seen from any one point or the periphery of the trees; but from the open sausage-back of Pilsdon there are tremendous panoramas over the three counties and the sea. Conversely the hill itself is a landmark, as Hardy was fond of remarking, for miles around. He may have called it 'little Pilsdon Crest' in his poem 'Wessex Heights', but all the evidence is that he did not think of it as little.

SOUTH WESSEX: *the coast from Lower Wessex to Budmouth*
(Dorset: the coast from Devon to Weymouth)

> ...The boats, the sands, the esplanade,
> The laughing crowd;
> Light-hearted, loud
> Greetings from some not ill-endowed;
>
> The evening sunlit cliffs, the talk,
> Hailings and halts,
> The keen sea-salts,
> The band, the Morgenblätter Waltz...

AT A SEASIDE TOWN IN 1869

In the 1820s and earlier the flat lands about the multiple head-streams of the Char and Simene were a good deal less well drained than now; Hutchins describes Marshwood Vale as 'hardly passable by travellers but in dry summers'. When the Tramp-woman and her 'fancy-man' were 'stung by every Marshwood midge', they were probably being plagued by mosquitoes, some still malaria-carrying. The peril of malaria has passed, but the dual legacy of unhealthiness and inaccessibility (the latter not vastly improved) accounts for the absence of development in this lush but sparsely-occupied and secretive quarter.

Also in the tramps' itinerary was ' "The Hut" renowned on Bredy Knap', an inn that stood north of the Dorchester–Bridport road (A35) in the angle formed by the lane leading down to North Barn. When Lea wrote, the building was no longer an inn, but in the old lane (traceable just east of the new one) Mary Ann Bull, the last reddle-seller, used to park her cart and dispense her wares. Finally, the ex-inn was demolished, but only a few years ago archaeologists came across its foundations and a number of old-fashioned bottles, unfortunately empty.

Farther east, where the A35 starts to curve toward Winter-bourne Abbas, stand the Nine Stones, the 'Nine-Pillared Crom-lech' passed by the rider in 'My Cicely'. This tiny prehistoric circle is now heavily shaded by trees, one of which has even imprisoned one stone in its roots. The site has been railed in by the Ministry of Public Building and Works.

The rider next went along the valley of 'the Bride-streams', the river Bride and its tributaries. There is now a minor road along the five miles of this old-world vale, west of the mouth of which lies West Bay, prominent in the story 'Fellow-Townsmen'. This is the little harbour so well fashioned by nature that it 'appealed to the passer-by as only requiring a little industry to finish it and make it famous'. But the apparently perfect harbour suffers from constant silting. West Bay has had a modest success as a holiday resort of a kind, but it has failed to grow. An enormous building, erected in 1885 as a boarding-house and residences, is now (since a fire in 1925) a block of flats; and in the season there is a large municipal holiday-camp.

As far as possible the harbour is still kept open; its main patrons are pleasure-craft, but it retains a little of its Scandinavian timber trade. Hardy's 'Harbour Inn' is in real life the little-altered Bridport Arms; but Barnet would not have had to take a boat to reach it from the east beach, nor would he to get to the other inn of the period, the George. The third inn, the West Bay Hotel, is more recent. There are some nondescript cafés, a church built in the 1930s, and even a sort of promenade. In 1887 the railway was extended from Bridport ('Port-Bredy'), only to vanish again a couple of generations later. On the whole West Bay still justifies Treves's description as 'probably the queerest seaport in any part of the British Isles'.

Inland, new villas and bungalows have all but closed the gap between West Bay and Bridport, and have so interspersed themselves among the surviving Victorian villas that it is no longer possible to pick out Lucy Savile's home, if indeed it existed outside the imaginations of Hardy and Lea. 'Château Ringdale' certainly never existed, but its site is real, and on it there was once a mansion of comparable importance. This was Wanderwell, and it stood on a rise just as did Château Ringdale; even the elm-trees really existed, and the only discrepancy is that the Bridport road passes to the west of the rise, not the east. Wanderwell has been demolished and the elms cut down, but the name lives on in one of the streets of the bungalow estate now occupying the ground.

As West Bay Road merges into Bridport's South Street— Hardy's 'long street . . . at right angles to the broad main street' —new buildings become fewer, and South Street itself can have changed only here and there. St Mary's church, where Downe and Lucy were married, remains as when Hardy wrote. The architect whose restoration work in 1860 drew his acid comment was Talbot Bury; and it must be admitted that he left precious little of the original fabric except the 'ancient font'. Near by, the Five Bells (its sign shows ringers on one side, bells on the other) is most probably the 'Ring of Bells' in the poem 'The Whaler's Wife'.

According to Lea, Barnet lived nearly opposite the church.

But Lea for some reason was totally defeated by Bridport. Barnet's house, sold in the closing phase of the story to the 'Congregational Baptist' trustees, 'who pulled down the time-honoured dwelling and built a new chapel on its site', was not in South Street at all, but where the Congregational church, built in 1860, stands today, in East Street. Hutchins says the church authorities bought a site that had not previously been built on; but an eighteenth-century map shows an unbroken line of houses on East Street's southern side, so Hardy is probably correct.

Nor is Lea much happier with Downe's house, which he places in Downe Street. Hardy, however, states that when Barnet was driving Downe home 'their route took them past the little town-hall, the Black Bull Hotel, and onward to the junction of a small street on the right'. This means they were travelling eastward along the main street; not only is Downe Street then on the left, but it is *between* the town hall and the Bull Hotel ('the Black Bull'). In fact, after passing the hotel the small street on the right to which the friends would have come is King Street. Many of its small houses have been pulled down, but enough remain to show the applicability of Hardy's picture. The reference at the end of the tale to the Downes having lived in East Street is clearly a slip.

The eighteenth-century town hall has acquired some public conveniences at its back, but is otherwise externally unchanged, and still dominates the town. The Savings Bank to which Barnet had recourse was at 36 East Street, near the Bull, in an eighteenth-century mansion that now has a cleaned exterior and solicitors within. The Bull itself has preserved its frontage but modernised its interior. A glass door still divides the porch from the hall.

The rope-making and net-making for which the town has so long been famous continue to flourish—the nets at Wimbledon are Bridport-made. The industry even lingers on to a limited extent in private houses, where special orders involving uncommon sizes or mesh are carried out. But the banks of the little river Brit (not to be confused with the Bride) are no longer devoted to the flax-growing that made Barnet's father rich, for the raw material used now is a synthetic fibre. In 1857 the railway 'invaded the town, tying it on to a main line at a junction a dozen miles off' (Maiden Newton). The Bridport branch still operates.

Close to West Bay is the western end of the Chesil Bank or

K

Beach ('pebble beach' in *The Well-Beloved*, 'Chesil Bank' in *The Woodlanders*). Hardy, however, bestows nearly all his attention on the Portland ('Isle of Slingers') end, where bank and so-called isle between them form the 'Deadman's Bay' of *The Well-Beloved* and *The Dynasts*. Here, close under Portland, lies the hamlet of Chesilton, today joined up with Fortuneswell ('the Street of Wells'). On the beachward side of the group of stone cottages there are still some roofless shells and broken walls, remnants of the houses destroyed, as recounted in *The Well-Beloved*, 'by the November gale of 1824' which swept the sea right over Chesil Bank and drowned some two dozen sleeping people. During the 1960s a similar gale, playing on a spring tide, caused waves to break over two rows of buildings into the roadway behind. Luckily an advance warning system is now in operation, and there was no loss of life.

Under an upturned boat on the beach hereabouts Jocelyn Pierston and Marcia Bencomb sheltered from the rain on their way to the mainland. In those days, before the making of the modern road, they had to walk along two miles of pebbles until they came to the 'precarious wooden bridge', now long replaced, that had itself supplanted the ferry. From here they continued round the 'Inner Bay or Roadstead'—Portland Harbour—past King Henry VIII's or Sandsfoot Castle. In 1906 (Treves) this Tudor fortress was still backed by a broad stretch of open downland; today Weymouth's suburbia has engulfed it, though the shore remains undeveloped and the ruin itself barely changed. Its rocky base, recently in danger of erosion, has been strengthened.

The railway to Portland has been closed to passengers, and the little station 'which stood as a strange exotic' close to Chesilton was demolished in 1969. Beside the line is a row of round, silver-shining fuel storage tanks, and beside that again a sizeable area of the vast harbour has been reclaimed and made into an extension of the Royal Navy's helicopter base.

The appearance of the peninsula has changed less than have many of its functions. What goes on in the rock-cut labyrinths belonging to the Ministry of Defence only those who work there know, but the set-up is very different from that of the old infantry garrison, for Portland is today a top-secret underwater-weapons centre. The Royal Naval Hospital is now civilian. The once-military Verne Citadel has become a civilian prison, the Victorian prison a Borstal. Improved techniques have invaded the quarries, but except for the large modern sheds the buildings where the stones are prepared look pure Victorian. The action of *The Well-Beloved*, 1852–92, begins a few years before and ends a few years after the immense harbour walls were built, yet this extremely conspicuous feature is not mentioned in the novel.

The Martinmas Fair lives on at Fortuneswell. So does the glare on the now tarred roads, for although the trees in the grounds of Pennsylvania ('Sylvania') Castle are no longer the only ones on Portland, others are still few. Hardy describes the old Roman road ascending 'in the stiffest of inclines' to the summit, while a modern road farther left led to the forts. Today a still newer route has been cut to the right of the Roman road which, however, remains unimpaired, except by a covering of grass in the upper reaches. The handrail by which Pierston eased his climb has survived.

The Caros' cottage is the last on the east side of the wide thoroughfare that leads southward from Easton ('East Quarriers') before one reaches the Pennsylvania Castle grounds. The cot is of stone, with a tiny stone-walled court or garden at the back; but the stone stile, pigsty and stable mentioned by Hardy were probably imaginary. During his lifetime the building fell into serious disrepair, but was purchased, rehabilitated and presented to the local authority to serve as a museum, by the late Dr Marie Stopes, who lived for many years in the older of the two Portland lighthouses. The cottage and its immediate neighbour, which was included in the purchase, now communicate internally. To make the museum loftier, the upper floor of the second cottage has been taken away, but the old bedroom fireplace remains.

Between this cottage and the castle grounds is the mouth of Church Ope (*not* Hope) Lane, no longer the 'dark little lane' of *The Well-Beloved* but with its small houses brightened and made fashionable. The church of St Andrew, or Old Ope church, was, as Hardy reminds us, first ruined and then obliterated by successive landslips. The churchyard too collapsed into what has since been a ravine, thickly covered with grass, shrubs, and a self-seeded extension of the Castle trees. One solitary arch of the church remains upright in its new site, and in the undergrowth it is still possible to read bits of the inscriptions on some of the tumbled gravestones.

Pennsylvania Castle itself—a pastiche built in 1880—is today an elegant hotel, with an agreeable circular bar in the principal tower. Beeches and chestnuts now add variety to the original elms, and a new entrance on the west side of the grounds has supplanted the earlier one close to the Caros' cottage. A few yards from this older gateway a curious little building built into and above the wall is probably the 'Elizabethan-style garden house' of the novel. Elsewhere along the wall a small door gives access by a rough path to the shore, and below the door a cavernous, water-filled opening at the base of Rufus Castle ('the Red King's Castle') must be what Hardy referred to as the 'dip-well'; certainly it supplied water to the fortress.

Immediately outside the south wall of the grounds there is a small holiday-chalet camp, which might well be an eyesore but in fact looks very pleasant. Far beneath it is a gracious little bay, Church Ope Cove, from which Avice Caro III and Leverre embarked on their flight, and where, some decades earlier, Anne Garland had boarded the Weymouth ferry (*The Trumpet-Major*). Two or three beach huts and a startling public convenience are the only modern intrusions into this nook, which is still reached by a long staircase-cum-footpath alongside the older path noted by Hardy. At the top of the paths, rising sheer from the rock, is Rufus Castle, or what is left of it, for much of this building too has fallen from its perch. The great blocks of masonry observed in *The Well-Beloved* continue to litter the lower slopes.

Easton, where Jocelyn's father had his quarrying business, is hardly a 'little' village, being after Fortuneswell the largest settlement on Portland; but whatever growth it may have seen in the twentieth century has not altered the appearance of its remarkably wide main street. South of Easton the scenery becomes open, although there is still one more village before the land descends toward the Beal or Bill. This famous headland, from which Anne Garland watched HMS *Victory* sail past, must have been more radically transformed since 1902, let alone 1805, than any other part of Portland. New's sketch almost agrees with the engraving in the first edition of Hutchins and the description in *The Trumpet-Major* of the 'wild, herbless, weather-worn promontory [where] saving the one old lighthouse about fifty yards up the slope, scarce a mark was visible to show that humanity had ever been near the spot'. In reality the second lighthouse was there as well, having been erected in 1789; but that Hardy had the older one in mind he made clear many years afterwards, when at the age of eighty-three he and Florence visited Dr Stopes, and for the first time he entered the edifice and climbed to the top.

The marks of humanity today include a large wired-off Ministry of Defence area, a car-park with its signs and ticket booths, a yellow-brick inn (in this all-stone world!), two wooden café-and-curio shacks, and an extraordinary row of black huts that from the back look like hutches on a turkey-farm, but prove on frontal inspection to be beach-chalets set on the cliff-top. Amid all this a small obelisk inscribed 'T.H. 1844' is not a product of Trinity House, but a monument to Admiral Sir Thomas Masterman Hardy, the Captain Hardy of *The Trumpet-Major*.

And yet the Bill has not entirely lost its magic. On a sweltering summer day it is as cool as the deck of a ship at sea, and on a wild day in winter one can forget the twentieth-century clutter and re-capture the atmosphere prevailing in the days of the three Avices or even of Anne. Out to sea, the patch of water called the Race, from which arose the spirits in 'The Souls of the Slain', is a turm-oil of frothing white crests. A view of the Race and the coast from the sea is to be found in *A Pair of Blue Eyes*. The Shambles lightship, also mentioned there, was replaced in 1971 by a new type of automatic lightbuoy and foghorn.

The Well-Beloved mentions the 'treacherous cavern known as Cave Hole'. This is on the east coast, a short distance north of the turkey hutches; part of the roof at some remote time fell in, leaving a bowl-shaped depression in the flat turf (as it now is) above, and in the bottom of the depression a hole through which the sea used to spout like a salt-water geyser, until spectacle was sacrificed to safety and stout iron bars were set across the hole. Prior to this, according to Wilkinson Sherren, notches cut in the rock made it possible to descend to a ledge in the cave.

On the west side of Portland the principal building is a large church surrounded by a most extensive churchyard. The church, St George Reforne, is where we are told in *The Well-Beloved* that 'the island fathers lay'. Hardy refers to its tower, and indeed it has a small one at the west end, but its main feature is the central dome. The masses of gravestones can still be seen in profile against the sea, but only just, so high has the grass grown around them, justifying still the epithet 'the bleakest churchyard in Wessex'. The church is no longer in regular use, and is locked most of the time. From this side of Portland one can look along the Chesil Bank to Abbotsbury ('Abbotsea', 'Abbot's Beach') and its two sinuous terraces of warm-tinted stone and thatch, seemingly immutable despite the ever-denser traffic threading between them.

The massive stone pillar erected on Blackdown ('Blackon') Hill, a National Trust property some three miles to the north-east of Abbotsbury, honours Admiral Hardy, but since it bears no inscription, it is not surprising that many visitors who drive up to it for the magnificent views believe it commemorates Thomas Hardy the writer. This Blackdown, one of several in west Dorset, tallies closely with Hardy's description in *The Trumpet-Major* and is also the 'Blackon' of 'After the Club-Dance', the third section of the poem 'At Casterbridge Fair'.

Captain Hardy's house stands at the foot of Blackdown Hill in the village of Fortisham ('Po'sham'). This little doll's-house of a manor faces one of the angles of what has become a bustling road-junction, but is unaltered except for windows modernised in Victorian times and the removal of creeper. Treves writes of a stuccoed front, but today we see it as it must have looked originally.

About three miles east of Portisham, and less than a mile west of Maiden Castle, stands Winterborne St Martin, more often known as Martinstown, scene of the great horse mart commemorated in the poem 'A Last Look round St Martin's Fair'. This fair is yet another that was already dwindling by 1914, although it lingered on until 1939, when the army took over the fairground. The site was a large paddock south of the church and divided by the village street. Today the smaller portion nearer the church has been retained as a green; the larger supports a housing estate.

South of Martinstown and east of Portisham, extending nearly to the Weymouth–Dorchester road, is Waddon Vale. Under the title of the poem 'The Lacking Sense' is the note: 'SCENE—A sad-coloured landscape, Waddon Vale'. But on a bright day it is cheerful enough with the Pucksey Brook threading its centre beside the embankment of the long-vanished Upwey–Abbotsbury branch railway. Most of it is lush pasture; there are farms and a plantation or two, but no villages at all. Amid the hills at its north-east corner, where the Wey has its source, stands Upwey, which has an interest for Hardy readers because of its mill. This, a splendid specimen of a watermill still in full commercial activity, has by some means become identified with 'Overcombe Mill' in *The Trumpet-Major*, although 'Overcombe' is admitted to be Sutton Poyntz. The evidence for believing that at best the assumption contains only a very small grain of truth will be found in the pages dealing with Sutton Poyntz (169ff).

Broadway and Upwey station is the scene of the poem 'At the Railway Station, Upwey'. Once the junction for the Waddon Vale line, the station is still open for main-line traffic. Although Upwey is half a dozen miles from Weymouth ('Budmouth', 'Budmouth Regis'), the houses of the resort have been extended along the A354 to form an unbroken link. Still nearer to Weymouth, but off the main road and therefore retaining much more of a village appearance, lies Nottington, the original of the anonymous spot where Anne Garland met King George III beside the 'sulphorous spring, good for various ailments'. Nottington is a spa that died. By the late eighteenth century treatises about its waters were already being published, yet it was not until 1830 that Thomas Shore built the so-called Round House—actually octagonal—for the comfort of patrons. By the turn of the next century it had become a laundry, and today it is a private house. The little spa's best time was when the spring was enclosed, as Anne saw it, only by a simple 'stone margin . . . to prevent the cattle treading in the sides'. The sole relic of that era is a short flight of steps, with Georgian handrail, where visitors bathed in the near-by stream.

The references to Weymouth in Hardy's prose and verse are many. George III and his family, whose visits are so prominent in *The Trumpet-Major*, stayed at Gloucester Lodge, the 'homely house of red brick' now somewhat expanded to form the Gloucester Hotel, but still Georgian in appearance. Next door stands the Royal Hotel. The present building is late Victorian, but its pre-decessor with the 'circular bays' passed by Dick Dewy and Fancy

Day was Stacie's Hotel, in which there were 'rattling good dinners' (*The Trumpet-Major*) while King George and his entourage danced in the Assembly Rooms below.

Except for the Gloucester and the Royal, almost the whole of this part of the seafront is unaltered Georgian, William IV, or early Victorian. The Victorian terraces consist entirely of small private hotels, among them the Belvidere at 3 Belvidere, Esplanade. Early in *Desperate Remedies* Miss Aldclyffe interviews Cytherea 'at the Belvedere Hotel, Esplanade'. The modern hotel of this name has been in existence only since World War II, but in 1867 number 13 Belvidere was listed as a lodging-house, which Hardy, who knew Weymouth well in the 1860s, evidently upgraded for his chatelaine. The spelling used by him is found in various contemporary documents. These terraces carried the new resort a fair distance eastward, but for three-quarters of a century the development had no depth. There are people still alive who recall when behind the terraces there were stables, and behind these the open fields bordering Lodmoor Marsh. In later Victorian times, when Weymouth experienced something of a renaissance, the area was rapidly built over. An early structure was the town station, near which stood the 'little Temperance inn' where in *The Well-Beloved* Marcia Bencomb put up. The inn's prototype if there was one, is not identifiable.

Weymouth had two sets of assembly rooms. Those featured in 'The Ballad of Love's Skeleton' were probably in the Royal Hotel. The other set, no less fashionable, were at the Old Rooms Inn across the harbour, where in *The Dynasts* burghers and boatmen discuss Trafalgar. The inn is situated in the oldest, most picturesque and least changed part of Weymouth beside the quays. Here old buildings remain on both sides of the water, their charm not diminished either by the modern cranes or by the sight, more familiar in Continental ports than in British, of passenger and goods trains making their way along the street with the motor traffic. Many of the 'heavy wooden bow-windows which appeared as if about to drop into the harbour by their own weight' (*The Trumpet-Major*) have not yet dropped, nor have they been eliminated by other means, except in the old High Street which was largely destroyed by bombs in World War II and is now the site of new municipal offices. There is even an illusion that green shutters still abound, until one perceives that the green belongs mostly to the window-paint and fascias of Messrs Devenish's many taverns.

The harbour-side is also the territory of the tale 'A Committee-Man of "The Terror" '. He put up at the Old Rooms Inn, the frontage of which has been modernised, but not inharmoniously; distinction is lent to it by baskets of flowers hanging above the ground-floor windows. The harbour bridge (more often called the Town Bridge) that he approached from St Thomas Street was modified in 1880 by the substitution of a flat swing section for the central arch, and finally replaced in 1930. In its original form this bridge was the subject of the poem 'The Harbour Bridge'. St Thomas Street is now a major shopping thoroughfare, but above the modern shop-fronts many of the houses still exhibit their bow-windows.

The 'office of the town "Guide" ' to which the Committee-Man went may have been any one of several establishments, since by 1804 there were already a number of guides. But if we assume the reference to be to the latest, then the office was Harvey's, probably in the same building as the library owned by him at 4 Charlotte Row on the sea-front, where the Dorothy Café now stands. The Committee-Man also called at the newspaper office, about which all that can be said is that the only local news-sheet circulating in Weymouth at the time was the *Sherborne Mercury*.

On the sea-front too was the theatre attended by Anne Garland and Bob Loveday in the King's presence, and in which the Committee-Man and Mlle V— watched Kemble in *The Rivals*. Hardy calls it 'a little building', and it must have been, for it occupied the site of the present Weymouth Hotel, a tall narrow inn that is now being expanded and upgraded. Fanny Kemble spoke of 'a doll's playhouse'. It appears at some time to have extended round the back of the houses to the east of it, with an entrance in Bond Street, perhaps where the Danish Bar is now. The last performance was given in 1859, ten years before Hardy worked in Weymouth for Crickmay. Today the only vestiges of the theatre are in the basement: a small room with a fireplace, probably a dressing-room; a staircase near it ascending to the former stage area (today service stairs behind a bar counter); and a large cellar extending under the street, where perhaps scenery was stored.

Behind the theatre, parallel with St Thomas Street, runs St

Mary Street, the 'Mary Street' of *Desperate Remedies* down which Manston's pursuers saw him making for the quay. At the end of this street too, near George III's statue, where 'the white angle of the last house in the row cut perpendicularly' into the seascape, Fancy Day met Dick Dewy for the drive home.

In the 130 odd years since the *Greenwood Tree* period the appearance of this corner has scarcely varied. The King's statue, brightly painted as a ship's figure-head and of about the same artistic standard, continues to gaze at the traffic-jams on the Esplanade; and the end house is still painted white. St Mary Street, like St Thomas, is now an important shopping centre, but many old upper bow windows survive.

Along the Esplanade the boatmen still offer skiffs for hire, as they did to those Crusted Characters the Hardcomes. The date of the Hardcome story can probably be set some time during the second quarter of the nineteenth century. The allusion to 'the pier', therefore, even if we have to concede a possible measure of anachronism, is likely to be to the first true pier, built about 1840. Further west, between the harbour and the new streets towards Sandsfoot, is the promontory called the Nothe, or in earlier times the Look-Out. Its dominant feature is still the great semi-underground fortress alluded to in *The Dynasts*; but the top is now laid out as pleasure-gardens, with lanes, rockeries and serpentine paths. When the Committee-Man walked there with Mlle V— it must have been like any other wild cliff-top. A year or two later Festus Derriman and Matilda, in *The Trumpet-Major*, also strolled there, and from its shelter the Melancholy Hussar and his companion rowed forth on their disastrous enterprise. Finally, the Hardcomes are seen upon the Look-Out with their fiancées.

Mlle V— and the Committee-Man had met by Cove Row, the terrace in which dwelt the boat-builder of whom Matilda had hopes. Cove Row nowadays is another of the unspoilt groups of little, mostly bow-windowed, houses unexpectedly surviving round the port; and there is a boat-builder there today.

Although so much nearer the sea, these old terraces are safer in bad weather than some of the buildings near the inner reaches of the harbour, at the back of the town. A song in *The Dynasts* treats of a wild night when the wind raved 'and the Back-Sea met the Front-Sea'. A footnote explains that the 'hind' part of the harbour was formerly called the Back-Sea. Today it is the Backwater; and when the wind whips up a spring tide the behaviour of the sea is sometimes no less alarming than in the old ballad.

At the northern (Radipole) end of Weymouth—in the period of *The Trumpet-Major* well outside the town—is the site of the cavalry barracks erected between 1795 and 1804. The barrack square, now built over, occupied the area bounded by Dorchester Road, Alexandra Road (on two sides), and Westbourne Road. The houses of Alexandra Terrace are thought to have been the officers' quarters, and the curious house facing into the elbow of Alexandra Road is also a barrack relic, as are one or two of the older villas in Dorchester Road.

SOUTH WESSEX: *the coast east of Budmouth*
(Dorset: the coast east of Weymouth)

Had I but lived a hundred years ago
I might have gone, as I have gone this year,
By Warmwell Cross on to a Cove I know,
And Time have placed his finger on me there:

AT LULWORTH COVE A CENTURY BACK

The route from Weymouth to Dorchester follows the ancient Ridgeway until, just north of the Upwey turning, it swings east and then sharply west again as it climbs to the crest of the downs. The old road, still present, ran nearly straight over the brow, along which a track also sometimes called the Ridgeway forms a white seam. While Laura Maumbry was living at Preston ('Creston') during the Fordington cholera outbreak, her husband used to meet her near where the road and this track cross; and dry-stone walls of the type that he kept between them still 'form the field-fences here'. When Lieutenant Vannicock turned up at the same spot Laura made him go down to the milestone 'on the north slope of the ridge, where the old and new roads diverge'. In fact the milestone stood a good quarter-mile north of the point of divergence; buried in 1940, it has not been disinterred.

A few yards up from the southern end of the old road stands the Ship Inn, 'with a mast and cross-trees in front', where Dick Dewy installed Fancy Day in 'a little tea-room', probably a private parlour. The inn continues to flourish, with minimal alteration, and the pole outside is still a ship's mast complete with fittings.

A stage-coach passenger in *The Dynasts* remarks that there seems to be a deal of traffic over Ridgeway. On a modern summer day there is an even greater deal of it, but it is also well peopled with Hardy ghosts, crowding forth from *The Dynasts*, *The Trumpet-Major* and the poem 'The Alarm'. Hardy's own visits are recalled in 'Old Excursions' (with Emma) and perhaps in 'Where the Picnic Was'; this poem has been generally assumed to belong to Cornwall, but on his copy Lea pencilled a note, ' "The hill to the sea"— ?Ridgeway'; and Bailey suggests a picnic in June of the last year of Emma's life, while the poets Yeats and Newbolt were both visiting Max Gate. He could also have drawn attention to the lines 'I am here / Just as last year'; for Hardy did not visit Cornwall in two consecutive years after Emma's death. Today the ridge track is a favourite resort of holidaymakers from Weymouth and the many caravan camps.

Just at the point of the V where the motor-road is joined by one end of the loop-lane through Bincombe, is the scene, with Bincombe Down, of the tale 'The Melancholy Hussar of the German Legion'. Near the junction, by Bincombe Farm, Phyllis met Corporal Tina before changing her mind. In the village a mood appropriate to the small sad story (mainly a true one) is not hard to come by, for Bincombe is a tiny forgotten place with a population half what it was a century ago, and still declining. Some bright new barns are conspicuous, but there are few new houses.

The country about is very hilly, and Phyllis's parental home indeed stood almost level with the top of the church-tower. In its latter years divided into two cottages, the house has now been pulled down but fragments of the floors and stones from the walls are easily observable in the long grass, together with vestiges of the cottage gardens. Across the tiny lane an ancient stone wall, probably dating from the time of the story, must look very like the wall on which Phyllis sat. The church was restored in the 1860s. In the south-east corner of its little churchyard lies the site of the two Hussars' graves, and in the parish registers the record of the burial may still be read.

The troops who loom so large in Hardy's Napoleonic stories were encamped all along the downs above Bincombe and Sutton Poyntz ('Overcombe'). But 'The Ballad of Love's Skeleton', although set in the 1790s, has no martial associations. In its opening lines the speaker invites his girl to Culliford Wood on Culliford Hill to 'watch the squirrels climb, / And look in sunny places there / For shepherds' thyme'. The wood is now merged in Came Wood (the 'Damer's Wood' where Miller Loveday bought his weather-vane mast); shepherds' thyme still grows there, but the red squirrel has long been ousted by the grey. On the eastern edge a round barrow, crowned by tall beeches and named Culliford Tree, is perhaps the 'hill-top tree' of 'The Walk'. Some of the unmodernised old chalk roads are still 'gated'.

Along one of the chalk tracks stands lonely Northdown Barn. Beside it are the ruins of a stone cottage that seems likely to have been the one with the bricked-up windows used by the troops in *The Trumpet-Major* as their powder-magazine. Some of the win-

dows are still filled in (with stone, not brick). The large barn intended for a hospital is no longer traceable, nor is the granary 'on
tall stone staddles' into which John Loveday saw his brother enter
with Anne.

'Overcombe Mill' has been the subject of an unnecessary amount
of confusion, the commonest belief being, as already mentioned
(see page 159), that it was modelled on the mill at Upwey. Certainly Hardy was familiar with Upwey Mill; he made several trips
to it, including one in 1879, the year in which *The Trumpet-Major*
was written. But it is very unlikely that he had any purpose other
than to refresh himself on the technicalities of the machinery, for
neither the buildings nor the environment are reflected in 'Overcombe'. The mill in the novel is a largely imaginary creation,
utilising, however, easily recognisable features of the two mills
then at Sutton Poyntz; and with a little industry it is not difficult
to distinguish which features are taken from which.*

The situation at the extreme end of the village, close under the
downs, the description of the mill and millhouse as forming a
single edifice, the details of the house and many features of the
garden, are drawn from the Upper Mill; the relative positions of
mill, millpond and cross, the statement that Anne ran out and
looked 'up and down the road', the reference to a bridge at the
mill-*head*, and the short distance Anne and Matilda had to carry
Bob to reach the 'little stream', are based on the situation of the
Lower Mill (see plan overleaf).

There is still a Lower Mill, though it is not the one in existence
in Napoleonic times (see plate, page 118). The Upper Mill was
pulled down in 1856 to make way for the Weymouth Waterworks
pump-house. Hardy is therefore unlikely to have seen it, but
twenty-three years later, during his researches in the neighbourhood, he must have found plenty of people to supply him with an
authentic picture; and his description of the millhouse is none
other than a portrait of the building that today is the home of the
waterworks superintendent. The house looks far too new, but its
appearance is deceptive. Its walls are much thicker than is to be
expected of a residence put up in the mid-nineteenth century, and
contain recesses and other features inexplicable in terms of that

---

* There was also a third mill on the south-western fringe of the village, but this
need not concern us.

L

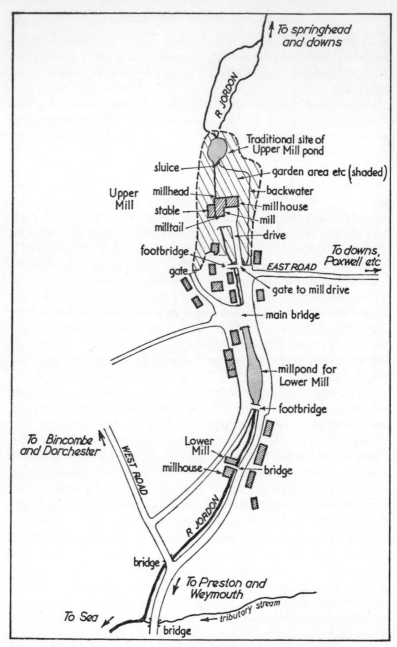

To springhead and downs

R JORDAN

Traditional site of Upper Mill pond

sluice

garden area etc (shaded)

Upper Mill

millhead

backwater

stable

mill house

milltail

mill

drive

footbridge

To downs, Poxwell etc

gate

EAST ROAD

gate to mill drive

main bridge

millpond for Lower Mill

footbridge

To Bincombe and Dorchester

WEST ROAD

Lower Mill

millhouse

bridge

R JORDAN

bridge

To Preston and Weymouth

tributary stream

To Sea

bridge

Sutton Poyntz before the building of the waterworks

time. The roof, though covered with modern slates, exactly fits
Hardy's picture. When certain modernisations were carried out
in Edwardian times (under the direction of someone still living
today) several antique structural features were found, indicating
that the house had been part of the mill. Hardy writes of four
chimneys; today there are two, but a pair were removed during the
work just mentioned. Plans drawn up for the pump-house show
the mill residence in exactly the position of the present dwelling.
The cover design, executed by Hardy himself, for the first edition
of *The Trumpet-Major* shows a building so similar to the house
there today as to compel belief that it was based on an imaginary
reconstruction of the missing mill half.

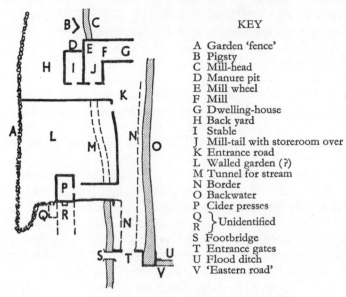

KEY

A Garden 'fence'
B Pigsty
C Mill-head
D Manure pit
E Mill wheel
F Mill
G Dwelling-house
H Back yard
I Stable
J Mill-tail with storeroom over
K Entrance road
L Walled garden (?)
M Tunnel for stream
N Border
O Backwater
P Cider presses
Q } Unidentified
R }
S Footbridge
T Entrance gates
U Flood ditch
V 'Eastern road'

Details of Sutton Poyntz Upper Mill

The real mill-house, like Hardy's, had a large garden, which
survives. By local tradition the millpond occupied the north-east
corner of the garden, above the point where one may still see the
site of the sluice that controlled the backwater. Hardy, however,
has clearly transferred the *Lower* Mill's great pool to the garden
site, together with the road junction, the cross, at its upper end.

There is no sign of the thorn-hedge so dense that the mill-boy could have walked along the top of it, but the 1856 plan shows the garden and forecourt bounded by a 'fence' of prodigious width. Two millstones recently dug up may have been the pair Hardy said were used for courtyard paving. The tree into which Bob leaped to make his escape belonged to the Lower Mill, and was recently felled.

The 'eastern road' by which the press gang returned to resume their search for Bob still exists in the form of a track that after leading east from outside the waterworks gate, turns north through some industrial premises and zig-zags up to the crest of the downs. Unless the traces of the zig-zag path cut by the cavalry have vanished only since Lea's day, it is probable that in claiming to have seen the path he was really looking at this road. The 'spring or riverhead' at the back of the mill is in fact some distance up the escarpment. The water authorities have built a brick surround, converting it into a miniature reservoir, and enclosed the neighbouring area with an iron fence.

The novel's many references to bridges are, with one exception, all but impossible to follow on the ground, and Hardy probably put bridges where he wanted them. The exception is the bridge under which the girls hid Bob, 'where a little stream passed under the road' about 200 yards from the mill. This has been variously identified with the footbridge at the southern end of the present Lower Mill pond, and the so-called Roman bridge a long way to the south-west, mistakenly sketched by New. The correct bridge is situated slightly south of the union of Sutton's two main lanes, and carries the road over the stream from Poxwell ('Oxwell') that joins the Jordon close by. The modern bridge is of brick, with parapets, but its predecessor may well have been unparapeted, and its arch, to judge from today's, would have been suitable for the concealment. Houses now flank either side of the road, but a little meadow surviving on the upstream side makes it easy to visualise the girls 'entering the opening by which the cattle descended to drink' on the down-stream side, and carrying their burden into the tunnel.

Modern Sutton Poyntz clings desperately to its former status as a pretty, old-world village, but it is losing the battle. At one end the best group of cottages looks across the pond at a very plain turn-of-the-century inn, just north of which is the monstrous excrescence of the waterworks. At the other end the fight is against the encroaching villas and bungalows of Weymouth's outer suburbs. Even the centre has its aesthetic handicap in the shape of a light-engineering factory.

Preston, astride the A353, forms virtually one village with Sutton Poyntz, sharing the church to which the miller's household were going when they noticed the proclamation on the elm tree. Here suburbia vies with groves of holiday caravans, and apart from the church, only a dozen cottages and the pleasant old Ship Inn (mentioned in *The Trumpet-Major*) remain from Laura Maumbry's day.

Between Preston and the real-life Overcombe is Jordon Hill, on which are the remains of a Roman temple first excavated during 1843 and the years following. Lea states that this is the 'Pagan temple' of the poem 'The Well-Beloved', without, however, explaining why Hardy should have transferred the site to Bere Regis. In any case, later research has shown that the temple was not dedicated to Venus, but (probably) to Aesculapius. The original discoveries were covered in, re-exhumed in 1932, and are now in the care of the Ministry of Public Building and Works.

The White Horse on the downs continues to be a landmark, as intended, though it would be more of one if the chalk were weeded and perhaps whitewashed; most of the white horses in Wiltshire put King George and his mount to shame. Not far away the Derriman home, Poxwell Manor, pictured in *The Trumpet-Major* in the last stages of dilapidation, had been somewhat rehabilitated, although still a farmhouse when Windle wrote. Today the mellow stone mansion has been fully restored, and is undoubtedly better kept and more beautifully furnished than at any time since the Hennings (Hardy uses the correct name) built it over 300 years ago. The main entrance is now at the back, where the fleeing Anne, after going through a door in the kitchen-garden wall, found herself on 'a rutted cart-track, which had been a pleasant gravelled drive'. This, like the last part of her approach from Sutton, is extremely hard to trace in any way that makes sense.

The short carriage-drive leading to the gateway at the front is yet in evidence, although no longer used. There are still fine trees nearby. The arched gateway with the porter's lodge over it has also been unobtrusively renovated; its outside stone stair is straight, not spiral. Within the walled 'quadrangle' where Old Derriman kept his livestock, beautiful flower-borders surround a smooth, rich lawn. In the façade of the mansion modern metal casements have replaced those stanchions worn away to 'mere wires'. Puzzlingly, there is no trace at all of the vertical sundial in the middle of the porch, nor were there ever any battlements.

Inside, the dining-room 'traditionally called the great parlour' has been superbly restored. The stone fireplace is separately scheduled for preservation, and the plaster ceiling and furniture are exquisite. Mellow farm buildings adjoin the manor. The only jarring note is the church with the circular tower, erected in 1868 to replace the ruined medieval church near by.

It was over the Pokeswell Hills (Hutchins's spelling) that the sea mists came which sent the bees fleeing in the poem 'The Sheep-Boy'. These coastal downs given an impression of utter changelessness, and it is surprising to discover that Clive Holland's photograph of 1899 (the New York *Bookman*) shows them, above Sutton Poyntz, criss-crossed with many hedges. All these have disappeared, although the downs are still scored by the old chalk roads, in contrast to which the only modern route is the A353.

Where this meets the A352 and continues beyond it as the B3390 is Warmwell ('Warm'll') Cross, mainly of interest for the ambushing of the Revenue men in the tale of 'The Distracted Preacher'. Nowadays the cross has become a large roundabout, and in place of the 'plantation which surrounded' the crossroads we have a group of tall conifers growing out of the central island itself. The old cross was not exactly in the position of the roundabout, but a little to the east. Several fragments of the former approaches survive; one even shows traces of a central white line—an indication of how recently it was superseded. Warmwell village is the 'Springham' of *The Trumpet-Major*.

The action of 'The Distracted Preacher' takes place mainly in Owermoigne ('Nether Moynton', 'Nether Mynton'), a quiet village just north of the A352. Though quiet, it has not been overlooked by the modern developer, and has many new houses of the smaller type, most of them lining a completely new street. The church was rebuilt in 1883, but the old tower remains; access to the platform at the top is still obtained just as in Hardy's account, except for the first stage, the 'singing gallery' having disappeared. Entry to the bell-loft is now gained by an enclosed spiral staircase attached to the tower.

The churchyard is, as described, higher than the road outside, but to the east a comparatively new wall now divides it from a farm-building enclosure. If Lizzie Newberry's garden was genuine, it has become separated from the churchyard by this agricultural intrusion; for her house, again assuming that it existed, must have been east of the church, and was probably one of the two attractive cottages still extant. Both accord with Lea's description, 'nearly opposite the Rectory'. On the opposite side of the churchyard there is an old, high-walled garden locally believed to be the prototype of Owlett's orchard, although it contains no trace of the famous hide-out, which was modelled on genuine examples. More or less facing this, at the corner of Holland's Mead Avenue, the new street already mentioned, stands the old forge; much altered and modernised, but still containing the smith's bellows.

There was never a Methodist chapel in Owermoigne, but up a narrow gravel track on the other side of Holland's Mead Avenue stands an ancient stone thatched house, Chilbury Cottage, where Methodist services were held during the last century. The cottage later fell on hard times, but has been excellently restored; the large parlour used for the meeting is now subdivided into kitchen and living-room. The old main 'street or lane' of Owermoigne is very long, and since it is not the principal theatre of modern development, it continues to display 'more hedge than houses'. At the far end stands the former mill, now a private house; even the stream has been diverted. The mill had previously been rebuilt in about 1850.

The other places in 'The Distracted Preacher' can easily be identified, Hardy having used many real names. Immediately across the A352 a lane leads over Gallows Hill to the tiny hamlet of Holworth, once a sizeable village but now consisting of two farms and a pillar-box. Lizzie Newberry took this route on her nocturnal expedition to Ringstead Bay ('Ringsworth Shore'). Beyond Holworth a chalk track leads directly over the magnificent empty downs to the bay. The latter too is magnificent—nearly a mile of golden curving beach backed by tumbled grassy hills rising to

500 feet, and in all of it scarcely a house or even a caravan visible. But just round the western horn a nascent holiday-villa and chalet colony stands ominously poised.

With the White Nothe and the Chaldons we come to territory associated more often with other writers, T. F. Powys, Llewellyn Powys and David Garnett, than with Hardy. Chaldon Herring ('Shaldon') appears in 'The Distracted Preacher' when Lizzie makes her second night journey. This time, after crossing the main road, she turns east along the hillside and then south over Lord's Barrow, which is at the intersection of two chalk lanes. Apart from the fact that the north–south lane, which leads to the Chaldons, has been given a modern surface, this landscape can hardly have changed in a single detail. Hardy says that the travellers reached 'Shaldon' Down, and then a ravine on the outskirts of 'Shaldon'. In fact, both Chaldons and the ravine linking them lie between Lord's Barrow and the down, so that Lizzie and the preacher must have come to them in the reverse order. The next landmark was the earthwork called Round Pound, a low circular enclosure on a hill-crest. There is a measure of shrub vegetation that obviously changes with time, otherwise yet again an unaltered scene.

From Round Pound Lizzie led the way to Dagger's Gate ('Dagger's Grave'), stated by Hardy to be 'not many hundred yards' from Lulworth ('Lulstead', 'Lulwind') Cove, but in fact about a mile off. Here was her rendezvous with the smugglers, who went on to the edge of the cliff and descended by rope. Dagger's Gate is simply a point in a shallow valley where the road from Winfrith Newburgh to the cove is crossed by a chalk track, the old chalk road along the hills; some farm outbuildings of various dates stand a short distance away. At the foot of a coomb between White Nothe and Durdle Door there is still to be seen an old wire rope, put in place by fishermen or smugglers, no one knows when, to give access to the beach.

Durdle Door, a much-pictured natural arch extending from the cliffs, is referred to by Hardy in the last stanza of 'The Bird-Catcher's Boy'. A rough stairway, blending with the rock, has been made over the neck of the arch to link the two small bays on either side of it; there are paths along and up the steep grass slopes above the cliffs; and on the level summit, partly masked by a grove of pine-trees, there is a caravan camp. In summer the area is crowded enough, but out of season it must be allowed that the scene has escaped serious disfigurement.

In *Desperate Remedies* the picture of Lulworth Cove, to which Owen took Cytherea, is preceded by a description of the excursion paddle-steamers that used to ply from Weymouth. The practice lasted well into the twentieth century, but nowadays the only visitors by sea come in motor-boats. There is, however, one link with the paddle-steamers: landing and embarkation were effected 'by the primitive plan of a narrow plank on two wheels—the women being assisted by a rope'. A contraption of this sort is still drawn up on the beach, and another, only slightly modified, stands beside it for use with the small launches that take excursionists for short round trips. The visiting vessels no longer land their passengers.

In Lulworth Cove the drowned bodies of Stephen Hardcome and his cousin's wife (*A Few Crusted Characters*) were cast ashore, and here Sergeant Troy set out for the swim that gave rise to the belief that he had been drowned. It is also the scene of the poem 'At Lulworth Cove a Century Back' and appears in *The Dynasts*. The Cove today is the victim of its own popularity. Old buildings include a terrace of fishermen's cottages, and some other cottages of charm, thatched and otherwise; but a large car- and coach-park right in the centre, a raw red-brick restaurant in the midst of this, various pieces of uninspiring construction in the lane leading down to the sea, and a general atmosphere of lollies and Cola bottles, squawking children and fat grannies with bad feet, do not make for picturesqueness or dignity, whatever their other virtues.

There are three hotels, but the inn mentioned in *Desperate Remedies* is none of these; it is somewhat toward the back of the village, north of the church, and is now a pleasant private residence, long and low, with two porches and colour-washed walls. The 'perfectly straight' road 'more than a mile in length' by which Troy approached the coast cannot be identified, because none of the approaches is straight.

The army camp at Lulworth is as hideous as the worst features of the cove village, with none of the latter's redeeming aspects. To add insult to injury, more than a thousand acres of some of

the finest coastal downland on our southern shores are denied to
the public because the military wanted it 'temporarily' as a firing-
range a quarter of a century ago and have it still, bizarrely supported in resistance to demilitarisation by naturalists who care
nothing for the pleasure of humankind provided the area be kept
safe for the commoner forms of wild life. As it chances, only one
of Hardy's settings is affected. This is Steeple, the 'Kingscreech'
of 'Old Mrs Chundle', which at firing times may be approached
only from the east. Pinion identifies 'Kingscreech' with Kingston
('Little Enkworth'), three miles to the east. But 'Kingscreech'
was in the charge of a curate, which Kingston was not and Steeple
was, under the rector of Tyneham (a rector is also mentioned in
the story). Steeple church, unlike either church at Kingston, used
to have a gallery like 'Kingscreech' and still has an octagonal
wooden pulpit, albeit not at the top of eight steps. The old lady's
cottage, near the parish boundary where a lane branched off to
Encombe ('Enkworth' or 'Enckworth'), was probably situated, or
imagined, slightly north of Smedmore Hill. Creech Barrow is also
on the parish boundary. Steeple today remains a tiny somnolent
place, amalgamated ecclesiastically with Church Knowle.

Encombe House, so prominent in *The Hand of Ethelberta*, is
a graceful eighteenth-century mansion in a fairy-tale setting, built
for one of the sons of George Pitt of Kingston Maurward and later
acquired by Lord Eldon, to whose family it still belongs. Disap-
pointingly, although Hardy describes both house and grounds at
considerable length, almost all his descriptive passages are spurious.
Some features (see page 43) are perhaps borrowed, like the anecdote that 'Enkworth's' original brick was faced with stone at the
insistence of George III, from Kingston Maurward. But Beatty
believes that Hardy simply devised for this mansion all that he
disliked in interior decoration.

Kingston, to which the brougham was ordered to be brought
for Ethelberta's flight, stands on a typical Purbeck ridge, and is
distinguished for G. E. Street's cathedral-like church of 1880.
The old church (1838) is now used as a village hall. About three
miles south, the coast pushes out to form St Aldhelm's or St
Alban's Head, mentioned in the poems 'At Lulworth Cove a
Century Back' and 'Days to Recollect'. The latter well evokes the
atmosphere of the huge grassy headland, round which it is still

possible to walk by a good footpath. The ancient chapel that once carried a light to guide seamen, and the coastguard station at the base of the promontory, were both there in the *Ethelberta* period; new are the quarters of the small RAF unit at Worth Matravers and the group of radar masts between that village and the point.

At the south-east corner of the Isle of Purbeck is Durlston Head, the 'old cliff' to which Hardy addressed himself in the poem 'To a Sea-Cliff'. Today the southward spread of Swanage ('Knollsea') has touched the headland and tamed its wilderness, but the un-tamed downs are not far off, and many a young couple—the majority, one hopes, happier than the 'twain' in the poem—con-tinue to frequent them.

Swanage looms large in *The Hand of Ethelberta*, and the short poem 'Once at Swanage' splendidly describes a rough sea wit-nessed here by Hardy and Emma not long after their marriage. The sea wall has been extensively rebuilt, in particular near the piers, where a fairly new hotel dominates the shore. The old pier remains in evidence, though reduced now to an irregular column of piles with a few cross-beams and planks. The 'new' pier, a magnificent piece of late Victoriana built in 1897, is close by. It still caters for excursion craft and in the summer there is still a regular service to Bournemouth, but it is many years since steamers for Cherbourg called.

Architecturally Swanage has come in for some justifiably harsh strictures, but it has retained its pre-resort nucleus intact, even to the old lock-up, the 'stone chimneys' mentioned by Hardy, the millpool, and several footways still paved with the original slabs. The church underwent Victorian restoration, but despite exten-sions in 1908 it still looks in keeping with its mellow surroundings. The tower with the unembattled parapet that impressed Hardy has been preserved.

Captain Flower's tiny cottage 'on a high slope above the town-let' is modelled not, as Lea states, on Durlston Cottage, but on West End Cottage, one of a pair at the end of a short cul-de-sac off Seymer Road. Here Hardy and Emma stayed early in their married life, the real owner being Captain Masters, first coxswain of the Swanage lifeboat. The cream, slate-roofed pair of cottages are still occupied and in good repair, but the 'orchard of aged [apple] trees' on the slope in front—the orchard garden of the

Royal Victoria Hotel—fell to the developers in the mid-1960s, and is now covered by a congeries of flats and bungalows that dismally limit the view of the sea from West End Cottage. Though the tiny cottage garden endures, 'The Lodging-House Fuchsias' no longer hang over the path.

The 'brilliant variegated brick and stone villa' to which Ethelberta and her sister moved was probably one of the houses in Park Road; and the Chickerells' last home, 'Firtop Villa', was one of the earliest houses in the rather upstage district on the heights south-west of the town, where there are still pines. Swanage began to be 'discovered' around 1880, after the period of the novel. The first visitors were authors, artists, and people in need of rest and quiet, whom the inhabitants were glad to lodge in their own cottages. Only some years later were the first few hotels and true boarding-houses erected—just in time, perhaps, for the miserable honeymoon on which Raye and Anna were setting out at the end of the story 'On the Western Circuit'.

The 'sinister ledge of limestones . . . like a crocodile's teeth' (*Ethelberta*), to avoid which steamers southbound from Swanage had to steam east at first, refers to the rocks off Peveril Point, at the southern tip of Swanage Bay. On the northern side of the bay the white cliffs, followed close in-shore during good weather by the Bournemouth steamers, are those between Ballard Point and Handfast Point; and at Ballard Point, still unbuilt on, one can see the vertical cliff 'rounding off at the top in vegetation, like a forehead with low-grown hair', as it is described in the novel, which is the 'Bollard Head' of the poem 'The Brother'. The great white cliffs are more than ever 'hollowed into gaping caverns', and the two famous pillars, Old Harry and his Wife (described but not named in the novel), have suffered a fatality, though whether it is Old Harry or the Wife who has collapsed into the sea depends on whether you accept the viewpoint of Swanage or of Studland.

When Ethelberta rode her donkey from Swanage to Corfe ('Corvsgate') Castle, she started along the shore and then climbed to 'the lofty ridge which ran inland', Ballard Down. From here, on a fine day, the views so graphically limned by Hardy, are hard to match, particularly northward across Poole harbour. In the foreground, including the harbour, they have changed little, save

for the line of cars snaking towards the Sandbanks ferry. But
the middle-distance scene is as different from what Ethelberta
saw as the ferry-bound cars are from her donkey: to the left of
Brownsea Island—still exhibiting 'fir-trees and gorse' and now
jointly administered by the National Trust and the Dorset Naturalists' Trust—the giant power-station chimneys and great square
blocks of industrial Poole ('Havenpool'); to the right of the isle,
the tall cliff-top hotels and apartment blocks of Bournemouth
('Sandbourne'); and behind both, the residential spread stretching
toward Wimborne and Verwood.

Ballard Down is continued eastward by Nine Barrow Down,
correctly named in *Ethelberta*. Although from the Swanage–
Corfe Castle road the tumuli make the ridge look like the back of
a prehistoric monster, they are less numerous here than on some
of the coastal heights farther west, and do not justify Hardy's
epithet of 'a huge cemetery'. As one nears Corfe, the 'brilliant
crimson heaths' (in season) round the head of the 'many-armed
inland sea' become increasingly evident; and because their sandy
base is pale, the paths that cross them still gleam white, in contrast
to the tarred roads. Hardy does not exaggerate when he suggests
that the more sombre climate south of the ridge encourages darker
vegetation than to the north; nor have the agricultural advances
of later times materially affected the contrast.

Corfe Castle stands on a high knoll in the only gap in the long
chain of Purbeck Hills. This celebrated place is noticed by Hardy
only in *Ethelberta* and 'Old Mrs Chundle'. Since the castle's partial
demolition in the Civil War it has remained uncommonly static.
Squat towers that lean at crazy angles over the valley and look as
if the next storm will send them crashing down can be seen
leaning at exactly the same angles in Hutchins's 200-year-old engraving.

The moat and first gateway remain as described by Hardy,
and despite the tread of tourists beyond number the 'green inclines' are green still. No genuine dungeons are in sight, but one
or two lower rooms with barrel roofs may include the 'dungeon'
entered by Ethelberta and the others, particularly since the rooms
are 'partly open to the air overhead'. At Corfe the skilled task of
preserving the ruins from deterioration is being privately under-
taken.

Corfe village is almost too pretty, as though constructed expressly for the summer coachloads. The only building identifiable in the novel is the Castle Inn, a small inn as stated. Situated on the highway to Swanage, it is unspoilt except for the presence of two petrol pumps. The 'village inn' elsewhere referred to is more likely to be the Greyhound or the Fox, both larger and more central—and also outwardly unspoilt.

Wareham and Lytchett Minster have already been dealt with in other sections (pages 73-4 and 86). Upton House, on the edge of Poole, is the prototype, in situation only, of 'Wyndway House' in *Ethelberta*. Neither the 'marble bas-relief of some battle-piece' nor the 'gilded and chandeliered salon' is to be found in the building; but the grounds do border a 'sheet of embayed sea', namely Holes Bay, a sort of lagoon (now bisected by the railway) at the back of Poole harbour. Except on this side, they are hemmed in today by the town's suburbs. During the 1960s the house, which belongs to Poole Corporation, was the home of an exiled Rumanian prince.

The 'paved wharf-side' of Poole harbour is the scene of that almost unbearable poem 'The Mongrel'. But Poole itself, although touched upon once or twice, is used as a setting only once, in the short story 'To Please His Wife'. In this, adopting a practice unusual with him, Hardy uses four surnames all of which, with minor spelling variations, are to be found on the walls of the parish church, St James. With its pillars of Newfoundland pine, St James is a charming example of its period, completed in 1820 and unmodified since. The 'Town Hall' from which Jolliffe escorted Emily Hanning home, is the Old Guildhall, occupying an island site in Market Street and still structurally intact, in spite of having been converted into public baths. The Town Cellar on the quay remains one of Poole's show pieces, with church-like buttresses and Gothic doorway and windows.

'Sloop Lane', in which stood the Hannings's stationery shop, does not appear in the annals of Poole, nor on Hutchins's town map. In the *Thomas Hardy Year Book* no 2 H. V. F. Johnstone argues credibly for Hardy having had in mind Bull's Head Lane (now Prosperous Street), close to which there used to be a little stationer's (Woodford's) that admirably fitted Hardy's description, even to the step down inside the entrance. Mr Lester's home was a 'large, substantial brick mansion' which 'faced directly on the

High Street'. There are one or two houses—one in particular, now a furniture emporium—that answer to this description, and inevitably Lea identified the 'right' one. On the other hand the former home of the real-life Lesters, in Thomas Street, some little way from the High Street, is also an exquisite red-brick Georgian house, splendidly kept today as the premises of a yacht club.

The 'long, straight road' that ascended 'eastward to an elevated suburb where the more fashionable houses stood' is the main road into Bournemouth, and the 'elevated suburb' is Parkstone, still the most elegant part of Poole. In the mid-nineteenth century, when Poole was smaller, Bournemouth was still so tiny that a fair stretch of heath separated them; today, though utterly unlike, they form a single urban mass.

Much industrial and residential new building has come to Poole, some of it, like the Poole Pottery establishment on the quay, in the very heart of the oldest quarter. Nevertheless, the place remains rich in old buildings, ancient alleys and quaint corners, despite the tardiness of the corporation in perceiving its duty to preserve them. Even Master John Horseleigh and his Edith, who lived here with her brother in the 1540s, would recognise more than a few scenes.

SECTION *10*

UPPER WESSEX
(Hampshire)

I joined in a jolly trip to Weydon-Priors Fair:
I shot for nuts, bought gingerbreads, cream-cheese . . .

A LAST JOURNEY

M

Southsea ('Solentsea') was where the Imaginative Woman and her husband ousted the poet Robert Trewe from Coburg House. Except for sundry new houses and flats, the seafront terraces are still predominantly Victorian. Of the several terraces and parades, St Helen's Parade displays unmatching houses with steps up to their entrances and small front gardens, but none particularly suggests Coburg House. Opposite the houses, trim public gardens with a bandstand have replaced a wild common. The excursion steamers used to tie up at Clarence Pier, completely rebuilt in 1961. The cemetery in the story was probably the one in Highland Road.

'The fashionable town on the island opposite' is Ryde, Isle of Wight, which in the last thirty years has doubled its population and halved its exclusiveness. Bonchurch, adjoining Ventnor on the south-east coast, is the scene of 'A Singer Asleep', verses in tribute to Swinburne. This small, steep resort also remains predominantly Victorian, and Swinburne's house and remarkably hideous tomb are in good preservation.

Portsmouth receives few mentions by Hardy; its most illustrious showpiece, HMS *Victory*, well described in *The Trumpet-Major*, was recently renovated. Southampton is alluded to more often, but is never used as a setting.

Bournemouth ('Sandbourne') Pier, mentioned in *Ethelberta*, was the old wooden pier opened in 1861, partly swept away six years later, and replaced by the present iron pier in 1880. The plural allusion to 'piers' in *Tess* takes account of Boscombe and Southbourne piers, both built in the 1880s, of which Boscombe, rebuilt after severe World War II damage, survives. Bournemouth pier has also been restored since the war. The groves of pines— authentic remnants of the heath—the promenades, the covered gardens, are more than ever a feature of this 'city of detached mansions' (*Tess*), which themselves have largely given place to huge blocks of flats. In Tess's day the population was 18,000; in

1961, 151,000, and today substantially higher. Yet a mile inland from the houses it is difficult to credit the proximity of a large town.

'The Herons' being imaginary, we do not know the starting-point of Tess's last independent journey; nor is the fugitives' route very clear. Angel walked from one of the Bournemouth stations—probably the western—toward the next one 'onward', that is westward, for he crossed a valley (the Bourne?) in that direction and was overtaken by Tess after turning north into the fir wood just beyond it. The couple continued north through the firs that 'here abounded for miles' but have now mostly given way to buildings as far out as Hurn Forest. The inn near which they stopped to eat seems to have been in the Hurn–St Leonards area. Afterwards they went on 'into the depths of the New Forest' to 'Bramshurst Court', an empty house that stood 'behind a brook and a bridge' and has been identified with Moyles Court, north of Ringwood. Correctly defined as 'an old brick building of regular design and large accommodation', the ancient manor had by 1860 decayed to a mere shell. Today, fully restored, it is a preparatory school for girls and boys. The brook and bridge are easily recognisable, despite the presence of a new concrete bridge nearby.

The New Forest ('the Great Forest') is the subject of the poem 'Throwing a Tree'; and inevitably the Trampwoman and her friends included it in their territory. It is not easy to say how different it looked then, or even at the later day when Tess and Angel passed through it. Roads, for instance, have increased in busyness but scarcely in number. Holiday-makers strow parts of the forest with caravans, but so did the gypsies. Its extent has remained roughly the same for the past 300 years, and the number of trees has actually increased since Hardy wrote. The verderers' courts and most of the old forest laws persist, though the Forestry Commission took over management of the timber in 1923.

Almost in Tess's and Angel's path lay Hurn Court, the 'Rookington Park' of *Ethelberta* and today a boys' school. The unchanged frontage (last modified in 1840) still looks on to a large 'expanse of green grass', near which are majestic vestiges of the once-plentiful 'fine old timber'.

Although no longer a lonely town 'hardly modified' by 'years of steam traffic', Ringwood is unmistakably 'Oozewood' of 'Master John Horseleigh, Knight'. It retains picturesque features, but petrol vapour has succeeded where steam (now departed) failed; the population has jumped by 70 per cent in the last few years, and most of the consequent new building is humdrum. The Walls' house is untraceable, as is the 'Black Lamb', though a plain Lamb (rebuilt) stands near the disused station.

The 'Noble Dame' story, 'Lady Mottisfont', is laid mainly in two mansions near Romsey. 'Deansleigh Park' is Broadlands, a buff-toned classical building in a gracious park on the town's outskirts. This was the birthplace and for long the home of Lord Palmerston, and in our own era is the seat of the Mountbattens. Hardy's reference to a 'pool fed by a trickling brook' is puzzling, for the river Test, which flows before the house, was broad even before its enlargement to form a lake. The other mansion, 'Fernell Hall', is the former Embley House, two miles to the west. Here for many years, whenever she could escape from London, lived Florence Nightingale; but the house was almost wholly rebuilt in the late 1960s, and is now yet another boys' school.

'Lady Mottisfont' opens in Winchester ('Wintoncester') cathedral, inside which the changes since Hardy wrote have been few. Outside, however, where the cathedral green lies to the north of the nave, recent excavations have revealed the complex foundations of the old minster—the Saxon cathedral—and below these part of the Roman forum. Nor is the site the only one in the city where ancient Winchester is being unearthed; yet, in contrast, so many new buildings have been put up that Angel Clare and 'Liza-Lu would have difficulty in recognising some areas, though not the gaol. A new wing has been added to this, the various frontages facing the road have been rendered and painted white, and no flagstaff now rises from the octagonal tower; but the other Hardy features, even to the 'yews and evergreen oaks' on their high bank above the roadside wall, are all present still. Only the white wicket through which the two visitors slipped out has gone, giving place to a metal barrier.

Farther up the hill the first milestone on the Romsey road continues to stand, legible if no longer white, on the 'green margin of the grass', near a bus shelter. But Angel and his companion would never have been able to see the panorama of Winchester from beside it, nor from less than several hundred yards nearer the city. Today trees have grown up to form a further barrier, and have also cut off the view from Lea's alternative viewpoint 'a little to the westward'.

North-east of Winchester there stood, until its demolition in the 1960s, Herriard House, Pinion's suggestion for the prototype of 'Icenway House' in 'The Lady Icenway'. Lea postulated Marwell Hall; but this is so nearly due south of Winchester as to seem hardly consistent with Hardy's statement that from Heymere House, between Bristol and Exeter, 'Icenway' lay 'beyond Wintoncester'—unless we assume Heymere to have been very near Bristol indeed. However, neither Herriard nor Marwell possesses any records showing a connection with the events in the story, nor do their churches hold a clue. Marwell Hall, built in 1816, was severely damaged by fire in 1969.

Creeping toward Herriard village is that rapidly developing industrial town Basingstoke ('Stoke Barehills'). Hardy's 'old town of nine or ten thousand souls' is now an overspill centre for many times that number, and has been completely redesigned; so that it is surprising to find all the features described in *Jude* surviving with minimal alteration, except for the site of the 'Great Wessex Show'. This was the once-celebrated Royal Counties Show, which began in 1854 as the Basingstoke Root and Stock Show and acquired its later name in 1861. Though its offices were always at Basingstoke, the show moved from town to town, the last being held at Kingsclere in 1966. The Basingstoke showground occupied the area of the present cricket ground alongside Bounty Road.

Both the railway routes mentioned by Hardy continue to operate, and the two westbound highways whose rival merits were debated have become the A30 and B3400. Their 'point of reunion' is Andover. Much of the refashioning of central Basingstoke has taken place just south of the station, immediately north of which you may still see what is left—after vandals overturned and smashed scores of gravestones in 1971—of the 'cemetery standing amid some picturesque medieval ruins'. The ruins are those of the thirteenth-century chapel of the Holy Ghost and the sixteenth-century guild chapel of Holy Trinity, both now freed of ivy but in danger of deterioration in spite of earlier repairs. At this moment funds are being collected for further restoration. The cemetery is no longer used except for an occasional burial in a family vault, and even before the recent vandalism the scene was somewhat desolate. Plans are under review for turning the area into a public garden. The chapels mentioned by Hardy were two flint ones, now demolished.

Where even Basingstoke's 'new red brick suburb' appears mellow amid the steel and concrete, the ancient parish church seems undeserving of the adjectives 'gaunt, unattractive'. It is unaltered except for the south aisle, rebuilt after a fire in the 1930s.

Barely separated now from Basingstoke is Basing; Old Basing House is the 'House of Long Sieging' in the poem 'My Cicely'—an allusion to the Royalists' four-year defence of it during the Civil War. In the 1960s army experts, using geiger counters, made an unsuccessful attempt to locate the large sum of money reputedly hidden in the grounds.

'Arrowthorne Lodge' in *Ethelberta* is probably imaginary, but from the references to road and rail would have stood in about the position of Breamore House, north of Fordingbridge. 'Farnfield' in the same novel, the park with a knacker's yard in place of a mansion, was evidently pictured near Farnborough, on the Surrey border.

Weyhill ('Weydon Priors'), west of Andover, where Henchard sold his wife at the fair, Hardy depicts as shrinking; and it is still shrinking, consisting of little more than a church, two inns, and a handful of cottages. Yet Weyhill Fair was among the great ones, and did not finally expire until 1947. Its site lies in and around the Y formed by the A303 and A342, but the 'winding road' of the novel is the lane that crosses these and leads to the nucleus of the village. The 'plantation' is still there, toward Ramridge. The nearer inn to the 'Fair-field', the Star, still has a room at the back with 'D R' on the door, for Drovers' Room, and a small room adjoining for their dogs.

NORTH WESSEX
and
CHRISTMINSTER
(Berkshire and Oxford)

Though the College stones
Are stroked with the sun,
And the gownsmen and Dons
Who held you as one
Of brightest brow
Still think as they did,
Why haunt with them now
Your candle is hid?

EVELYN G. OF CHRISTMINSTER

J ude and Sue spent a considerable time in Reading ('Aldbrick-
ham'). It then had 60,000 or 70,000 inhabitants, and today has
at least double the number. Twentieth-century houses encircle the
original town, and there is much redesigning of the centre, where
even the two railway stations have become one. Yet a fair amount
of old Reading remains, including the George Hotel, where the
couple first stayed and where Jude had spent his night of reconciliation with Arabella. The George is still one of the leading
inns of the town.

Jude and Sue lodged for most of their sojourn in a little lane
far from the station and 'almost out in the country'. This can be
placed with near-certainty in the area of small streets and Victorian
two-storey red brick terrace houses west of Southampton and
Whitley Streets. There is no 'Spring Street' on the nineteenth-
century maps, but there is a Spring Gardens, off which leads
Spring Terrace. These roads still exist, and a short distance from
the end of Spring Gardens some unbuilt-on ground merges even
today into the open country.

The inn in which Arabella stayed overnight, 'The Prince', is
lost among many possible prototypes; the Royal William (recently
closed) in Spring Gardens is typical. The region is part of St Giles
parish, the clerk of which from 1871 to 1885 lived and worked at
66 Horn Street. Jude and Sue wished to marry in a 'Superintendant
Registrar's office', yet went to 'the office of the district'. There were
two of these, the nearer and likelier being at 24 Southampton Street
on the corner of Mundesley Street, in a house now converted into
a kitchen furnisher's shop. Mundesley Street could well be the
'unfrequented side alley' up and down which the couple walked
after Sue's courage had failed her. The church where they saw a
wedding would be St Giles itself (restored 1873).

Somewhere near Reading is the 'Gaymead' of 'The Son's
Veto', a 'pretty village, with its church and parsonage'. We are
told of a white gate to the parsonage garden, trees in the vicinity,

and a glebe. The church had communion-rails, a roof held by tie-beams, and a 'fine peal of bells'. Several prototypes have been suggested (as well as that there was none), and selection might be easier if one could identify the 'church out by Gaymead' of the Devil and Ten Commandments legend related in *Jude*. This cautionary tale, however, seems to have been borrowed by Hardy from another part of the country. The Wessex Edition map, showing Gaymead in the position of Theale, can scarcely be accurate, since Theale meets none of the descriptive points.

The most probable prototype is one that has not, I believe, been put forward in print before: Sulhampstead or Sulhampstead Abbots, about three miles south of Theale. I am told by one who knew her that a certain Sulhampstead lady, long dead now, was once introduced to Hardy at a social gathering, and that on learning where she lived, he said that he had put her village into one of his stories as 'Gaymead'. I have so far been unable to obtain corroboration of this claim, but at least it is true that although Sulhampstead is scattered and not notably attractive, its former vicarage and especially its fine church tally exactly with Hardy's few descriptive hints.

Inkpen ('Ingpen') Beacon, named in the poem 'Wessex Heights', and in fact England's loftiest point south of the Cotswolds and east of the Mendips, is today a popular, but so far unspoilt, viewpoint for motorists, especially from nearby Newbury ('Kennetbridge'). This, like Reading, is a fast-growing industrial town in the heart of which one can nevertheless still find the remnants of an older place, justifying Hardy's phrase 'a quaint old borough'. To Newbury came Jude, seeking the composer of the new hymn he had heard near Salisbury. The hymn appears to be imaginary, but for the composer Hardy probably had in mind Henry Godding, organist from 1865 to 1894 at the parish church of St Nicholas ('I think he plays in the large church there') for which he composed several chants. He had no known connection with Oxford, but the Goddings did own a shop, though not a wine business. Today there is a memorial window to the organist in the church, which stands behind a trim sward amid the shops.

The Jack and the Chequers, at either of which Anny would rather have stayed than at the (untraceable) temperance hotel, can both be seen: the Chequers still as a hotel, the Jack as a modern fashion-shop, retaining, however, a first-floor Tudor room with a fine oriel window looking on to a side alley. The new chapel, to see the laying of whose foundations Arabella came to New-bury, was the Baptist chapel opened in 1859 (somewhat postdated by Hardy). It stood in Northbrook Street not far from the Jack, on the spot now occupied by Richard Shops and John Collier, and has been rebuilt at St Mary's Hill.

When Arabella and Anny left for Wantage they must, to pass within sight of Jude's birthplace, Great Fawley ('Marygreen'), have taken what are now the B4000 and A338. At Fawley Hardy alludes to cottages pulled down, trees on the green felled and the old church replaced by a new one, all prior to the start of the novel. These changes seem to have exhausted the local capacity for in-novation; modern Fawley is an unattractive little village, its green a lumpy grass waste, its roofs flaunting great stretches of cor-rugated iron, its new buildings few and ugly, like the new class-room tacked on to the Victorian school in the wrong-coloured brick, or the uninspired stabling of the only important newcomer, the Fawley Stud. Ironically, by far the most striking feature is the church 'of German-Gothic design, unfamiliar to English eyes . . . erected . . . by a certain obliterator of historic records [G. F. Street] who had run down from London and back in a day'. Its construction was begun, as a tablet on the wall testifies, in 1863, once more upsetting Weber's chronology, which places the open-ing of the story in 1855.

The vicarage, no longer a church property since the amalgama-tion of the parish with Chaddleworth, dates, like the school, from the 1860s. The well still exists but has for many years been covered by what seems to be the lid of a vault from the old churchyard: not without a certain relevance, since the shaft is reputed to be filled with skeletons, albeit of sheep and pigs. The old graveyard is now a small, melancholy area of rank grass, out of which enough gravestones protrude to excite speculation on how many were really 'obliterated' and replaced by those 'ninepenny cast-iron crosses warranted to last five years'. The crosses have all duly vanished. A short distance north of the cemetery lay the pond (now filled in) where, according to Jude's great-aunt, the young Sue had so impudently paddled.

Just opposite the graveyard, on the edge of the green, there used

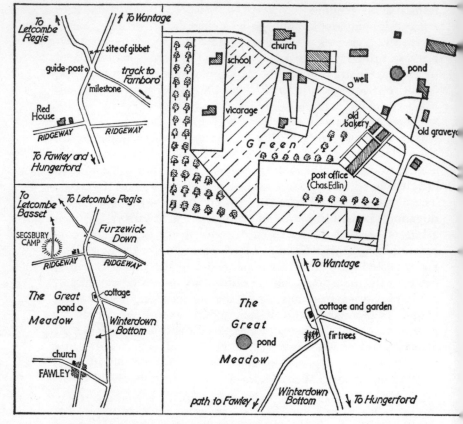

(*Top right*) Fawley Magna ('Marygreen') in the nineteenth century; (*bottom right*) the cottage occupied by Jude and Arabella after their marriage; (*bottom left*) between Fawley and the descent to Wantage; (*top left*) site of the milestone on the back of which Jude cut his inscription

to stand, well within living memory, a pair of thatched cottages of which one was the old village bakery and in all likelihood the prototype of Great-Aunt Drusilla's home, though this cannot be proved. I have seen a photograph of the cottage, which does not show the diamond-leaded window described in *Jude*; but this might well have had to be replaced, and in favour of the building there is a lean-to at the end of it that could have been old Drusilla's 'great fuelhouse'. The claim of the old bakery would be greatly helped if we knew that Mary Head, Hardy's grandmother, who spent thirteen of her early years (from 1772) at Fawley, had spent them under this roof.

Close to the site of the vanished building stands a terrace of nineteenth-century brick cottages, the farthest of which has long been the village store and post-office. Whether Hardy thought of this as the Widow Edlin's home we cannot tell, but between 1854 and 1876 the storekeeper-postmaster was a Charles Edlin.

The 'great meadow', scene of Jude's bird-scaring, remains wide and lonely, and the path across it later taken by him to visit Arabella is still in use. Their nuptial cottage, near the junction of this path with the Wantage road, was either pulled or burnt down at the turn of the century; a little thicket projecting into the field from the roadside hedge occupies the site of its garden. The 'unhealthy fir-trees' near by survived some years longer. The pond in which Jude tried to drown himself, but could not break the ice, lay in a fold of the 'open down' about 350 yards west of the path. Some 35 feet in diameter, it was filled in many years ago.

The former 'hedgeless highway' to Wantage now has substantial hedges along much of both sides nearly all the way from the Fawley turning. At the crest of the hill, where the Ridgeway crosses the road, a pair of twentieth-century cottages stand behind a small lawn, and a few dozen yards west stand two more, rendered. Between the pairs is the site of the Red ('Brown') House, of which

THE BROWN HOUSE

no trace is left. Hardy errs in identifying the Ridgeway with the
'Icknield Street and original Roman road'. Both roads are long pre-
Roman, and the Icknield Way traverses the northern escarpment
at a lower level, along the line of the A417 and B4507. The Ridgeway, described in *Jude* as green, is today gravelled along this reach.
The 'circular British earthbank' just north of it, where the court-
ing Jude and Arabella walked, is Segsbury Camp or Letcombe
Castle, a grassy fort still undisturbed apart from the lane across its
centre, and that was already old in Jude's time.

'Cresscombe' is Letcombe Bassett, a valley village mainly
notable for the watercress beds (now disused) that occupy much
of its centre. Alongside these stands a detached, elegantly kept
thatched cottage locally known as Arabella's; but its identity is
open to considerable doubt, for it is not isolated, and its position
at the bottom of the dip and on the same side of the stream as
the road is wholly incompatible with Hardy's precise account of
Jude's and Arabella's first sight of one another. Nor can it be
easily reconciled with Jude's route from Fawley, which Lea
(who initiated the claim of the cottage) professes to have followed.

The gibbet that Drusilla said used to stand where the 'Fenworth'
(also spelt 'Fensworth') road left the highway by a handpost, was
situated where the Letcombe Regis road branches off opposite the
track over Furzewick Down. Although 'Fensworth' suggests
Furzewick, the name probably stands for Letcombe Regis. There
is still a handpost.

Nearby stood the celebrated milestone on the back of which
the Oxford-besotted youth carved his inscription. Removed
during the 1939 anti-invasion measures, the stone was subsequently
believed lost, until in 1969 it turned up, with two others, as the
result of a clear-out at the Wantage Urban District Council yard.
It was decided to reinstate all three stones, but by the end of 1971
this had still to be done.

When Arabella walked back to Wantage after meeting Phillotson on the Fawley road, she 'practised dimple-making . . . from
where the pollard willows begin to the old almshouses in the first
street of the town'. The willows are still flourishing, unpollarded
now and faced across the road by new houses. The seventeenth-
century almshouses, of red brick and cream-painted stone, are
splendidly maintained.

Page 201 (*left*) Narrobourne: the close resemblance to the description in 'A Tragedy of Two Ambitions', and the absence of any similar site, points to this spot near Holywell Mill, West Coker, as the scene of Old Halborough's drowning. In 1970 the waggon-bridge (out of sight to the left) was unfortunately replaced by one of concrete

(*right*) Plymouth: no 9 Bedford Terrace, home of the Giffords during some of Emma's early years, is the 'high new house' of the poem 'During Wind and Rain'. It is the only one of her Plymouth homes still standing

Page 202 (*left*) Targan Bay: although it figures in *A Pair of Blue Eyes*, the Pentargan Bay waterfall is perhaps better remembered for its association with several of the Cornish lyrics composed after Emma's death

(*right*) St Launce's: the vendor and player of 'flutes, and fiddles, and grand pianners' at Launceston in *A Pair of Blue Eyes* was based on a noted piano-maker and instrument-seller named Hayman, whose shop between High Street and Church Street has now become this café

In the town itself, an uninspiring place, the only identifiable *Jude* building is the Bear Hotel, from which Sue took a 'little car' to return to Fawley. The Bear stands back from the Market Place, its interior pleasantly modernised behind a frontage that Sue would have no difficulty in recognising. She had travelled by train to Wantage Road ('Alfredston Road') station—opened in 1863, demolished just over a century later—and had covered the two miles into the town by steam tram. This vehicle, called the Grantham Car, was the first of its kind in England; there is a model of it in the Science Museum, South Kensington. It had supplanted a horse-tram in 1876, this date reinforcing the evidence of Fawley Church and Hertford College (see page 206) that the action of *Jude* should be placed at least a decade after the dates suggested by Weber. In time the Grantham Car was superseded by a somewhat senile train, which continued to carry passengers until 1925 and freight until 1946, when it made a last dramatic journey, tearing up the track behind it.

Just before the road from Wantage reaches Oxford it skirts Cumnor ('Lumsdon'), the village to which Jude and Sue walked to call on Phillotson. Cumnor was then separated from Oxford by a stretch of 'prettily wooded country'. Today the route is bordered by houses on both sides; but they are detached, and stand in large, well-timbered gardens. Cumnor church tower is 'embattled', as stated, but there is no turret, nor ever was. There is a large new school, but the buildings of the former one are kept in repair, as is the still-occupied 'homely little dwelling' in which Phillotson lived. The 'old house across the way' that sheltered Sue also survives. Cumnor, much extended, is now one of Oxford's wealthiest residential suburbs.

New building of a more industrial sort is in evidence when one crosses out of Wessex and enters the city through Botley and Osney, but there is far less here than to the south-east where the Nuffield car-building empire sprawls. In 1928 Cowley and several other districts were brought within the city bounds, so that with still later editions academic Oxford has been reduced to a tiny nucleus. Not that it did not know the pains of expansion long before; in 1887 complaints were already being made about the increasing barrier between city and countryside, one of the areas involved being the so-called Jericho ('Beersheba'), after Jericho

N

Road (now Walton Street), its chief artery. There are still a Jericho Street and a Jericho Inn—the latter very smart, a good example of the change that is beginning to overtake more and more buildings in this once entirely (and still mainly) working-class quarter of two-storey red-brick terrace houses, very similar to the Spring Gardens quarter of Reading.

Here Jude had his first lodgings, and almost his last meeting with Sue. Hardy wrote a key to many of his 'Christminster' names, identifying Jericho positively with 'Beersheba'; so why did he describe the view from that first room of Jude's as though the house were on the southern edge of central Oxford instead of the north-western? The 'raw and cold air from the Meadows' came from Port Meadow, and the church of 'St Silas' is St Barnabas, designed by Hardy's one-time employer, A. W. Blomfield. As high-church (up to the time of writing) in fact as in fiction, it still has a large cross suspended above the chancel steps, though the design differs somewhat from the cross in *Jude*.

During the Fawleys' family visit to Oxford Sue and the children occupied lodgings that looked toward where, 'at some distance opposite, the outer walls of Sarcophagus College—silent, black and windowless—threw their four centuries of gloom, bigotry and decay into the little room'. The restricted view included the 'outlines of Rubric College beyond the other' and the tower of a third. If we are to take all this literally, 'Sarcophagus' was a fifteenth-century foundation near to Brasenose, and it is tempting to think Hardy had in mind All Souls, especially since the name itself has some affinity with a sarcophagus. But if the suggestion is correct, Hardy must have imagined the windowless walls: unlike several of its neighbours, All Souls exhibits none. The inn where Jude slept, and also 'Mildew Lane', are not identifiable. The cemetery where the children were buried was surely St Sepulchre, reached by a short path between the houses of Walton Street. The burial-ground, virtually disused since 1954, lives on at a peaceful public garden, crossed by a winding path between trees that in summer form a green tunnel.

The most striking innovation in the university area is the cleaning of the older stonework. By 1970 most colleges, the Bodleian, the Sheldonian Theatre, and many other landmarks were exhibiting details that had been masked for generations. Prior to the cleaning, most of the alterations to the older colleges had been effected (under Gilbert Scott) just before the *Jude* period, and the greatest change following it had been the construction of the New Foundations, succeeded in the present century by the addition of still more buildings (some very striking in design) to meet the ever-increasing pressure on accommodation. Nor has the process ended: for the 1970s there is a massive programme of new faculty buildings, museums and libraries.

Among Hardy's code-names not already quoted are 'Cardinal'—Christ Church; 'Biblioll'—Balliol; 'Crozier'—? Oriel (but according to Lea, Merton); 'Old Time Street'—Merton Street or Oriel Street. The 'Cathedral-church of Cardinal College' is Oxford Cathedral, still accessible across the vast green quadrangle of Christ Church. When Jude heard the 101-stroke curfew that sounds every evening at five past nine on the great bell in Tom Tower, it was still rung by hand. In our own lazier age it is operated electrically.

His first rendezvous with Sue was near the cross in the roadway marking the spot where the martyrs were burnt at the stake; and, despite resurfacing, the place is still so marked. The 'singularly built theatre' into whose lantern he climbed was the Sheldonian, and the great library before it, the Bodleian, now eclipsed by the New Bodleian at the corner of Broad Street and Parks Road.

The Sheldonian was also the focus of attention when Jude, Sue and the children stood in the rain to watch the procession on 'Remembrance Day'—the Commemoration or Encaenia. The family had come from the railway station, at that time one of a pair side by side: the Midland Region station has now been abandoned. At Carfax ('Fourways') Jude led the way along the High Street ('Chief Street') as far as the 'church with the Italian porch, whose helical columns were heavily draped with creepers'—St Mary the Virgin, now cleaned and creeperless—where they 'turned in on the left'—up Catte Street—and came to the 'open space' between the Sheldonian Theatre and 'the nearest college'—Hertford—where the crowd were gathered. It is Hertford College that displays the carved frieze (a stag motif) and the Latin motto that Jude explained to his fellow-bystanders: *Ad fontes aquarum sicut cervus anhelat*—'As pants the hart for cooling streams'. He is stated to have studied the carving 'years before', but in fact this part of Hertford was not built until 1887.

Of Oxford's more famous inns, several are changing their function as the colleges that are their landlords cast about for extra accommodation. Thus the Mitre ('Crozier') retains its restaurant (now a steak-house) and bars, but has turned over its hotel quarters to Lincoln. The 'low-ceiled tavern' where Jude recited the creed in Latin, and which on his return to Oxford he found had become an enlarged, modernised and fashionable rendezvous, is the Lamb and Flag, adjoining its landlord, St John's College. The Flam, as the students call it, has been further enlarged and altered a number of times, in keeping with changing tastes. The typical gin-palace of Jude's later visit has therefore disappeared; but the 'low-ceiled tavern' remains easily recognisable in the central section, much frequented for down-to-earth evening meals. When this low part was the whole tavern, entry was made a short distance up the adjoining alley—the 'court' or 'lane' of the novel—across the mouth of which the St Giles Street frontage extends to form an arch. With the enlargement, a second doorway became available under the arch itself, and it must be this that Hardy called a 'spacious and inviting entrance'. (See plate on page 135.)

Carfax, with its ancient St Martin's Tower, is still a popular rendezvous. The High, as the university calls it, remains broad and reasonably undisfigured, a street of many shops and some interesting taverns. South and west of it, on either side of St Aldate's, lies the area that best justifies Hardy's vivid picture of obscure alleys, jutting porticoes, oriel windows, and florid doorways. But today these corners show little of the 'rottenness' which formerly made it 'impossible that modern thought could house itself in such decrepit chambers.' West again lies more rebuilding.

In *Jude*'s closing pages Arabella goes to 'Oldgate' College, entering under an archway and walking 'along the gravel paths and under the aged limes'. Although the most celebrated limes at the time were in the grounds of Trinity, the allusion to the archway establishes 'Oldgate' College as New College; not only is the entrance arched, but an arch spans New College Lane just outside. Limes grow in two parts of the gardens; those in the nearer are recent replacements; but at the far end of the remoter garden there is still a row of older trees.

The lodging in which Jude died, that house so wistfully and vainly sought by Lea, remains as elusive for us as for him. After Jude's death Arabella and her friends made their way down St Aldate's to Folly Bridge and thence 'passed by a narrow slit down to the riverside path'. The bridge is the same today, and the steps and slopes down to the two towpaths are bordered by the iron railings that bordered them then. Nor has Christ Church Meadow ('Cardinal Meadow'), having escaped a project to drive a sunken road across it, materially altered. It is the banks of the river that are changing, as the 'gay barges' of the boat clubs are steadily replaced by modern boathouses.

Hardy denied that 'Christminster' was to be wholly equated with Oxford. Outside *Jude* and *The Life* the city is hardly mentioned, and always under its real name. In the only Oxford poem, from which the lines at the head of this section are taken, 'Evelyn G.' is Mrs A. D. Godley (*née* Gifford, Emma's cousin and the wife of the Public Orator). She died in 1920 at Arlington House, today known simply as 27 Norham Road. Situated near the Parks, the yellow-brick Victorian house is now converted into flats.

MID-WESSEX
(Wiltshire)

The grey Cathedral, towards whose face
Bend eyes untold, has not met yours;
Your shade has never swept its base,

Your form has never darked its doors,
Nor have your faultless feet once thrown
A pensive pit-pat on its floors.

IN A CATHEDRAL CITY (SALISBURY)

Win Green ('Wingreen'), already mentioned (page 95) in relation to Tess's journey with Alec, is also touched upon in the poem 'The Vampirine Fair'. The hill is part of the Wiltshire area of Cranborne Chase that when Hardy knew it had been redeemed from a wilderness and turned into farmland. As such it was much affected by the lean times of the mid-nineteenth century and again by those of the 1920s and 1930s. In the period of *Tess* Win Green and its surrounding coombs must have looked very much as they did in our own century before Rolf Gardiner of Fontmell Magna restored large tracts of the reverted land and clothed the bare hills with forests.

The 'Manor Court' of 'The Vampirine Fair' is Rushmore, a large early-nineteenth-century mansion south-west of Win Green, former home of the remarkable General A. H. Lane Fox Pitt-Rivers. This house, shabby but outwardly unmodified, has now become a boys' preparatory school. Primroses still border the long drive. The 'churchyard home' of the poem is at Tollard Royal, where the church still bears a 'steeple-cock'.

Hardy and Emma stayed at Rushmore during the 1890s, and paid a visit to the most fantastic of the general's enterprises, the Larmer Gardens: an experience later used for the poem 'Concerning Agnes'. General Pitt-Rivers had laid out these grounds as a place of public recreation. An ornamental pool was dug, a 'temple' built, a caretaker's house, bandstand and theatre erected. 'Quarters' were constructed—wooden picnic houses, in various Indian styles, about a large lawn for dancing. The whole was approached by a broad avenue of magnificent trees festooned with lamps, the 'faery lamps' of the poem. At the peak of the venture 24,000 people visited the Larmer Gardens on a single Sunday. But the enterprise had the evanescence of all faery things, and after the general's death the gardens fell into increasing decay. Mr Michael Pitt-Rivers has now restored the scene as much as may be, although the bandstand and two of the fragile 'quarters' were past redemption; but in the current economic climate any hope of reopening the grounds remains in abeyance.

Not surprisingly, the Wiltshire scene most frequently met with in Hardy's work is Salisbury. He had a great affection for the cathedral, despite his rejection of its creed in the poems 'The Impercipient' and 'A Cathedral Façade at Midnight'. It figures prominently in *The Hand of Ethelberta*, in one passage of which Christopher plays the organ while Ethelberta inspects the 'sallow monuments'. The monuments are the same today, with a minor addition or two, but the organ was replaced in 1876, a few years after the action of the novel: Christopher would have played th e instrument presented by King George III in 1792. This is still in use in Salisbury, for it was re-erected in the church of St Thomas of Canterbury, the scene of Sue's wedding with Phillotson. Following the havoc wrought in the eighteenth century by Wyatt on 'the fair fane of Poore's olden episcopal see' ('My Cicely'), Gilbert Scott carried out further restoration in the 1860s and 1870s —work used by Hardy to provide Jude with his term as mason —and in 1939 the upper part of the spire was strengthened. It is now surmounted at night by a red warning-light.

The Close remains unspoilt, as well it ought, for there is no more spacious or gracious setting for a cathedral in western Europe. On the western side the Training College ('Melchester Normal School'), attended so ingloriously by Sue and rather more successfully by Hardy's sisters, has undergone extensive alteration and enlargement, but the 'ancient edifice of the fifteenth century, once a palace' has been preserved, and is now the school headquarters. The garden still runs down to the Avon, and in front of the house the courtyard survives, with its wall much lowered. Beyond the lane 'trees of emerald green' shade the sward as they did in 'The High-School Lawn'. The Theological College, also mentioned in *Jude*, a large seventeenth-century building on the north side of the Close, remains virtually unaltered.

Another visitor to the 'damp and venerable Close', a few years later than Ethelberta and her friends, was Swithin St Cleeve (*Two in a Tower*). His goal was the Bishop's Palace, which has now become the Cathedral School. The trees in the palace grounds, and the rooks that nested in them, were both said by Hardy to seem 'older, if possible, than those in the Close'. Some of the trees near the palace are certainly very old, but others have died and been replaced. The rooks have died and not been replaced.

The description of the city of Salisbury in *Jude* hardly applies today: '. . . a quiet and soothing place, almost wholly ecclesiastical in its tone; a spot where worldly learning and intellectual smartness had no establishment'. Perhaps the change was already beginning when Hardy wrote, for he made Sue say that the centre of life had moved from the cathedral to the railway station. Now it has moved again, to the central car-park.

On market days the focus was probably always the Market Place. Round this, inevitably, various twentieth-century structures have appeared, but many highly diverse buildings from earlier epochs remain, among them, fairly certainly, the original of the Harnhams' house in 'On the Western Circuit'. The 'dignified residence of considerable size' stood at the 'remotest corner' from that nearest to the cathedral, that is at the north-east angle. Two houses are possible: the *second* (Georgian) house along the north side (Blue Boar Row), the ground floor of which is now occupied by a music shop; and the corner house at the meeting of Endless Street and Winchester Street, now a hardware shop.

Markets are still held twice a week, though livestock is now sold in a new market a few streets away. On three October days each year the square teems, by ancient right, with a fun fair, as in the story. At the south-east corner stands the Guildhall ('the Town Hall') where Ethelberta and the others attended Christopher's concert in 'a large upstair assembly room' (the Banqueting Room). Concerts are still held there, but two courts of justice maintain the official character of the building, from which the city corporation transferred its deliberations in 1927.

When Ethelberta and Picotee left the Guildhall they made their way up 'a long street' (Fisherton Street) to the railway station. Jude, too, must have known this thoroughfare, though the 'street leading from the station' in which he found a temperance hotel may have been Mill Road. The 'town bridge' that he crossed was Fisherton Bridge, rebuilt in 1961. Fisherton Street today is a street of mean architecture but many and varied shops. It also contains the city's theatre.

The unnamed 'junction' where the whip incident occurred in *Two on a Tower* is not identified as 'Melchester' because this would

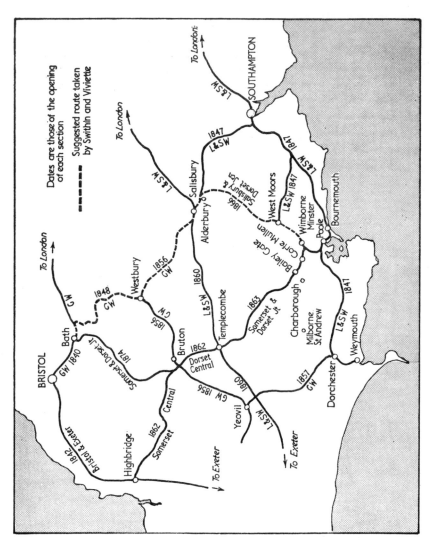

The railway network in the period of *Two on a Tower*

not at all have suited certain aspects of the story, nor would Salisbury's busy twin stations have permitted the episode to take place without attracting a large crowd. But Hardy's data concerning the 'junction's' relationship to 'Welland House' (Charborough) are so explicit that Salisbury is the only possible location. After stating (correctly) that 'Warborne' (Wimborne) station lay five miles from 'Welland House': and 'the next station above that nine miles' (again correctly), he continues: 'They [Swithin and Viviette] were bound for the latter: their plan being that she should there take the train to the junction where the whip accident had occurred . . . and return . . . as if from Bath'. Since Wimborne is east of Charborough, the 'next station' can only be farther east, and was in fact at West Moors, where the Salisbury & Dorset Junction Railway (opened in 1866) branched off from the London & South Western, to run north and join another of the L & SW lines two miles outside Salisbury.

The words quoted above make it plain that West Moors itself was not the 'junction'—and in any case passengers from Salisbury to Wimborne did not have to change there. Coming from Bath, the only change necessary was at Salisbury, which therefore was the real 'junction' behind Hardy's careful veil. This, too, is where Viviette's brother would have changed on his journey from London—though in practice he would have been more likely to have travelled to Wimborne direct through Southampton. Today the little S & DJR line has long been closed and the track torn up. Salisbury is still a junction for other routes, but the old GWR station has been closed and converted into a van depot.

On returning from the station, Ethelberta and her sister booked in at the Red Lion, a large coaching inn that remains one of the principal hotels and a prominent showpiece. Here, too, Phillotson stayed before his marriage, and nearly a century and a half earlier the first Countess of Wessex (*A Group of Noble Dames*) had secret appointments with her own husband. Ethelberta's Lord Mountclere stayed round the corner at the White Hart, where in the story 'A Committee Man of the Terror' Madame V— had left the coach. The White Hart is an eighteenth-century hostelry that has similarly retained its original appearance.

Both Jude and Charles Raye, in 'On the Western Circuit', had lodgings in the High Street, a relatively short thoroughfare that has managed to remain old-world at the North (or Close) Gate end while becoming wholly twentieth-century at the other. A stone's throw from the modern end stands the church of St Thomas of Canterbury, already mentioned. The Phillotson–Sue wedding preceded by only a few years the discovery over the chancel arch of a 'doom', a medieval mural portraying the Last Judgement (an omen that would have been a gift to Hardy), which had lain hidden under whitewash since 1573. In other respects St Thomas's continued much as at the time of the novel until the 1960s, when most of the stonework of the large Perpendicular windows was replaced.

The Market House in which Jude told Sue of his marriage to Arabella faces on to a small extension of the Market Place called the Cheese Market, and is a lofty affair of stone and much ironwork, built in 1859. One wing has now been sealed off and made into a covered footway to the central car-park; the rest is hired out for exhibitions.

The 'cemetery on the hill' where Jude first worked is on the eastern outskirts, bordering London Road. A hundred years ago it looked upon open meadows, most of which have now been built over. Also on the city outskirts stands Old Sarum ('Old Melchester'), until well into the present century heavily overgrown, swarming with rabbits, its deep ditch choked with trees and shrubs: a worthy setting for Anna's seduction in 'On the Western Circuit'. Today the whole area is in the trim condition one expects of properties in the care of the Ministry of Public Building and Works. The ruins of the castle and the ground-plan of the razed cathedral are well signposted, and in 1954 Salisbury City Corporation acquired some forty-four acres adjoining, in order to keep the site clear of building encroachment.

Close to Salisbury is Wilton, a small town living mainly on its memories. Lea and Pinion both give Wilton House, seat of the Earls of Pembroke, as the scene of the principal events in 'The Marchioness of Stonehenge'. Certainly Hardy's meagre clues suggest this. But neither the most recent (and therefore least inhibited) account of the Pembrokes, Tresham Lever's *The Herberts of Wilton*, nor the researches of the late earl—no mean authority on the history of his family—have produced evidence that the story concerns any real occupants of Wilton.

Salisbury was the starting-point of Mr George Crookhill's strange journey, the adventurous part of which, as we have already seen (page 91), began as he toiled up Coombe Bissett Hill (still in rural surroundings, now numbered A354). Tess and Angel also went through the city on the journey that ended at Stonehenge, and few Hardy passages so accurately evoke the spirit of a place as his description of their arrival at the monument in the dark. Today, after a period as the private property of the local lord of the manor, it is protected from vandals by a wire fence and maintained by the Ministry of Public Building and Works. Outside the fence the area is the concern of the National Trust, which in 1969 put underground most of the accretions inseparable from public popularity.

Since the *Tess* episode (about 1889) there have been several changes in the great circle themselves. In 1899 two monoliths in the outer circle keeled over. In 1901 the upright of the central trilithon, which for centuries had been tilting inward, was straightened. In 1958, at the end of half a century of skilled archaeological work, many of the fallen stones were correctly replaced. The surrounding ditch, too, has been partly excavated during this century; and just inside it a ring of blocked-up pits, the Aubrey Holes, has been incompletely dug out. Less than a mile north of Stonehenge lie Larkhill camp and its artillery ranges.

For their excursion from Salisbury to Wardour Castle Jude and Sue took the train to, presumably, Tisbury (the line is still in operation), from which the walk is about two miles. In discussing the project Sue had confused the 'new' Wardour Castle with the old. The later building, Palladian in style, was finished in 1776 for the eighth Earl of Arundell, and its beautiful circular central gallery did in fact become the home of a fine collection of paintings by the masters Hardy names. But after the death of the last earl in 1944 the mansion began to fall into disrepair, and one by one the pictures were sold off. The Arundells finally sold the castle to a religious order for conversion into a seminary; but 'conversion' included stripping out the decorated ceilings and wall-panelling, followed by a proposal to pull down the mansion altogether! Luckily the secular authorities were able to intervene, and Wardour Castle, repaired and with the survival of its remaining decoration assured, has since 1960 been occupied by the Cranborne Chase School for Girls.

On leaving the castle Sue and Jude walked across the 'open country, wide and high' to a station on another line, 'about seven miles off' to the north. This was evidently Boyton or Wylye (both now closed) on the Warminster line. All this region of Wiltshire continues to be one of the least spoilt parts of the county, with vast views. The walkers crossed the 'old road from London to Land's End', now the A303, which suggests that they were making for Boyton. The shepherd's cottage where they were accommodated for the night is probably fictitious. Another 'mid-Wessex' railway station is mentioned in *A Pair of Blue Eyes*. This is Chippenham (still in service), where Knight and Smith saw the waggon bearing Elfride's coffin attached to their train.

North of Salisbury Plain (the 'Great Plain') are the Marlborough ('Marlbury') Downs, scene of 'What the Shepherd Saw'. The focus of the tale is an arch of three stones, the Devil's Den ('Devil's Door'), standing in a shallow cultivated valley, Clatford Bottom, immediately north of the Bath road (A4) two miles west of Marlborough. The stones, with two more, recumbent, formed part of a Stone Age tomb. Hardy describes the arch as it is today—two uprights bridged by a horizontal. They stood thus when Bradley wrote in 1907, but later one of the uprights developed a crack, and the cross-stone was in grave danger of falling until repairs were carried out in 1921. Hutton's description of the monument in *Highways and Byways in Wiltshire* (1917) is incorrect.

'Lambing Corner', where the shepherd boy had his hut, had a real existence, but for many years now has been just part of the rolling farmland. This has become much more domesticated in appearance notwithstanding lingering tracts of furze and a vastly diminished number of sheep. The duke and duchess lived at 'Shakeforest Towers', a name unmistakably suggested by Savernake Forest; and indeed 'the old park entrance . . . now closed up and the lodge cleared away', close to the 'great western road', is a reference to the gate (now open again) leading into Savernake's Grand Avenue from the A4. The 'ancestral trees' are no doubt the avenue's famous beeches. But the house itself must have been suggested by Clatford House, immediately across the A4 opposite Clatford Bottom. This extraordinary building is a gabled

Page 219 Endelstow House: Lanhydrock House, near Bodmin, is the principal model for Lord Luxellian's mansion in *A Pair of Blue Eyes*. This print shows it before the fire of 1881 destroyed all except the north wing; but the reconstruction exactly followed the original design

Page 220 Endelstow House: the more ornate features in Hardy's description are not to be found at Lanhydrock, but are borrowed from Athelhampton, close to Puddletown, Dorset, a house well known to the novelist in his

farmhouse of brick and tile on three sides, but the side facing the highway is of stone, Georgian in design, and extended upward to form a dummy top storey, with painted-in windows, to hide the gables. The house is now empty, though not ownerless, and is in some danger of demolition.

In the heart of Savernake Forest stands Tottenham House, for long the seat of the Marquises of Ailesbury and today yet another boys' preparatory school. (For its association with the story 'The Duchess of Hamptonshire' see note (page 256) on *A Group of Noble Dames*.)

> Well: when in Wessex on your rounds
> Take a brief step beyond its bounds,
> And enter Gloucester . . .

This invitation introduces 'The Abbey Mason', Hardy's account in verse of the legendary invention of the Perpendicular style by the mason in charge of rebuilding at the abbey church, Gloucester, which later became the cathedral. No one knows the degree of truth in the story; but in a much changed and uglified city the unknown mason's 'petrified lacework' stands intact.

o

OUTER WESSEX
(Somerset)

Beneath us figured tor and lea,
From Mendip to the western sea—
I doubt if finer sight there be
    Within this royal realm.

A TRAMPWOMAN'S TRAGEDY

O ne brief scene in *The Dynasts* is laid just on the Somerset side of the border with Wiltshire, at Shockerwick House, now the seat of the Dukes of Newcastle. A previous occupant had become a close friend of the painter Gainsborough, and William Pitt the Younger was visiting Shockerwick from Bath to see the mansion's Gainsborough paintings when the news of Austerlitz reached him. Hardy combined the receipt of the news with Pitt's famous injunction to roll up the map of Europe, although in fact that remark was made while he was being conveyed, seriously ill, back into his own home at Putney. But the tradition that the incident took place at Shockerwick persists there to this day.

Of Hardy's allusions to Bath the most familiar is the description given by Bathsheba Everdene's young farmhand, Cainy Ball. It was not until afterwards, in 1878, that the Roman baths, the most extensive outside Italy, were disinterred, discoveries continuing far into the twentieth century. The water 'ready boiled for use' flows hot as ever. The city remains an elegant shopping centre, but the prototypes (if any) of the shops named by Cainy defy identification. The 'clock with a face as big as a baking-trendle' may have been the abbey's, though the dial is not really large. The abbey, featured in the poem 'Aquae Sulis', was last restored extensively between 1864 and 1871, so that it remains very much as when Hardy wrote, with the exception of a covered cloister added to the nave in 1923 as a war memorial.

In *Far from the Madding Crowd*, *Two on a Tower* and 'The Marchioness of Stonehenge', weddings take place at Bath, but none of the churches or lodgings is specified. The poem 'Midnight on Beechen, 187–' evokes a panorama of Bath on a night in mid-June. This high bluff just south of the railway has wooded flanks, and near its summit runs a footpath from which the view is now almost hidden in summer, except at two points, by the growth of Cainy's 'old wooden trees'. Apart from the riverside in the foreground the spectacle has not so far lost too much of its period character; but there is, nevertheless, a steady erosion, for the authorities, though ready enough to protect individual buildings, seem unable to grasp that it is the homogeneity of the eighteenth-century whole that makes Bath unique.

From Bath it is a natural transition to the other half of the see, Wells ('Fountall'). Here Maumbry, in 'A Changed Man', and the Halborough brothers in 'A Tragedy of Two Ambitions' studied at the Theological College in the close, old Halborough was sentenced, and the cathedral 'by Mendip east of Dunkery Tor' saw the attempted robbery recalled in the poem 'The Sacrilege'. Today even the eighteenth-century thief would find cathedral and close very little different, though in 1969 fears were aroused by the erection, just outside the close, of a small estate of box-like and grossly inappropriate houses. It is to be hoped that the 'grand conservation scheme' for central Wells, approved by the city council a year later, will prevent further aesthetic affronts.

There was, and still is, a small prison behind the Guildhall, but it has always been used only for prisoners awaiting trial; in real life old Halborough would have served his seven days at Shepton Mallet.

Some miles east of Wells, and next to a hamlet with the improbable name of Vobster, is Mells ('Falls'), the home of Squire Dornell (really Horner), whose daughter became the First Countess of Wessex. The Horners held Mells until 1917, when the building was all but destroyed by fire. The present mansion, designed in 1923 by Sir Edward Lutyens, was built for another owner.

Mells Park, however, continues to be graced with many fine trees that in their youth must have shaded Squire Dornell, though the long avenue of beeches that he compared favourably with the Melbury Park oaks has recently had to be uprooted as the result of age and disease. But the ride itself, asphalted now, is still the drive to the house.

Glastonbury (Glaston), a graceful town despite its growth, is briefly mentioned as the place where the Trampwoman's friend, Mother Lee, died. This little company faced 'the gusts on Mendip ridge', and it was in certain Mendip caves that the adventures in Hardy's only children's story, 'Our Exploits at West Poley', took place. West and East Poley themselves, and the cavern 'Nick's

Pocket', are imaginary; but Priddy, at whose annual fair the unhappy protagonist of 'The Sacrilege' 'snatched a silk-piece red and
rare' is a true Mendip village. The fair is still held, and it is not
just a fun-fair; sheep and a few cattle change hands. A Mendip
village that has lost its fair is Binegar, to whose revelries old
Halborough and his new wife went after visiting Joshua. The
field near the church in which a horse fair was held until the 1950s
is still pointed out.

Wills Neck—the 'Wylls-Neck' of 'Wessex Heights', and the
highest point in the Quantocks—has escaped desecration except
by stag-hunting, which continues undiminished nearly half a
century after Hardy sent a message of encouragement to a Taunton
gathering of the League for the Prohibition of Cruel Sports. Much
of the range now belongs to the National Trust. Beyond the
Quantocks lies Dunster, the principal setting of *A Laodicean*. The
evidence that, in situation at least, Dunster Castle is 'Stancy
Castle' and Dunster village 'Markton' is provided by Hardy's
Wessex map and also by the similarity of 'de Stancy' to de Lancy,
the name of a family with a seat near by. But there is no resemblance
between the castles of fact and fiction—even less than Hardy indicates in his preface. Beatty has made out a very plausible case
for contending that Hardy, forced to dictate *A Laodicean* from a
London sick-bed, modelled Stancy on Corfe Castle (page 181) and
took its paintings from Hutchins's list for Kingston Lacy. Today
Dunster Castle, thrusting its complex lineaments, the colour of a
Golden Russet apple, high above the trees, retains an agreeable
touch of fairyland; the Victorian restoration was unusually discreet.
Below the hill the village has been very carefully protected from
anything out of harmony: perhaps too carefully, making it a little
precious.

'Toneborough Deane' in 'The Sacrilege' is Taunton Deane, a
first-class dairying region. At Taunton ('Toneborough'), in *A
Laodicean*, Somerset's rival Havill had his office, and Captain de
Stancy was quartered in the cavalry barracks. In 1879 these were
demolished and replaced by infantry barracks, from which the last
combatant troops departed in 1959; their quarters became offices
for the Army Pay Corps and other units, and there is also a small
military museum. At 'Toneborough' too the Honourable Laura
(*A Group of Noble Dames*) was secretly married in the church of

St Mary, notable today for the resplendent colours of its interior where all the painted woodwork has just been restored.

As to Exmoor and Dunkery Beacon, respectively 'Exon Moor' and 'Dunkery Tor' in 'The Sacrilege', Dunkery, like Wills Neck, has been spared twentieth-century embellishments; but Exmoor is the subject of some concern because of the steady conversion of marginal areas into farmland.

From one meaning of 'moor' to another: 'sad Sedge-Moor' was 'skirted' by the Trampwoman's party, and 'Sedgemoor' is mentioned in 'Molly Gone'. In the days before skilled drainage turned it into pasture, enough of the moor was marshland for many parts to need 'skirting'. The drainage was begun centuries ago, but even now a wide strip on either side of King's Sedge-moor Drain is covered only by the coarsest grass and sedge, its appearance probably differing little from what it was in the Trampwoman's day.

Like a backbone along these fenlands runs the narrow ridge of the Polden Hills. It was while the Trampwoman and her friends were climbing 'toilsome Poldon [*sic*] crest' that the teller of the tale began her fatal flirtation. They were making for the spot where the tragedy was to occur, the inn 'far-famed as Marshal's Elm', almost at the eastern extremity of the range. Marshal's Elm became a farmhouse before the turn of the century; today, in that it offers bed and breakfast, it has returned in some measure to its original function. There appear to be few alterations inside, but there is no visible evidence that it was ever an inn. Hardy referred in a footnote to the former 'fine old swinging sign'. This was still recalled locally when Lea wrote; now it is not even a memory.

In the jail at 'Ivel-chester' (Ilchester) the Trampwoman's lover was hanged. Hardy supplies a footnote referring to the terrible conditions in the jail, which he describes as demolished. It was not entirely pulled down, however, for half-hidden today behind a petrol station there is a low building with odd cross-shaped windows, now used as a storehouse, and this was once part of the boys' prison quarters. Behind this again are two semi-detached stone houses, still known as Gaol Cottages, which were in fact the prison bakery and wash-house. On the other hand, according to J. Stevens Cox, the tall, narrow building by the river Yeo popularly believed to be the 'hanging chamber' (and photographed as such by Lea) is nothing more than a garden summer-house built after the demolition of the prison.

A few miles west of Ilchester the Yeo passes under a humped bridge that unites the villages of Long Load and Little Load. On the Little Load side the mouth of a tributary stream has been widened to make a bay for a barge, and this is the spot referred to in the introductory note to the poem 'Vagg Hollow'. Here, and at a now vanished wharf on the Long Load side, barges from the Bristol Channel off-loaded into waggons that carried their merchandise 'inland', that is to Yeovil and Sherborne. The waggon route, however, was by Ash and Tintinhull, and did not pass through Vagg Hollow. It therefore seems likely that 'Load Bridge' was a slip for Pill Bridge, which still spans the river Ivel midway between the Loads and Ilchester, and where barges also unshipped. From Pill Bridge (itself too narrow for vehicles) a road, still partly in evidence, led into Ilchester, after which the waggons would have travelled, as Hardy says, down 'the old Roman Road' (now the A37) as far as the Halfway Inn. Here today the A37 swings east, but the old road ran straight on toward Preston Plucknett, and indeed continues to do so as a little-used lane, surprisingly verdant in an area fast becoming a Yeovil suburb. Vagg Hollow is a very deep depression just north of the intersection with the route from Tintinhull. Hallucinations are still occasionally experienced there.

To some extent the suburban atmosphere has spread to Tintinhill, a straggling village noted for the presence of Tintinhull House (or the Mansion) the 'manor' of 'The Flirt's Tragedy', 'Embowered in Tintinhull Valley / By laurel and yew'. Today it belongs to the National Trust. The garden (redesigned in 1900) still boasts a fine old yew. Close at hand is Montacute ('Montislope') House, familiar to readers of Llewellyn Powys. Hardy is on record as having told Lea that Montacute was 'Elm-Cranlynch' in 'The First Countess of Wessex'. But Hardy was confusing two branches of the Phelips ('Phelipson') family. The Phelipses indeed held Montacute from the Dissolution until the early 1930s, and *Richard* Phelips whose daughter Edith married Sir John Horsey ('Horseleigh') belonged to Montacute, which is therefore the 'Montislope' of 'Master John Horseleigh, Knight'. But *Charles* Phelips, the Charles 'Phelipson' of 'The First Countess', belonged to a lesser branch that had been banished in some disgrace in 1587 to the family's small manor at Corfe Mullen near Wimborne, and it is this manor that is 'Elm-Cranlynch' (see page 101).

Montacute, a National Trust property now, is a big, curiously impersonal house—perhaps because the furniture is an assemblage of gifts made to the Trust and never formed a home. A feature of great interest to Hardy readers is a plaster frieze in the hall, depicting a sixteenth-century version of the skimmington ride (*The Mayor of Casterbridge*). In the time of Sir John Horsey the present house did not exist; it was begun only in the 1590s by the nephew of the Edith Phelips who married Sir John. Nearly two hundred years later, when Edward Phelips of Montacute was planning his modifications, he bought the drawing-room chimneypiece, some windows, and the whole of the ornamental stone façade of Clifton Maybank (see page 142) for re-erection. There is a reference in 'Molly Gone' to 'Montacute Crest'. This is St Michael's Hill, the conical tree-clad eminence immediately west of the house.

Between Montacute and Clifton Maybank lies West Coker, the 'Narrobourne' of 'A Tragedy of Two Ambitions'. 'Narrobourne House' is described as a 'gloomy' manor house with a conservatory, a gravel terrace on the east side, and a view across the meads to a point where the local stream encounters a weir with a footbridge over it, then narrows to 'pass under a barrel arch or culvert constructed for waggons to cross into the middle of the mead in hay-making time'. There are trees round about, and a footpath leading past the weir from a point on the main road between the village and Hendford Hill—the real name of a hill leading southwestward out of Yeovil ('Ivell').

Several manor houses adorn the Cokers, and many weirs used to serve mills along the stream. But only one locality meets virtually all Hardy's points. In the hamlet of Holywell, between West and North Coker, there stands a disused mill, now renovated in part as a private house; and in the former watermeadows behind it there lay until 1970 a combination of sluice, footbridge, culvert and narrowing stream so closely resembling Hardy's picture that identification is unavoidable. In 1970 the culvert and waggon-bridge were replaced by a stone and concrete structure carrying the drive to the house; and to my great regret the opportunity for recording the old bridge in a photograph was lost.

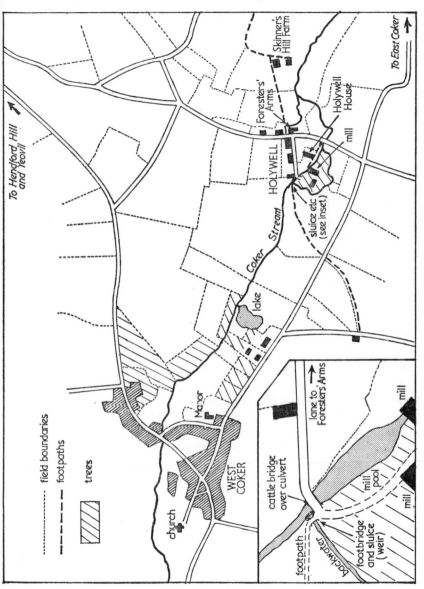

To illustrate *A Tragedy of Two Ambitions*

field boundaries
footpaths
trees

To Hendford Hill
and Yeovil

Skinner's Hill Farm

Foresters' Arms

Holywell House

HOLYWELL

mill

sluice etc
(see inset)

Coker Stream

lake

Manor

WEST COKER

church

To East Coker

lane to
Foresters' Arms

cattle bridge
over culvert

footpath

footbridge
and sluice
(weir)

backwater

mill pool

mill

mill

Close to the site grow trees through which the brothers could
have seen the lights of West Coker Manor along the mead upstream. The modest size of the 'Coker Rill', as it is called in the
poem 'The Pat of Butter'—a 'narrow bourne' in truth—makes it
hard to find spots where even a drunken man in the dark could
drown; but here the channel is so deep and steep-sided that with
the brook in spate, as we are told it was, the episode becomes
entirely credible.

There are minor objections. 'Narrobourne' church had three
bells; both Coker churches have eight. The weir had 'hatches',
whereas there is really only one (making the structure technically
a sluice). The drowning man's cry, if it reached Rosa in the manor,
must have been audible in the millhouse and in Holywell House.
But these are small points, reminders that Hardy saw no reason why
he should not take liberties in a piece of fiction. That he took some
in this tale is evidenced by his references to the 'stile by a bridge'
past Hendford Hill, for none is traceable on even the largest maps
of the time. Possibly Hardy 'moved' the manor: it was stated to be
close to the footpath.

Suburbia has encroached from Yeovil in this direction too;
bungalows come to within a few yards of the weir. Yet West
Coker remains a pretty place. The manor, cheerful enough now
and delightfully modernised within, could well have had a 'gloomy'
appearance in Victorian times. There is neither trace nor recollec-
tion of a conservatory (except at St Juliot all Hardy's conserva-
tories seem untraceable), but the 'broad gravel path' can be recognised. The church, little changed, is chiefly of interest for the
name of a former rector: Halberton, significantly like Halborough.

Yeovil itself, the sprawling helicopter- and glove-making town,
bears little resemblance to the place where old Halborough pro-
posed to stay at the (fictitious) 'Castle Inn', and Mr Cope ('For
Conscience' Sake') lived in 'St Peter's Street' and was a curate
at 'St John's Church' (both imaginary). Apart from the parish
church, the few old buildings look overwhelmed.

A dozen miles west, beside the tree-lined A30 that here runs
along a 700ft ridge, stands Windwhisle Inn, yet another 'lone
inn' favoured by the Trampwoman and her friends. Until the
1950s this was still a rough public house, with benches and scrubbed
tables, not much changed from the tramps' and highwaymen's

haunt of old. Now it has been made elegant and comfortable, and it is only for those with a romantic and quite impractical love for the squalid past that a spell is broken. Nevertheless, Windwhistle retains a more antique appearance than, say, the Horton Inn; and there is a woman's ghost seen from time to time on the road outside, even by those who have not yet been in.

Windwhistle lies between Chard and Crewkerne. The poem 'Growth in May' bears the footnote 'Near Chard', the country around which is the rich pasture-land described in the poem. Tracts of 'elbow-high green' that cause even the hedges to 'make a mean show as a fence' have not entirely vanished, praise be. Crewkerne is mentioned in the poem 'At Wynyard's Gap'. Today, despite the presence of one of the country's largest cheese factories, it still appears old-world; these small Wessex market centres do not change much with the decades, or even with the centuries. In the same poem there is also an allusion to Pen Wood. This is a large, irregular-shaped tract on the slopes of Birt's Hill a few miles east of Crewkerne, with the Dorset–Somerset boundary across its middle. Its main distinction, and the reason for its remaining unspoiled, is that at no point is it touched by even a minor road.

Corton Hill is one more of the landmarks listed in 'Molly Gone'. Corton Ridge and Corton Hill are two steep heights, grassy and gorse-strewn, about four miles north of Sherborne, forming part of the western edge of the uplands that here bound the plains of the Yeo. A little to the north is Cadbury Castle, a circular hill supporting an earthwork that is the 'Camelot' of the poem 'Channel Firing'. In the late 1960s extensive excavations were made there in an attempt to establish a historical basis for the Arthurian association, but results were inconclusive. The same poem alludes to 'Stourton Tower'; this is Alfred's Tower, a late eighteenth-century brick landmark on the wooded heights dividing Somerset from Wiltshire. Now a National Trust property, the tower is in good repair.

Hemmed in on all sides but the north by the Dorset boundary is Milborne Port ('Millpool'), once among the properties of the squire in 'Squire Petrick's Lady' (see page 128). Today the little town, if no longer what it was, is far from moribund, and its attractive old houses are surrounded by much new development.

Where the road from Bristol to Poole (A357) crosses that from London to Land's End (A30) stands Henstridge Ash. In a note to 'By Henstridge Cross at the Year's End' Hardy refers to 'this centuries-old cross-road', but it must have undergone greater modification in the half-century since he called it so than in all its prior existence. Originally the poem bore the name 'Mellstock Cross', but the four arms are in any case symbolic. The 'white handpost' has given place to traffic lights.

LOWER WESSEX
(Devon)

A very West-of-Wessex girl
    As blithe as blithe could be,
    Was once well-known to me,
And she would laud her native town,
    And hope and hope that we
Might sometime study up and down
    Its charms in company.

THE WEST-OF-WESSEX GIRL

The only Hardy work in prose or verse to have a North Devon setting is the Noble Dame story 'The Honourable Laura'. From his own map it is not difficult to identify 'Cliff-Martin' with Coombe Martin, and to place the (imaginary) Prospect Hotel in the region of Woody Bay. The waterfall in the story, though not corresponding in detail, is based on the Hanging Water that cascades down the wooded slopes into this inlet. To suit his tale Hardy narrows the flanks, increases the final drop and eliminates the trees that might have checked Northbrook's fall. He may also have invented the rock-hewn steps; today the descent is by a broad gravel path that zigzags across the stream. But the cascade remains spectacular. The shore is boulder-strewn, but probably displayed enough sand to make it suitable for a duel. The Woody Bay Hotel, however, cannot be identified with the 'Prospect', which lay some way inland near the turnpike road. The 'nearest railway town' was Lynton, on the Barnstaple & Lynton Railway.

Coombe Martin, straggling inland along North Devon's only coastal road, has never made up its mind whether or not to become a full-blown resort. Barnstaple, also mentioned, may be defined as an industrial growth round a beautiful and historic centre; in the late 1960s it was suggested as an 'overspill' town for London, unsuccessfully.

In South Devon the 'Silverthorne Dairy House', home of the milkmaid of the 'Romantic Adventures', was (according to Hardy's supplementary information to Lea) 'probably' near Silverton, north of Exeter ('Exonbury'), in a still superbly lush dairying area. At Exeter, in 'For Conscience Sake', Mr Milborne discovered his former betrothed and their daughter running a dancing-school in a 'central and open place'; he took rooms opposite. Since much of the city centre was damaged beyond repair by World War II bombing, the odds are against the survival of any particular buildings Hardy may have had in mind. But old houses are still to be seen, sometimes where least expected: one of the charms of contemporary Exeter is that antique corners are to be found hiding amid imaginative post-war reshaping.

The allusion in 'The Carrier' to 'Sidwell Church and wall' refers to St Sidwell's in the north-east sector of the city, and suggests Cullompton as the carrier's destination. The church seen today is new, its predecessor having been destroyed in the air raids; but the churchyard walls are the old ones.

There is some slight evidence, much inflated by those who believe Hardy's life to have been dominated by Tryphena Sparks, that 'My Cicely' was inspired by events at Topsham, where Tryphena was living with her husband and his mother. Bailey even suggests, citing the line 'Where Exe scents the sea', that the 'graveacre' is meant to be Topsham churchyard (Topsham is near the head of the estuary). But since the preceding line runs '. . . to the gate of the city / Where Exe . . .', this theory is hardly tenable. The Exe is plainly scenting the sea at Exeter. In truth the 'graveacre' is much more probably the city cemetery—disused since 1871 and now a public park, but retaining a number of tombstones amid its many trees—that overlooks the river on the line of the old city walls.

The 'Lions-Three' of 'My Cicely' stood 'beside the great highway (now the A30) 'ten miles from Exeter'. There is no record of a Three Lions at the time anywhere in Devon, but at Honiton— fifteen miles from Exeter—one of the old coaching inns is called the Three Tuns. The present narrow stuccoed frontage on the main street—relatively peaceful since the coming of the by-pass— conceals an old building that rambles back to a great depth. By no means peaceful today is the nearby stretch of the 'Highway' called Fairmile Hill, whose traffic-racked slope would scarcely be walked now by the fresh maiden of 'The Dear'. On the coast to the south stands Sidmouth ('Idmouth'), the resort near which Baron Xanten's yacht was moored in 'The Romantic Adventures of a Milkmaid'. The short but charming Victorian seafront is still much as Hardy knew it.

That scenes should have altered since Hardy described them is to be expected, but Plymouth had already undergone great alteration between the time when Emma was brought up there and Hardy's visits following her death. This is made clear in the poem 'Lonely Days'. But the tramlines and 'electric ropes' have vanished as though they had never come, and the 'duller and dingier tone' of the house-fronts has been countered by the bright freshness of so much new building since the devastation of the last war. The 'Three Towns' of 'Places'—Plymouth, Devonport and Stonehouse—were amalgamated in 1914, since when nine other territories have been engulfed. The Hoe as known to Hardy was not very different from the Hoe today, although in Emma's childhood, the period conjured up in so many of the Plymouth poems, it was still a bluff of crude rock, with no promenade. The latter and the various paths and roads have been asphalted since Hardy wrote, and inevitably new monuments have appeared. Across the Sound the Breakwater, after the lapse of a century, would occasion no surprise to Stephen (*A Pair of Blue Eyes*), but farther out the present Eddystone Lighthouse was put up in 1882, and the one he saw has been re-erected on the Hoe.

A recent addition to the Hoe is the Hoe Theatre, in which the band now 'booms' in summer instead of in the open as in 'The Marble-streeted Town'. The 'marble' was limestone paving that when worn smooth looked like marble, especially during rain. There is still some in service. West Hoe Pier, from which the suitor rowed to Cremyll in 'The Second Night', continues to extend its crab-claw arms below Grand Parade. (For Cremyll and Edgcumbe see page 243.)

St Andrew's church, the premier church of Plymouth, was gutted by fire-bombs, only the shell and tower, with its splendid carillon and chimes of ten bells, surviving. The church has been fully restored, but its churchyard with the 'multifarious tombstones' noticed by Stephen has given place to a gracious terrace bordering Royal Parade, the wide new avenue that has replaced Plymouth's chief pre-war thoroughfare, Bedford Street (also noted by Stephen). St Andrew's bells, said in 'Places' to chime 'the quaint old Hundred-and-Thirteenth tune . . . Night, morn, and noon', really played fourteen tunes, a new one each day for a fortnight, every four hours. This has been discontinued (it must have driven nearby residents nearly mad at night), but the bells are often rung by hand, and one day in 1969 a Dorset visitor heard them playing another of Hardy's favourites, the Sicilian Mariners' Hymn.

St Charles church was also gutted, and its shell has been kept as a permanent memorial of those fearful nights. It stands, nearly inaccessible, on the centre island of a busy roundabout. At night the interior is floodlit. Here, Hardy states in *The Life*, Emma long wished to be buried in the Gifford vault, until on attending her father's funeral she found the sepulchre had been 'broken into, if not removed' to improve the church entrance.

Most of the houses in which she passed her childhood have also now disappeared. Several of them can be identified in the Plymouth poems. Her birthplace, alluded to in the opening stanza of 'Places', was 10 York Street, a thoroughfare that suffered so much in the air raids that it has been swept away in the re-planning. The 'room by the Hoe' in the following stanza was in her next-but-one home, 9 Sussex Street. On her manuscript of *Some Recollections* Hardy set a query by the number, but 'John Gifford, Solicitor' is entered for number 9 in Brendon's *Directory* for 1852. Close to the Hoe Park, Sussex Street is a short road now closed at the northern end, but formerly linking Saltram Place (Citadel Road) with Princess Place. Again the air raids annihilated most of the houses, including the Gifford residence, which stood on the east side, at what has now become the top of the cul-de-sac. Its garden, already destroyed by a new road (Sussex Place) when Emma wrote *Some Recollections*, is the scene of the second and third stanzas of 'During Wind and Rain'. The 'high new house' in the last stanza, to which the family moved from Sussex Street, is 9 Bedford Terrace, an even shorter cul-de-sac off Tavistock Road. This little backwater survived the war, and still conforms in almost every detail to Emma's own description. It was probably this house to which Hardy pictured her returning late in life and hearing the dancers 'through the party-wall' as recorded in 'Lonely Days'.

OFF-WESSEX
(Cornwall)

Does there even a place like Saint-Juliot exist?
  Or a Vallency Valley
  With stream and leafed alley,
Or Beeny, or Bos with its flounce flinging mist?

A DREAM OR NO

For Hardy Cornwall remained almost exlusively the county of his courtship. Even Cremyll, already mentioned in connection with Plymouth (page 239), is linked by Bailey with this, for he believes that 'The Second Night' was inspired by a detour Hardy made to Plymouth, where Tryphena was then headmistress of a school, during the return from one of his visits to St Juliot. Cremyll has altered little, but at Mount Edgcumbe (the girl in the poem was an 'Edgcumbe lass') the glorious Tudor mansion—now partly rebuilt—was ruined by the bombing of 1941.

St Juliot ('West Endelstow') is the focal point of Hardy's Cornish writings; and precisely because it was of such personal moment, he disguised much of the topography in a way that even now we cannot entirely rectify. One scene, however, that he described with complete fidelity in *A Pair of Blue Eyes* is the rectory ('Vicarage' in earlier editions), and his description fits almost as well today. The house stands in a 'little dell like a nest', and traces of a quarry are still visible in the vicinity. 'A thicket of shrubs and trees' of no small charm encloses a smooth lawn, and the conservatory, subject of 'The Frozen Greenhouse', has been restored by the present occupants of the house. The french window that figures in both the novel and the poem 'At the Word Farewell' (in which the lawn also appears) continues in being, but the verandah is no more, although its floor still extends along the south wall. Gone too is the subject of 'The Sundial on a Wet Day'; it stood a little way out from the south-east angle of the house. In the poem 'A Duettist at her Pianoforte' Emma, by then Mrs Hardy, is looking back on the duets she used to play with her sister, Helen Catherine Holder, in the rectory drawing-room. The house is the 'dwelling' of 'The Seven Times', and is the theme or setting of several other poems that do not touch upon individual features. Grey-roofed, grey-walled, with deep blue woodwork, it displays no architectural modifications but is no longer a rectory, tiny St Juliot having been

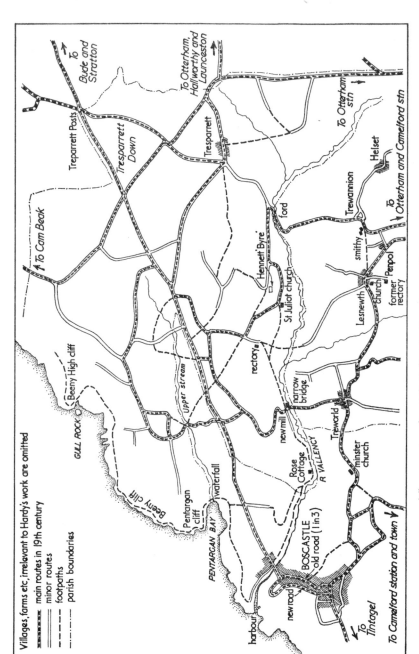

Villages, farms etc; irrelavant to Hardy's work are omitted

▬▬▬ main routes in 19th century
– – – minor routes
· – · – footpaths
· · · · · · parish boundaries

To Bude and Stratton

To Otterham, Halworthy and Launceston

To Ottarham stn

To Otterham and Camelford stn

Treparrett Posts

Tresparrett Down

Tresparrett

Helset

Trewannion

smithy

Penpol

former rectory

church

Lesnewth

ford

Hennett Byre

St Juliot church

To Cam Beak

rectory

Beeny High cliff

GULL ROCK

Upper stream

narrow bridge

Treworld

minster church

Beeny cliff

Pentargan cliff

waterfall

new mill

Rose Cottage

R VALLENCY

PENTARGAN BAY

harbour

new road

BOSCASTLE
old road (1 in 3)

To Tintagel

To Camelford station and town

The country about St Juliot in the nineteenth century

amalgamated with no fewer than six other parishes under Boscastle ('Castle Boterel').

When we leave the rectory grounds the verisimilitude of the picture ends; for the novelist represents the village as being much nearer the sea than it is, which explains why he says of the church-yard that 'not a tree could exist up there', although the trees that now ring it were there when he wrote, as Emma's sketch (now hanging in the church) proves. Other trees make it impossible to see the church from the rectory. (According to Lea, the position of 'West Endelstow' is a mixture of those of St Juliot and Forra-bury.) Emma's picture shows the graveyard indeed 'serrated with the outline of graves and a very few memorial stones'. Since then the number of headstones has increased, although the 'mono-tonous grey-green grass' is still unkempt.

The 'tower owning neither battlement nor pinnacle' is shown in Emma's pre-restoration sketch to have owned both; nor does the new tower differ. The 'six-and-thirty old seat-ends' that Hardy saw decaying in an aisle were removed during the restoration, but another sketch now in the church shows what they looked like. The west gallery was also removed. The most interesting feature of the present church is the two tablets on the north wall, one recording that Emma laid the first stone of the rebuilt aisle and tower and directed the church music, the other testifying to Hardy's supervision of the restoration in 1871. There is a third tablet in memory of Emma's brother-in-law, the Reverend Charles Holder. The tablet to Emma is the subject of the poems 'The Marble Tablet' and 'The Monument-Maker'.

The principal original of 'Endelstow House' (*A Pair of Blue Eyes*) is Lanhydrock House (now a National Trust property) in the Fowey valley south of Bodmin. Here one may identify the 'spacious court', the many-mullioned windows, the 'ancient gate-house of dun stone' (spanned, however, by a rounded arch, not 'high-shouldered Tudor'), the avenue of sycamores beyond, and the long, barrel-vaulted picture-gallery described in the novel. The gallery and the wing it occupies are in fact the only remnants of the mansion seen by Hardy, in 1881 the central and southern blocks were destroyed in a fire and replaced by exact replicas.

Lanhydrock, however, is not the only model for 'Endelstow House'. The latter had mullioned dormer windows, surmounted, like the gables, by grotesque figures; tall 'octagonal and twisted' chimneys, surpassed in height, however, by the trees behind them; polygonal bays in the angles of the court, their surfaces 'entirely occupied by buttresses and windows'; and over the main entrance a 'far-projecting oriel springing from a fantastic series of mouldings'. None of these features appears at Lanhydrock, or elsewhere in Cornwall. But in Dorset, within a few miles of his home, was a mansion he had several reasons for knowing intimately* and which displayed all the missing features—Athelhampton, already considered in an earlier section (page 70) as the prototype of 'Athelhall'. Here are the mullioned dormers and roof-gables with the grotesque finials; the tall (but not twisted: a slip?) chimneys overtopped by the trees behind, a polygonal bay, all buttress and window; and when a gatehouse stood to the south of the present frontage, above the gate (which had a 'high-shouldered Tudor arch') projected a magnificent oriel supported on a truly 'fantastic series of mouldings'. (See plate, page 220.)

'Endelstow Park' is probably based on that of Lanhydrock, but the Smiths' cottage and its little bridge are an invention. The 'faint outline of ditch and mound' indicating the site of an earlier house appears to be an allusion to Prideaux Castle, an ancient earthwork five miles south of Lanhydrock above the Luxulyan valley that provided Hardy with the name Lord Luxellian.

'Endelstow House' was situated at 'East Endelstow'—Lesnewth, a village even smaller (if possible) than St Juliot, and in reality not east but south of it, across the valley. Because Hardy placed St Juliot nearer the sea, the contrast in scenery between the two 'Endelstows' is purely fanciful. 'East Endelstow' church (the scene, according to Hardy's own note, of the poem 'The Young Churchwarden') reflects aspects of these at both Lanhydrock and Lesnewth. 'Not forty yards from the mansion' accurately places Lanhydrock church in relation to the house, but 'in a little dell' relates to Lesnewth, for Lanhydrock church stands on a small rise. Today neither graveyard is demarcated by square boundary-stones, but they are shown in the old print of Lanhydrock reproduced on page 219. Yews are not conspicuous round either

* His father had worked on the restoration; he himself had sketched it in water-colour in 1859 (the painting is now in the Dorset County Museum); and he had written an article on the new church for the *Dorset County Chronicle*.

church. The 'Luxellian vault' is another Dorset importation, being based on the tomb of the O'Briens in Stinsford Church (see page 39).

'East Endelstow', we are told, lay on two sides of a ravine, the halves being united by a bridge from which a steep ascent led to 'West Endelstow'. Lesnewth parish is indeed divided by a ravine running south from the Vallency valley, and the road referred to can still be followed, although it has long ceased to be a principal link between the two villages. It descends eastward from Lesnewth church, crosses the picturesque stream at the bottom of the ravine by a concrete bridge built about 1960 to replace a stone one destroyed by a flood, then breasts the ridge carrying Treworld Farm. From here a lane drops down to a bridge over the Vallency near Newmill, but remembering Hardy's *imaginary* position for St Juliot, he was probably thinking of the lane to Minster and Forrabury.

The route by which Knight and Stephen followed the hearse from Camelford ('Camelton') station to Lesnewth church is mainly imaginary—inevitably so, if Hardy was to maintain his fiction that St Juliot lay much nearer than Lesnewth to the sea. But there are still one or two people who recall the smithy in which, in the novel, the two men took shelter. It is not named on the 25in OS map (which marks most smithies), although it was still functioning when the first edition was published; but those who knew it remember that it stood east of Lesnewth church, where the track from Helset joins the St Juliot road by Trewannion. It ceased operations around 1904, when the smith left to join a colleague at Tresparrett Posts. The 'Welcome Home' inn, by contrast, never existed.

Camelford station now lies derelict beside the railless track. Camelford itself remains a small, most attractive townlet, in which the 'Luxellian Arms' was probably a pseudonym for the Darlington Hotel.

The 'Manor House' or 'The Crags' has no counterpart in or near St Juliot; but the feature from which it took its name, the 'jutting angle of a wild enclosure . . . which almost overhung the valley' has several possible models farther down the Vallency gorge. This beautiful and thickly wooded ravine figures in a number of poems. It runs just west of St Juliot, between interleaving hills, at the foot of which the river purls along, as pretty to the ear as to the eye; and the footpath so prominent in the novel is still walkable, albeit with certain stretches often under water. Much of the woodland on the south side of the valley is now National Trust property, as is Newmill. In addition to this last there are several cottages, one of them in ruins; but which, if any, are we to pick for Mrs Jethway's house? When she is found crushed under the fallen church tower at 'West Endelstow', Knight wants her to be carried to the 'nearest house', the rectory; but Lord Luxellian suggests that since a surgeon will have to be summoned from Boscastle, it would be better to carry her to the first house in that direction; and when they do so, it proves to be her own home. In reality the rectory, Newmill, and the cottages mentioned above all lie in the direction of Boscastle from the church; but Hardy's shifting of St Juliot blurs all such realities. Mrs Jethway's home was rather large, had a set of rock-cut steps leading to the water, where there was a hollowed-out basin, and stood alone under 'a row of scrubby oaks'. None of these features, except the solitude, belongs to any of the real cottages. The indefatigable Lea settled for the easternmost, Rose Cottage, pretty enough for a calendar but of doubtful probability.

Toward its mouth the Vallency valley widens out, and the river disappears behind the houses to flow at last into Boscastle harbour. This little haven, where Stephen landed from Bristol, is now a National Trust property wholly given over to small pleasure-craft and fishing-boats; but there are many people in the little town who can recall when, before the days of proper roads, the port took in much of their coal and general supplies.

Boscastle has not had many additions: the inevitable car-park, a wider bridge, new buildings on the fringes, souvenir shops. All too often 'the drizzle bedrenches', as in the poem 'At Castle Boterel'; and in winter 'Upon Boterel Hill, where the waggoners skid' as Hardy wrote in 'Places', the motorist sometimes fares little better, although an easier route now bypasses the terrifying 1 in 3 gradient that he and Emma knew.

The north-east road out of Boscastle arrives in due course at Bude, the 'Stratleigh' of the novel, no longer 'a small watering-place' but a major resort. Long before this the route passes near two cliffs prominent in novel and verse. One is the cliff to which Elfride rode, with Stephen accompanying her on foot, and where, in a natural alcove, they exchanged their first kiss and she lost her ear-ring; she returned much later to this same cliff with Knight and found the ear-ring still in the alcove. Let us call this cliff A. Cliff B is the cliff that Elfride reached on foot by crossing a hill behind the rectory and following a stream until it ended in a waterfall with the cliff on the right; here she met Knight, and after they had seen the *Puffin* steaming to Boscastle with Stephen aboard, they experienced the terrible adventure that nearly cost them their lives.

Hardy describes cliff A and its approach by saying that to reach it Elfride and Stephen left the lane and crossed some fields. They then followed an irregular path that eventually ended in a flat ledge passing round the face of the 'huge blue-black rock' about halfway up. Here they found the alcove and sat down. Below them, gulls screamed on detached rocks. Only when referring to Elfride's second visit, this time with Knight, does Hardy suddenly give the cliff a name, 'Windy Beak', and calls it the second-highest along that coast, with the popular reputation of being the highest of all. Elfride mentions that it is farther from St Juliot than the cliff of their misadventure.

Now to cliff B. After describing the stream followed by Elfride as 'smaller than that in her own valley' and at a higher level, flowing past a green carpet at the bottom of a shallow bush-lined trough, Hardy remarks that toward its mouth the ridge to left of it 'dwindled lower and became insignificant', while that to the right rose steadily higher until it ended in a clearly defined edge. Presently the bed of the stream reached a similar edge, and the stream tumbled to its death in a cascade. The cliff was 'visible like a concave wall', and consisted of 'blackish-grey slate, unvaried in its whole height by a single change of shade'. A grassy path 'wound along inside a bank, placed as a safeguard for unwary pedestrians' to the top of the cliff, and thence inland. The height of this cliff was locally believed to be 700 feet, but was actually 650. Perpendicular 'from the half-tide level', the rampart formed no headland, but one wall of an inlet, with a promontory at a lower level on either side. In the novel this cliff is referred to as the 'Cliff Without a Name', but in his Preface of 1895 Hardy admitted that it had one, and later still he allowed it to be identified with Beeny Cliff, so marking it on his own map.

This is where the confusion starts. All the attributes, except
the height, of cliff B, the scene of Knight's near-tragedy, belong
not to Beeny Cliff* but to a very similar one nearer to Boscastle,
forming the north wall of Pentargan ('Targan') Bay. This cliff,
too, is black, sheer, concave in horizontal section, and curving
toward the left of anyone looking seaward. To it belong the
summit path, now sadly overgrown, the protective bank, still
traceable, the waterfall with its miniature meadows near the base,
and the stream that has its source in the shallow vale of the Vallency
valley. Even the freak air currents that Knight was demonstrating
are familiar to local people. Beeny High Cliff, while sharing many
of these features, never had a bank protecting the path over its
top, and though there is a small waterfall beside it, this wells out
of the ground a few yards from the drop; there is no stream.

Now let us consider cliff A, 'Windy Beak', the scene of the lost-
and-found ear-ring. The loss of the ear-ring is based on a genuine
experience of Emma's at Beeny High Cliff. 'Windy Beak', moreover, has all the characteristics of Beeny: it is black, sheer, locally
believed to be the highest rampart on the coast but is actually the
second-highest, and it is confronted by an isolated dome in the
sea called Gull Rock. In short, cliff A *is* Beeny. But Beeny having
been subsequently mis-identified as the scene of Knight's folly,
'Windy Beak' had to be assigned either an imaginary status, or a
prototype elsewhere: hence the identification with the Strangles
(Lea), which is not sheer, and Cam Beak (several writers), which
is not black. Nor had either of these ever been considered the
highest cliff in the district. If only Hardy had admitted that his
'Cliff Without a Name' was the Pentargan cliff, to which he had
given Beeny's height, and that Beeny was 'Windy Beak', all
would have been plain.

The flat ledge and the alcove with its natural seat have now
disappeared; rock-falls from the cliffs are frequent, and the details
of the cliff face must have changed many times in a century. The
'distant light-ship' seen after the finding of the ear-ring must refer
to the lighthouse on Lundy; in 1870 this would have been just
within range, but the nearest light*ship* was well outside it.

* More often known locally as Beeny High Cliff. The OS map marks the whole
stretch between the Pentargan and Beeny inlets as Beeny Cliff. There is also a High
Cliff, *tout court*, a mile north of Beeny High Cliff.

The 'shallow, bush-lined trough' of the stream that Elfride followed to Pentargan Bay has become so thickly overgrown, in addition to having its banks blocked by stone walls, that progress along it is now all but impossible, even in the upper reaches above St Juliot, but the path giving access from the rectory can still be made out. Perhaps the route was never practicable outside Hardy's imagination, for Emma records that he and she normally approached the bay by the (still used) path from Boscastle harbour.

Bay and waterfall appear in several poems, including 'Best Times', 'After a Journey' and 'Under the Waterfall'. Hardy made rough sketches here, and also at the lovers' other picnic site beside Beeny High Cliff. The 'Figure in the Scene' describes one sketch, and 'Why did I Sketch?' looks back on it. 'Where the Picnic Was' may be set here or in Dorset (see page 167). 'If You had Known', 'The Phantom Horsewoman', the lilting, exquisite 'Beeny Cliff': these are examples only of the spate of poems that hark back to this strip of coast or to St Juliot.

'A Man was Drawing Near to Me' depicts Emma's feelings as she awaited the young architect's first visit to the lonely rectory. He passes Hallworthy, Otterham, Tresparrett Posts, Hennett 'Byre'. Of these, Otterham is still a very drowsy village, deprived now of its railway station; Hennett, a magnificent old stone-built farm near St Juliot church; Hallworthy a village yet, though at a busy road junction; and Tresparrett Posts, the most altered of all to judge from the portrait of it in 'Where Three Roads Joined', is an even busier junction. Between Tresparrett village and Posts lies Tresparrett Down, the 'Parrett Down' of *A Pair of Blue Eyes*. It remains open pasture, but where the main road skirts the village many bungalows have recently appeared.

At most seasons Bodmin Moor today fully lives up to the dreary picture that met Stephen on his drive from Launceston ('St Launce's'). In the poem 'St Launce's Revisited' the 'Castle and keep uprearing' (where in *A Pair of Blue Eyes* Mrs Smith as a girl had looked for owls' feathers) still 'uprear' above a plethora of 'quaint gables and jumbled roofs'. Opposite the castle bailey, now laid out as a small park, stands the town hall built in 1881; its predecessor, in front of which the young lawyer removed Mrs Smith's bramble, was the curious building still to be seen between the main part of St Mary Magdalene church and its tower.

In the valley north of the town is the now passengerless railway station, beyond which the old packhorse bridge continues to carry pedestrians across the river, while wheeled traffic thunders over a newer bridge close by. Up the hill again, the 'Falcon' where Elfride changed her clothes is the White Hart, a pleasant inn on the Market Place which is also the 'inn / Smiling nigh' of 'St Launce's Revisited'. 'Hill Street' in *Blue Eyes* is a fictitious name, but the shop once kept by the versatile seller and player of 'flutes, and fiddles, and grand pianners' occupies the angle between Church Street and High Street. It was run by one Hayman, who not only sold and played instruments but manufactured his own 'pianners', which enjoyed a wide reputation. After his death his shop and studio became a clothier's, and are now a restaurant. But over a doorway in High Street you may still see the stone-cut likeness of two musicians.

In a dell off the Launceston–Halworthy road snuggles St Clether ('Cleather'), scene of 'The Face at the Casement'. Conjectures that this refers to one Charles Raymond, who died in 1873 or 1874, aged 38, may now be discarded, for they stem from a monograph by Kenneth Phelps in the Toucan Press series (no 32), based solely on a few entries in the church registers, plus a good deal of conjecture. By the time Hardy could have seen him, Raymond was a married man with several children; moreover he was apparently illiterate—hardly a probable friend, let alone suitor, of Emma's. Mr Phelps now concurs that a much more likely subject, of the few who qualify, is William Henry Serjeant, the son of the curate, who died at the vicarage on 26 January 1872, at the age of twenty-three. His youth seems finally to dispose of the rumour that the owner of the 'face' had sought Emma's hand, but it is easy to believe that the vicar of St Clether knew his colleague of St Juliot, and that Emma and Hardy (with or without the Holders) drove over during Hardy's third Cornish visit in May–June 1871 to inquire after the young man's health. If, as they left, Hardy glanced back in time to see the invalid turn away from an upstairs window, the incident would have been all he needed to engender his narrative. Today the vicarage is a private house, for the parish has been combined with Tresmeer and Laneast, where the present vicar lives. The building stands opposite the entrance to the church.

In the early 1870s Emma stayed with friends near Lanivet, a large village on the Bodmin–St Austell road (now A391). Hardy visited her here, and during a walk they experienced the curious incident related in 'Near Lanivet, 1872'. There are several junctions where the handpost, which Hardy noted as 'on the St Austell road', may have stood; but they seem unlikely to include the one suggested by Bailey. Most of the old posts have been replaced by international-style metal signs. The subject of the poem 'By the Runic Stone', so long a mystery, appears to have been solved by Miss Evelyn Hardy in an article in the *London Magazine* for February–March 1972. There is no space here even to summarise Miss Hardy's arguments, but using the clues in the verses she visited all likely sites until she felt certain that the right cross now stands, mutilated, outside the Wharncliffe Arms at Tintagel ('Dundagel'). In 1870–4 it was serving as a gatepost at Trevillet Farm, near St Nectan's Kieve, behind Tintagel. Hardy, Emma, and her sister would have passed the spot in March 1870, on their way to Penpethy quarries, and may well have stopped there to picnic. The inscription on the cross commemorates a Saxon, which for Hardy would justify the mild licence of 'runic'; and the nearby site of St Nectan's Oratory and a holy well would account for the phrase 'in such a place'.

'Where the grass sloped down' refers, in this interpretation, to the steep, grassy sides of the upper reaches of Rocky Valley, the defile that runs from St Nectan's Kieve down to the sea at Bossiney Haven. Near the haven lies the scene of 'The Self-Unconscious', though whether Bossiney or Boscastle is the 'Bos' of other poems is open to argument. A few miles inland Rough Tor, a 1,300ft peak on Bodmin Moor, is the 'Rou'tor' of 'I Rose and Went to Bou'tor Town'. The 'town', nevertheless, is not nearby Camelford but Bodmin; the subject of the verses is the displeasure of Emma's father, then living near Bodmin, at her engagement.

Tintagel castle, in which Hardy and Emma were once trapped, is much better cared for than a century ago, the Ministry of Public Building and Works having equipped it with plenty of paths, staircases and lawns. Hardy set his verse play *The Famous Tragedy of the Queen of Cornwall* in the Great Hall, but neither text nor stage directions offer descriptive matter. Not far away on the cliffs stands Tintagel's large church, restored since Emma sketched it but before

Q

Hardy and Florence had the unhappy experience there recorded in
The Life.

Trebarwith ('Barwith') Strand, a rectangular bay three-quarters
of a mile in breadth, to which the Swancourts and Knight drove
'along a road by neutral green hills', accurately fits Hardy's picture.
Seen from its north-western extremity, the whole expanse of cliff
and shore reveals no sign of humanity except a glimpse of white
buildings in the south-east angle. In reality, the cleft through
which the only road descends contains a moderate colony of
bungalows and small hotels. One hotel has been converted out of
what in Hardy's time were coastguard cottages, but the little
cottage cited in *Blue Eyes* is probably the one behind the modern
hut called The Surf Shop.

A short way inland along the Trebarwith road are cliffs of a far
more bizarre appearance, formed by the slate-quarrying near
Penpethy. Hardy's visit just mentioned to see about materials for
St Juliot church is commemorated in the poem 'Green Slates'. The
quarries worked then are now abandoned, but others in the group
remain in vigorous operation.

We are left with Hardy's one Cornish setting, in prose or verse,
that is not associated with Emma. This is the scene of the story
'A Mere Interlude', which takes place further west than the other
'Off-Wessex' localities. Using an assortment of real names and his
own modifications, Hardy alludes to Truro ('Trufal'), Mousehole
and St Clement's Isle, St Michael's Mount and Redruth ('Red-
rutin'); but the main action is laid in Penzance ('Pen-Zephyr'),
which is perfunctorily sketched, and in the Scillies (the 'Isles of
Lyonesse'), which are not described at all beyond the mention
that they include St Mary's ('St Maria's') and its town, Hugh
Town ('Giant's Town').

Thus, at the extreme end of 'Off-Wessex', we also come to the
end of this survey. But though the book is at a close, its subject is
not. New clues continue to come to light, upsetting old beliefs,
solving old mysteries. Perhaps all the keys to Hardy's Wessex will
never be found. And that, if galling to us, is how Hardy would have
preferred it.

Note on
A Group of Noble Dames

The degree of historical truth in these stories has been the subject of argument ever since they were published. At the one extreme the eminent W. R. Rutland derides the notion of any reality underlying 'such far-fetched tales'—including, presumably, those based on Hutchins; at the other there are Hardy's own statements and the rather over-dramatic testimony of Sidney Heath. Three times at least Hardy declared the tales to be substantially true: in a letter to Edward Clodd, in which he said 'most' of the stories were 'founded on fact'; in a letter offering the American serial rights to Harper's, in which he included the parenthesis 'names disguised but incidents approximating to fact'; and, according to Weber in *Thomas Hardy and the Lady from Madison Square*, in conversation with Rebekah Owen.

Sidney Heath was the author of an apparently unpublished article under the title 'How Thomas Hardy Offended the County Families of Dorset' (1906), of which the typescript is now in the Dorset County Museum. Written somewhat in the vein of a *chronique scandaleuse*, the article declares *all* the stories to be no less than a 'transcript of official documents put into the form of fiction'. These documents are said to have been found, interspersed among deeds, by H. Moule during his curatorship of the museum, and to have been copied out by Hardy, who took the copies to Max Gate. The article recounts how some of the heads of the families involved reacted to publication of the tales, one ordering all Hardy works in his house to be burnt in the courtyard, another threatening with dismissal any employee found bringing a book by Hardy on to the premises, a third forbidding the local bookseller to stock the Wessex novels. Heath of course gives no names, though it is evident they were all in the documents. But when Professor Bailey recently looked for these they had disappeared, perhaps not entirely by accident; and Hardy's copies would beyond doubt have been destroyed. One intriguing aspect of the article is that Heath makes no reference to the fact that several of the stories are set in other counties; on the contrary, his implication is that each tale refers to a Dorset seat. Are we to infer from this that the non-Dorset locations are just part of Hardy's method of concealment? This is hard to believe of 'Lady Mottisfont', but it could explain why the present owners of several of the conjectured sites in the 'outside' counties have, at my request, searched their family papers without finding anything to suggest the source of Hardy's material.

My impression is that in at least one or two cases—perhaps those in which he felt the discovery of the real protagonists would be most damaging—Hardy adopted a double disguise, fictionalising a setting that, even if identified, would be found to have nothing to do with his *dramatis personae*. The most interesting of the mysteries involves 'The Duchess of Hamptonshire', not only because it contains the most detailed topographical description, but because Hardy seems to have been so deeply impressed by the realities behind it that he wrote the tale three times, under different titles and for different magazines (see Weber, 'A Masquerade of Noble Dames', *PMLA*, June 1943). In the other versions the 'Batton Castle' of 'The Duchess' becomes 'Stroome Castle' and 'Croome Castle'. Now, 'Batton' is very like a Hardy substitution for Badminton, and Badminton is very near Castle Combe. The 'Batton' mansion does not resemble either the present or former Badminton House, but the fictional park could pass for that of Badminton. 'Emmeline', the heroine's name in all three story versions, is not found in the church there, but 'Emily' appears on a number of memorials. I am assured by the family historian that Hardy's tale has nothing whatever to do with the Beauforts, who own Badminton; but did Hardy use this area as the basis of his topography, doubly hiding the fact that the true happenings he found so interesting had been enacted somewhere much nearer home? Or is this theory itself a red herring?

Bibliography

This list includes the great majority of books most likely to help the topographical student, and all the works to which reference has been made in the text. Apart from the three principal biographies, the many studies concerned primarily with Hardy's life and place in literature have had to be omitted. Nor has it been possible to cover the great array of local histories, ranging from large volumes to pamphlets, many of which have proved invaluable in the preparation of this volume. For these, readers are recommended to the public reference libraries in the appropriate areas.

Biographies
Hardy, Evelyn. *Thomas Hardy: a Critical Biography* (London, 1954).
Hardy, Florence Emily. *The Life of Thomas Hardy*. Originally published as *The Early Life* (1928) and *The Later Life* (1930). Now recognised beyond dispute as Hardy's own handiwork, edited and completed by his second wife.
Weber, Carl J. *Hardy of Wessex* (New York and London, 1965, revised).

Books of outstanding topographical interest (in order of publication)
Hutchins, John. *The History and Antiquities of the County of Dorset*. (1st ed 1774; 2nd ed 1796–1815; 3rd ed, corrected, augmented and improved by William Shipp and James Whitworth Hodson, 1861–73.) Hardy's principal historical source. The engravings differ in each edition; the Dorset County Library (reference room) contains a pamphlet tabulating the variations.
Windle, B. C. A. *The Wessex of Thomas Hardy*, with illustrations by E. H. New (1902). Almost the earliest attempt at a key

to Hardy's settings, and in many respects the most charming. Some bad mistakes, offset by surprising accuracies.

Harper, C. G. *The Hardy Country* (London, 1904). Windle without the charm, and New without the grace. Nevertheless, a fuller picture at nearly as early a date, with some interesting engravings.

Treves, Frederick. *Highways and Byways in Dorset* (1906). Sir Frederick Treves, Bt, was the surgeon who performed a secret operation on King Edward VII just before his coronation. His book contains many references to Hardy's works, and is adequately illustrated.

Lea, Hermann. *Thomas Hardy's Wessex* (1913). Reprinted as *Highways and Byways in Hardy's Wessex* (1925). Reprinted in facsimile, Guernsey, 1969. Despite its reputed infallibility, Lea's now almost legendary book contains a number of mistakes (as well as some curious gaps) which cannot be glossed over by maintaining that because he obtained his information direct from Hardy (who also corrected the proofs), error is impossible. Hardy's own memory in later life was not immune to lapses, and the closer one studies Lea *in the field*, the deeper grows the suspicion that during the two men's strenuous journeys Hardy's concentration sometimes wavered, leaving the questioning topographer to take for assent a silence that was merely, in the phrase of one of my helpers, a quiet failure to disagree. Nevertheless, Lea disseminated much fascinating information, and his photographs remain the fullest pictorial record ever made of the Hardy scene.

Purdy, R. L. *Thomas Hardy: a Bibliographical Study* (London, 1954). The origins of Hardy's prose and verse.

Douch, Robert. *Dorset: a Handbook of Local History*, with additions and corrections to 1960 (Bristol, 1962). An indispensable guide to the local histories, including pamphlets.

Lea, Hermann. *Thomas Hardy through the Camera's Eye*, edited by Cox, J. S. (Beaminster, 1964). Supplementary information dictated by Hardy, covering the stories collected in *A Changed Man* and in the verse volumes *Satires of Circumstance* and *Moments of Vision*. One or two blunders in identification again show that Hardy did not always recollect accurately.

Pinion, F. B. *A Hardy Companion* (London, 1968). Contains a long

alphabetical list of virtually every character and place in
Hardy's prose and verse, with a full key to the Wessex nomenclature including some identifications not previously offered.
Information much condensed but of great usefulness. A few
inaccuracies.

Bailey, J. O. *The Poetry of Thomas Hardy: a Handbook and Commen-
tary* (N Carolina, USA, and London, 1970). Includes the sum-
total of knowledge to date about the topography embodied
in Hardy's verse, with special attention to the present condition of the scenes. A very few minor errors and one or two
very odd judgements, but indispensable.

An Inventory of the Historical Monuments in Dorset: West Dorset
(1952), South-East Dorset (1970), Central Dorset (1970). To
date, this is the only county in Hardy's Wessex fully surveyed
by the Royal Commission. The North Dorset volume has still
to be published.

Beatty, C. J. P. *The Part Played by Architecture in the Life of Thomas
Hardy (with Particular Reference to the Novels).* PhD thesis,
London University, 1963; unpublished, but currently undergoing revision for publication. Exhaustive and in general
reliable on the scenes it covers. Some original identifications.

Cox, J. S. (general editor). Illustrated Monographs on the Life,
Times and Works of Thomas Hardy. Some seventy of these
pamphlets have now been published, first at Beaminster,
Dorset, later at St Peter Port, Guernsey. Their interest for
the topographical student varies according to subject.

The Thomas Hardy Year Book (Guernsey, 1970 and annually). A
most valuable publication in which Hardy scholars set forth
their latest views and report the results of the latest researches.

Pevsner, Nikolaus (and others). *The Buildings of England.* All the
relevant counties except Dorset have now been covered in this
famous series, and the Dorset volume is in preparation.

Some books of minor topographical interest (alphabetically listed)
Barber, D. F. *Concerning Thomas Hardy* (London, 1968).
Beatty, C. J. P. (editor). *Thomas Hardy's Architectural Notebooks*
(Dorchester, 1966).
Bradley, A. G. *Rambles in Wiltshire* (London, 1907). Especially
good on Cranborne Chase and the Marlborough area.

Brayley, E. J. and Britton, John. *The Beauties of England and Wales* (1803).

Cassey, Edward & Co. *History, Gazetteer, and Directory of Berkshire* (1868).

Cochrane, C. *The Lost Roads of Wessex* (Newton Abbot, 1969).

Cockerell, Sydney. *Friends of a Lifetime* (London, 1940).

Collinson, John. *History and Antiquities of the County of Somerset* (Bath, 1791). Collinson is to Somerset what Hutchins is to Dorset.

Cox, J. S. *Identification of Fictitious Place Names in Hardy's Works* (Guernsey, 1968). Little more than an index to Lea's two works listed above, repeating all their mistakes and making no serious attempt to fill in their omissions.

Deacon, Lois and Coleman, Terry. *Providence and Mr Hardy* (1966). Tries to supply a good deal of topographical background to Hardy's poems. Whether the findings are acceptable depends on the reader's estimate of the authors' general argument.

Delderfield, E. R. *West Country Historic Houses and their Families*, 2 vols (Newton Abbot, 1968, 1970).

Flower, Newman. *Just as it Happened* (1950).

Gerard, Thomas. *Survey of Dorset* (1732). Written nearly 100 years earlier, the real authorship was lost sight of and the book was published as the work of John Coker. Contains a few points of interest.

Gilbert, C. S. *An Historical Survey of the County of Cornwall* (1820).

Gilbert, Davies. *The Parochial History of Cornwall* (1838).

Goode, Ronald. *The Old Roads of Dorset* (Bournemouth, 1940; revised 1966).

Hardy, Emma Lavinia, edited by Evelyn Hardy and Robert Gittings. *Some Recollections* (1964). Very useful for Emma's Plymouth and early Cornish years.

Hardy, Evelyn (editor). *Thomas Hardy's Notebooks* (London, 1955).

'Holland, Clive' (C. J. Hankinson). *Thomas Hardy, O.M.: the Man, his Works, and the Land of Wessex* (London, 1933).

Thomas Hardy's Wessex Scene (Dorchester, 1948).

Hoskins, W. G. *Devon* (London, 1954).

Kerr, Barbara. *Bound to the Soil: a Social History of Dorset 1750–*

1918 (London, 1968). Some direct topographical bearing, but of most value for depicting living conditions.

Lucking, J. H. *The Railways of Dorset* (Lichfield, 1968).

Maxwell, Donald. *The Landscape of Thomas Hardy*, paintings (London, 1928).

Mayo, C. H. *Bibliotheca Dorsetiensis* (1885). 'Printed books and pamphlets relating to the history and topography of Dorset'.

Millgate, Michael. *Thomas Hardy: his Career as a Novelist* (London, 1971).

Orel, Harold. *Thomas Hardy's Personal Writings* (Kansas, USA, 1966; London, 1967).

Oswald, Arthur. *Country Houses of Dorset* (1959, revised).

Parker, W. M. *On the Trail of the Wessex Novels* (Poole, 1924).

Phelps, W. *The History and Antiquities of Somersetshire* (1836).

Phillimore, W. P. W. and Blagg, T. M. *Berkshire Parish Registers*.

Pinnock, W. *The History and Topography of England and Wales* (1825).

Pouncy, John. *Dorsetshire Photographically Illustrated* (Dorchester, 1857). Truly remarkable photographs excellently reproduced.

Powys, Llewelyn. *Dorset Essays* (London, 1935).

Somerset Essays (London, 1937).

Rutland, W. R. *Thomas Hardy: a Study of his Writings and their Background* (Oxford, 1938).

Saxelbye, F. O. *A Thomas Hardy Dictionary* (1911).

Sherren, Wilkinson. *The Wessex of Romance.* (1902). Chiefly interesting for being almost as early as Windle, with some additional information.

Southerington, F. R. *Hardy's Vision of Man* (London, 1971).

Thomas, D. St J. *Regional History of the Railways of Great Britain: the West Country* (Newton Abbot, 1966).

Twycross, E. *The Mansions of England and Wales* (1847–50).

Tyndale, Walter. *Wessex* (1906). Paintings, with descriptions by Clive Holland.

Weber, Carl J. (editor). *Dearest Emmie* (New York and London, 1963). Selected letters from Hardy to Emma.

Weber, Carl J. *Thomas Hardy and the Lady from Madison Square* (Waterville, Maine, USA, 1952). The lady was Rebekah Owen, an American who paid many visits to England from

R

1886 onward and established a close association with the Hardys.

Weinstock, M. B. *Old Dorset* (Newton Abbot, 1967).

Wightman, Ralph. *Abiding Things* (1962). Useful observations on the Piddle valley, and on bygone agricultural methods and ways of life in Dorset.

Maps

ORDNANCE SURVEY 1in to 1 mile, first edition. Reprinted, with editorial notes by J. B. Harley (Newton Abbot, 1970–1). The original survey for the Wessex counties was made from 1811 onward.

25in to 1 mile, first edition. The relevant areas were surveyed in the 1880s.

TITHE MAPS, dating mostly from the 1840s, and ESTATE MAPS of a variety of dates, are to be seen in the archives of the appropriate counties.

ADDENDA

Section 6, p. 120. Hartfoot Lane: the 'Lane Inn' where Angel dismissed the fly in *Tess* is the Fox, since renovated.

Section 13, p. 229. The poem 'On Martock Moor' refers to a flat expanse, now rich pasturage, a few miles west of Ash. 'Weir-water' was probably a weir on the River Parrett.

Section 14. In 'A Mere Interlude', 'Tor-upon-Sea' is Torquay, the now much-enlarged south Devon coast resort.

In 'The Honourable Laura' Hardy's name for Barnstaple is 'Downstaple'.

Index

Place-names are shown in capitals: Hardy place-names in italic capitals. Poems are listed under that heading. Names of Hardy characters are not indexed, but references are covered under the titles of the appropriate works.

FONTMELL MAGNA, 95, 211
'For Conscience' Sake', 237
FORDINGTON, 25–7, 167
 CHURCH, 19; CROSS, 25; FAIR-
 FIELD, 27; FIELD, 22; MILL LANE
 (*MIXEN LANE*), 27; STAND-
 FAST BRIDGE, 25–6; STANDFAST
 CROSS, 25; street names, former,
 25–6
Forestry Commission, 57, 62, 71, 188
FORRABURY, 245
FORTUNESWELL, 154
FOUNTALL, see Wells
FRAMPTON, 138
Frampton family, 86
FROME (FROOM), river, 12, 27, 53,
 81–3
FROME HILL, 35, 78
FROOM-EVERARD, see West Strat-
 ford
FROOM PATH, see Stinsford
FURZEWICK DOWN, 200

Gainsborough, Thomas, 225
GALLOWS HILL, 84
Gardiner, Rolf, 95, 211
Garnett, David, 176
GAYMEAD, 195–6
GILLINGHAM, 112
GLASTON, see Glastonbury
GLASTONBURY, 226
GLOUCESTER, 221
Godding, Henry, 196
Godfrey, A. D., and Mrs, 207
'Grave By the Handpost, The', 138, 142
GREAT FOREST, the, see New
 Forest
GREAT HINTOCK, see Minterne
 Magna
GREAT PLANTATION, the, 84, 86
GREAT MID-WESSEX PLAIN,
 see Salisbury Plain
GREAT POOL, the, 81–2
GREAT WEIR, see Stony Weir
Great Wessex Show, the, 190
GREENHILL, see Woodbury Hill
GREENHILL POND, 61–2, 67
GREENWOOD TREE, the, 63
Grey family, 40
GREY'S WOOD, 52
GRIMSTONE DOWN, 137

Group of Noble Dames, A, 23,128, 130–1,
 255–6

HALFWAY INN, 229
HALLWORTHY, 251
HALSTOCK, 61
HAMBLEDON HILL, 109
Hambury family, 43–4
HANDFAST POINT, 180
HANDLEY HILL, 95
Hand of Ethelberta, The, 43, 73, 86, 178–
 82, 188, 212–13
Hardy, Emma Lavinia, 34, 119, 167,
 179, 201–2, 207, 211, 238, 240, 243,
 245, 248, 251–4
Hardy, Florence, 35, 254
Hardy, Henry, 79
Hardy, James, 41
Hardy, Kate, 41, 79
Hardy, Mary, 79
HARTFOOT LANE, 119–20
Harvey, Major, 141
HAVENPOOL, see Poole
Hayman (of Launceston), 202, 252
HAZELBURY BRYAN, 116, 119–20
Heath, Sidney, 255–6
HEEDLESS WILLIAM'S POND, 59,
 61
HENDFORD HILL, 230–2
HENSTRIDGE ASH, 234
HERMITAGE, 133
HERRIARD HOUSE, 190
HETHFELTON FARM, 86
HETHFELTON HOUSE, 83–6
HEYMERE HOUSE, 190
Hicks, John, 23, 31
HIGHER BOCKHAMPTON
 CUCKOO LANE, 52; *ELIZA-
 BETH ENDERFIELD'S COT-
 TAGE*, 52; *LEWGATE*, 48;
 THOMAS HARDY'S BIRTH-
 PLACE, 48, 51–2
HIGHER CROWSTAIRS, see Hog
 Hill
HIGHER FORSTON, 138
HIGHER HYDE HEATH, 84
HIGHER JIRTON, see Higher Fors-
 ton
HIGHER KINGCOMBE, 143, 145
HIGH STOY, 131, 133
HINTOCK HOUSE, 131; see also
 Turnworth House

The following names were coined by Hardy for *An Indiscretion in the Life of an Heiress* and subsequently discarded: